Relating in Psychotherapy

In John Birtchnell's last book *How Humans Relate*, he proposed a new theory as the basis for a science of relating. *Relating in Psychotherapy* explains how the relevance of this theory relates to the practice of psychotherapy. The theory cuts across all schools of therapy, and is a way of describing each school in terms of relating in both the client and the therapist.

The theory is constructed around two major axes; a horizontal one concerning the degree to which we need to become involved with or separated from others, and a vertical one concerning the degree to which we choose to exercise power over others or permit others to exercise their power over us. With numerous clinical examples, John Birtchnell explains how we need to be competent in all four relating positions (close, distant, upper and lower), and argues that people who seek therapy usually lack competence in one or more of them, but through the course of therapy, their relating capabilities can be improved.

Relating in Psychotherapy can have applications in psychotherapy and in couple and family therapy, and will be an invaluable resource for therapists, counsellors and other mental health professionals.

John Birtchnell is Honorary Senior Lecturer at the Institute of Psychiatry and Honorary Psychiatrist at the Maudsley Hospital, London. He is the author of *How Humans Relate: A New Interpersonal Theory*, Psychology Press 1996.

Relating in Psychotherapy

The Application of a New Theory

John Birtchnell

First published in hardback 1999 by Praeger Publishers
88 Post Road West, Westport, CT 06881, USA

First published in paperback 2002 by Brunner-Routledge
27 Church Road, Hove, East Sussex BN3 2FA

Simultaneously published in the USA and Canada
by Brunner-Routledge
29 West 35th Street, New York, NY 10001

Brunner-Routledge is an imprint of the Taylor & Francis Group

Typeset in Times by RefineCatch Limited, Bungay, Suffolk
Printed and bound in Great Britain by
T.J. International Ltd, Padstow, Cornwall

British Library Cataloguing in Publication Data
A catalogue record for this book is available from the British Library

ISBN 1-58391-275-4

To Maggie

CENTRE	Lincoln
CHECKED	X
ZONE	~~Blue~~ Green
ZONE MARK / SUFFIX	616.89 BIR
LOAN PERIOD	1 month

Contents

Figures

Preface to the paperback edition

I am pleased to have this opportunity to provide some continuity between the hardback version of this book and the present paperback version. It is clear from some of the reviews (see, for example, Harris, 2000) that there remains some confusion over the extent of the originality of the ideas that I am proposing. I have to accept some of the blame for this, for I do vacillate on this point myself. Of course, no views are ever entirely original and, in several places, I point to continuities between my own ideas and those of others. The origin of the confusion most likely lies in the interplay that is apparent between two distinct points of view: the first is that the interpersonal processes with which I am concerned already are enshrined within most established forms of psychotherapy, which is why I have devoted so much space to describing them as they present themselves within a range of different therapies; the second is that, to do full justice to the principles of therapy that I am enunciating, it would be necessary to introduce what would amount to an entirely new form of therapy, which would incorporate these principles. Since already there exist so many different therapies, all of which have their devotees, and all of which can, in their separate ways, be highly effective, this did not seem a possibility worthy of serious consideration. However, as the book proceeded, the idea of introducing a form of therapy that would represent for me the ideal became increasingly appealing, and so, towards the end of the book the term *relating therapy* began to emerge. So this then is what it is: a way of wrapping up in a single package the various strands of therapy that focus on improving a person's relating competence, and, incidentally, of taking measures along the way to determine how the therapy is progressing; but I would not wish to present it as something superior to, or that should supplant, all that has gone before.

Obviously, the single, central and uniting feature of the book is the theory of relating and how it is applied to psychotherapy, but there are secondary features, some of which merit further comment. The first is the attention that I pay to the part that others play both in bringing about, and in reinforcing and maintaining, a person's defective relating. A mother who needs her daughter to stay close to her will, both initially and for the rest of her life, sabotage her daughter's attempts to function as an independent person. Coupled with this, her daughter will seek out people and situations with whom, or in which, she never needs to act independently; so by the time she comes to therapy she has become imprisoned within a social system in which any form of independent existence has become an impossibility for her. No amount of therapy, on its own, will undo all this; so the role of the therapist will have to be to reveal what has happened and is continuing to happen to her, and to support her while she tries to disentangle herself from these restraints.

This ties in with the idea, first introduced in my previous book (Birtchnell, 1996), that while being related to is as important as relating, relating gets more attention. Being related to can be defined, classified and measured as precisely as relating can. People do not always know they are being related to, and sometimes they think they are being related to when they are not. People are related to as much by internalised others from their past as by real others in the present, and sometimes they project on to others in the present the relating of internalised others from the past. This leads me to the issue of interrelating. This is another term first introduced in my previous book, and it is the theme of Chapters 7 and 8 of this one. I was surprised by how confusing some readers have found this term. It is simple enough really: Where relating refers to what one person does to another, interrelating refers to what goes on between two people. When two people interrelate each both relates to and is related to by the other; that is four separate processes are going on at the same time.

The second feature I wish to expand on is the functioning of what I call the outer brain and the inner brain, both in normal, everyday life and in psychotherapy. Tirril Harris (2000) described this as being ". . . surprisingly reminiscent of the distinction between the Conscious and Unconscious . . ." (p. 567), and Bateman (2000b) wrote, ". . . I was unconvinced that the new formulation added very much although it carries less baggage than the conscious and unconscious of psychoanalytic theory" (pp. 449–500). It is true that it is unencumbered by traditional psychoanalytic theory, dominated as it is by the issue of repression; but it is much more than this. Firstly, it is firmly rooted in evolutionary theory, and secondly, while there are, as yet, no proven links between the outer brain and the inner brain and specific brain structures, the formulation is much more closely aligned to the theories of neuroscience and contemporary psychology. Within my theoretical framework, the inner brain is the hypothesised location of the relating objectives: It generates relating needs, and determines when and whether these objectives have been met; and most important of all, it, and it alone, is capable of releasing the emotions that convey to the individual whether, in a relating sense, s/he is on course or off course.

So what then of the outer brain? It is an astonishing development because it has the quality of objectivity: It can somehow rise above us and watch ourselves in action. It rides the inner brain like a rider rides a horse. The outer brain would be lost without the inner brain just as the rider would be lost without the horse, and yet the outer brain is able to improve the functioning of the inner brain just as the rider is able to improve the functioning of the horse. The outer brain is able to suss out what the inner brain is trying to do and can even see how the inner brain has got things wrong, and somehow, and this is part of what happens in psychotherapy, it is able to get the inner brain back on track. This analogy of the horse and rider is an interesting one because the psychoanalysts write of the conscious taming the unconscious. My understanding of the relationship between the outer brain and the inner brain is that the outer brain does not try to tame the inner brain; it is much more respectful of it than that; rather it tries to understand what the inner brain is trying to do and tries to play its part in enabling it to do it better. Only the inner brain truly understands the rules of the game, and all the outer brain can do is try to pick up these rules by watching the inner brain at work.

Since completing the book, I have devoted much time trying to understand better the nature of the outer brain and the inner brain, and this has taken me into hitherto unexplored territories (Birtchnell, in press). Much of what I have read about the evolution of the brain, neuroscience, neuropsychology and even neurology, has resonated with what I first formulated in Chapter 2, and I remain more than ever convinced of the relevance of all of this to psychotherapy. It is becoming ever clearer that the greater part of our decision making takes place at an unconscious level and that much of what we do at a conscious level is simply rationalising after the event. Despite this, the role of the outer brain in comprehending what the inner brain appears to be up to, and correcting it when it appears to be taking the wrong path, is crucial to the psychotherapy process.

The third important feature I wish to take up is the integration of psychotherapy with measurements of relating deficits. The instrument based on relating theory, which some centres are now using in individual psychotherapy, is the *Person's Relating to Others Questionnaire*, currently in its revised form, the *PROQ2*. All the reviewers have considered this to be a valuable development. Jill Savege Scharff (2000) wrote, "His therapeutic strategy is designed to address areas of incompetence that the trained therapist can easily recognise, but which the questionnaire makes more specific for purposes of assessing change" (p. 119), and Anthony Bateman wrote, "The author should be congratulated for his painstaking work in developing a theory, putting it into practice, and producing meaningful measurement. This is a formidable attempt to produce an evidence-based psychotherapy" (p. 500). What I wish to stress is that the PROQ2 is useful even with conventional forms of psychotherapy, that is psychotherapy in which the therapist does not focus on relating deficits and their correction. Samples of psychotherapy patients consistently show higher mean scores than non-patients and these mean scores have been shown to drop significantly over the course of therapy.

This strongly suggests that psychotherapy patients do have relating deficits and that these, quite incidentally, get corrected in the course of conventional psychotherapy. Obviously, the ideal (which I now call relating therapy) is for the therapist to use the PROQ2 to reveal those areas in which there are relating deficits, direct the therapy towards correcting them and repeat the PROQ2 to determine how successful the therapy has been.

Following on from the PROQ2 is the development of instruments for measuring interrelating. Since in interrelating there are four processes going on at one and the same time, there have to be four questionnaires to measure these four processes, and together, these are called the *Couple's Relating to Each Other Questionnaires (CREOQ)*. With these, it is possible to compare how each person considers s/he relates to the other with how the other considers s/he is being related to. The disparity between the self-relatings of the one and the other relatings of the other is sometimes striking, and shows how mistaken people can be about how they think they are being related to. A recent review of these instruments and their application to individual, couple and family therapy is provided in Birtchnell (2001).

Research on relating instruments continues. In Chapter 9, it is stated that while significant changes in PROQ scores were reported for psychodynamic psychotherapy, no such changes were reported for the more time-limited cognitive analytic therapy. In a new trial of cognitive analytic therapy, in a different centre, significant changes in PROQ2 scores have now been reported. A recent study (Birtchnell and Shine, 2000) showed significant correlations between PROQ2 scores and scores on the *Personality Diagnostic Questionnaire (PDQ-4)* (Hyler, 1994), suggesting that most personality disorders are classifiable in terms of relating deficits. Shorter versions of the PROQ2 (the PROQ2a and PROQ3) are being tested, as is an objective measure of relating called *Observations of Relating Behaviour (ORB)*.

Where then does all this leave us? Some still have difficulty with the book. For example, although Kiesler (2000) acknowledged that "Contemporary interpersonal theory most assuredly needs conceptual elaborations" and that "[my] presentation of ideas at times suggests potentially attractive and necesssary elaborations of interpersonal theory," he found it impossible to ascertain why anyone should "invest the inordinate effort required to master and adapt it as a guide to future theory and research." However, I think there is growing evidence that the ideas expressed in the book, which may have seemed strange when the book was first published, are really not so far removed from more conventional thinking. Anthony Bateman (2000a) argued that much of what I was recommending would already be considered to be good psychotherapy practice, and in a lecture he gave in 1999 (2000b), he acknowledged that psychoanalysis is becoming more concerned with relational and interactional perspectives, particularly as mediators of change. He revealed his grasp of the message of the book when he wrote, "I concluded, rightly or wrongly, that the real point is that the therapy makes the therapist think about what he or she is doing in relation to the other in terms of upper and lower and closeness or distance. This can then be used to inform interventions as well as helping the therapist and patient identify where each of them is on the axes at any given moment" (p. 499). Perhaps then, the book now is more acceptable than it was when it first came out. Try it and see.

References

Bateman, A. (2000a) Book review. *British Journal of Psychiatry*, 176, 499–500.

Bateman, A. (2000b) Integrative developments in analytic psychotherapy. Paper presented at the Joint Conference of the Royal College of Psychiatrists and the British Psychological Society, October 9, 1999. Published in the *British Psychological Society, Psychotherapy Section Newsletter*, 27, 12–24, June, 2000.

Birtchnell, J. (1996) *How Humans Relate: A New Interpersonal Theory*. London: Psychology Press.

Birtchnell, J. (2001) Relating therapy with individuals, couples and families. *Journal of Family Therapy*, 23, 63–84.

Birtchnell, J. (in press) *The Rational Outer Brain and the Emotional Inner Brain*. (Provisional title). Hove: Psychology Press.

Birtchnell, J. and Shine, J. (2000) Personality disorders and the interpersonal octagon. *British Journal of Medical Psychology*, 73, 433–448.

Harris, T. (2000) Book review. *British Journal of Medical Psychology*, 73, 567–568.

Hyler, S. E. (1994) *Personality Diagnostic Questionnaire, (PDQ-4)*, (4th ed.). New York, NY: New York State Psychiatric Institute.

Kiesler, D. J. (2000) A "relating circumplex" by any other name . . . Book Review. *Contemporary Psychology: APA Review of Books*, 45, 676–679.

Savege Scharff, J. (2000) Book Review. *American Journal of Psychotherapy*, 54, 118–120.

Preface to the hardback edition

This book is a sequel to my previous book, *How Humans Relate: A New Inter-personal Theory*. The previous book was about a theory. This book is about an application of that theory. The theory grew out of a preoccupation with the concept of psychological dependence. The breakthrough came when I realized that dependence had two parts, one to do with getting close and one to do with being lower. Once that became clear, I could see that there had to be other kinds of relating that involved becoming distant and being upper. It occurred to me that being close, distant, upper and lower must be the only possible ways we could relate. So that was it—everything we do has to involve becoming either close or distant, or lower or upper.

It does not diminish the study of relating to point out that it can be reduced to these four activities, any more than it diminishes the study of mathematics to point out that it can be reduced to the four operations of adding, subtracting, multiplying and dividing. In fact, there is almost a correspondence between being close and adding, being distant and subtracting, being lower and dividing and being upper and multiplying. Relating, just like mathematics, can become extremely complicated, but it helps to understand both relating and mathematics if one can identify the basic processes upon which that complexity is constructed.

It can be, and has been, said that there is nothing original about my ideas about relating. In the opening paragraph of the previous book I wrote that Newton did not discover gravity. It was always there. He simply drew our attention to it. In the same way, I did not discover relating. I simply drew the reader's attention to it. In his review of the book in the *British Journal of Psychotherapy*, Robert Royston (1995) pointed out that we have always known that people are aware of the distance, and the power asymmetry, between themselves and others. "The theory then," he said, "appears to be not a new explanation but a point around which descriptions of human behavior can be organised" (p. 638). I would not argue with that. One sunny Saturday morning in Perth, Australia, a woman came up to me at the end of a lecture I had given, and said, "It's obvious when someone points it out to you, isn't it?" I agreed with her. Something of the same can happen in psychotherapy. At the end of a course of therapy a client can say, "You haven't taught me anything I didn't already know." I would agree with that too.

There have been many responses to the first book, some favorable, some not so favorable, but the one that troubles me most is "So what?" meaning, how does it help to be aware that people are sometimes close, sometimes distant, sometimes lower, and sometimes upper? It is mainly to answer questions like this that I decided to write this book. I cannot expect people to be impressed by my assertion that relating can be reduced to these four states unless I can demonstrate how useful it can be to conceptualize forms of relating in terms of them, and what advantages there are to describing the processes involved in psychotherapy in terms of overcoming our difficulties in attaining them.

In my more grandiose moments, I thought of calling the first book "What life is all about." Within the psychotherapy literature, little is written about this topic. It may seem odd that psychotherapists should set about their task of helping people adjust to life while showing so little interest in what the objects of life might be. Freud's famous expression "loving and working" is neither fundamental enough nor comprehensive enough. Mapping out people's problems in terms of the directions in which they are moving has provided for me a clearer idea of what to do in therapy. Because of this, therapy has come more naturally and flowed more easily.

In the preface to the first book I wrote, "Theories take a long time to grow." In this preface I could write: Theories take a long time to catch on. Even though it is five years since the publication of the first book, I cannot assume that the reader is familiar with the theory, and yet I cannot incorporate a full account of it in this book. The compromise I have chosen is, following the first two introductory chapters, to alternate chapters describing the theory with chapters describing its application to psychotherapy. This way, the reader will not have to wade through a long account of the theory before proceeding to consider its application. Thus, each theoretical chapter will prepare the reader for the chapter on psychotherapy that is to follow.

Chapter 2 began as a paragraph of Chapter 1, but gradually grew to become a separate chapter. It has a bearing on the content of the other chapters. The germ of it appeared in the first chapter of the first book. It proposes the existence of an inner and an outer brain. This can now be considered a second theory, though one that grew out of the first theory. Like the first, it has its roots in evolution. It complements and enhances the first theory and, particularly in the last chapter, the two theories have become closely interwoven.

In books on psychotherapy, there is always the problem of what to call the person who is seen and worked with. It does not seem right to consider someone who has interpersonal problems as being ill. Therefore I am averse to using the term "patient." The common alternative is "client." While this carries the unfortunate assumption that the person is paying for what is being provided, it is the preferable term, and the one that I have used throughout the book.

There is also the matter of gender, which in descriptions of relating crops up all the time. Readers of the previous book complained about my use of the terms s/he, her/his, her/himself. Despite this, I believe it is right to acknowledge that there are two genders, so I have used them again in this book. I think they are preferable to writing she or he, her or his, herself or himself and them or their.

Finally, a few acknowledgments: In Chapter 9 I am indebted to Kim Twigger, at Nene College, Northampton, for collecting the student data; to Mark Dunn and his staff at the Munro Clinic of Guy's Hospital, London, for collecting the data on clients receiving cognitive analytic therapy; to Julie Roberts and her colleagues in Northampton, Graham Rehling and his colleagues in Canterbury and Rob Eyres and his colleagues in Redhill for collecting the data on clients receiving psychodynamic psychotherapy; and as always, to my son, Bill, for writing the programs for scoring the questionnaires, for preparing the diagrams and for constant advice on all matters concerning computing.

Chapter 1

Relating and its relevance for psychotherapy

This book is written around a theory that was fully described in an earlier book (Birtchnell, 1993/1996). The object of the present book is to explain the relevance of the theory to psychotherapy, but it will not be possible to do so without taking up some considerable amount of space explaining the theory itself. Since the theory is about how humans relate, it is to be hoped that even the most psychotherapeutic of readers will find the theory interesting in its own right. It is promised that, from the outset, every effort will be made to establish links between the theory and the practice of psychotherapy. This book, like the first book, adopts the theory as its central and uniting theme, but since the theory is not, first and foremost, a theory of psychotherapy, it may frustrate some readers who are looking for a new psychotherapeutic approach. However, if they persevere, they should not be disappointed. The theory will affect the way they think about relating and, since relating is a predominant concern of psychotherapists, it will also affect the way they both think about and practice psychotherapy.

Within the psychotherapeutic session there are two separate though inter-locking processes: (1) the therapist and client are involved in relating behavior that is directed toward each other, and (2) the client is describing to the therapist relating experiences that s/he has had, or is having, in the world outside. The therapy proceeds by focusing attention upon and trying to make sense of both of these; and while it can quite reasonably be maintained that, both within the therapeutic session and in the world outside, human relating can be an extremely complex process, there are advantages to breaking it down into its simpler components. Since relating is so central to what goes on in, and to what is talked about in, psychotherapy, providing a theoretical system within which to describe and comprehend it should provide a more rational basis upon which to conduct the business of psychotherapy.

The theory with which both the previous book and the present one are concerned is firmly set within an evolutionary context. It considers the relat-ing of humans to be an extension of the relating of all other life forms. Viewing humans as just another life form has its advantages, and setting human relating within the broader context of animal relating provides a theoretical framework within which to explain it. This is not to say that human relating is the same as the relating even of other animals, for many features of human relating have no clear equivalent in the relating of other animals, but even these are made more meaningful by demonstrating continuities between them and those forms of animal relating from which they would appear to have evolved.

Evolution

Evolution works by, every so often, generating within the gene pool of an organism a chance variation of some established feature of that organism. If the offspring that carry this chance variation survive and reproduce, this advantageous variation becomes a permanent characteristic of the organism in succeeding generations. Because evolution has a way of discarding everything that carries no advantages, every part of every organism must have a function (or in rare instances, like the appendix, must once have had a function) and everything an organism does must be done (or must once have been done) for a purpose. There are no surplus parts to organisms, and organisms do not waste time doing things for no reason. Strictly speaking, the logic of this argument is back to front. Parts of organisms do not really have functions, and the activity of organisms is not really purposeful. In the course of evolution, only those organisms that had advantageous parts, or that acted in advantageous ways, survived. Surplus parts and useless activity, which had no survival value, were a waste of space or a waste of time and simply got bred out. However, it is convenient for us to speak of parts as having functions and of activities as having purposes, and this is the way it will be put for the rest of the book.

The human organism is no exception to this rule. All our parts are (or exceptionally, were at one time) functional and all our actions are (or exceptionally, were at one time) purposeful, because that is the way we have evolved. Each organ and each part of each organ has a job to do; from the moment we are born, all of our organs swing into action and continue to function in their allotted ways until the day we die. Nobody has to tell them what to do or teach them how to do it; from the very start, they all function perfectly, because that is the way that evolution has shaped them.

Similarly, and perhaps more surprisingly, our brains know, within certain broad parameters that will be described shortly, what objectives we should be striving toward and direct our behaviour into certain actions that are most likely to attain them. Nobody has to tell our brains what these objectives should be, or how best they should organize our behavior to enable us to attain them. From the moment we take our first breath, our brains set us on track along certain behavioral pathways and keep us on track for the rest of our lives.

Life forms as living machines

One could liken the parts of an organism to the parts of a machine. Each part has a function; and when all the parts perform their functions together, the machine runs smoothly. Machines, like for example television sets, have sub-systems that are analogous to organs. They interconnect and interact in order to attain the machine's ultimate objectives, just as organs do to attain the organism's ultimate objectives; but organisms are much cleverer than machines, because they can, to varying extents, repair broken parts, replace worn-out parts and even produce brand-new versions of themselves that are able to take over when they come to be beyond repair.

If machines have ultimate objectives, then organisms should as well; so what are the ultimate objectives of organisms? Why do they exist? Since we ourselves are organisms, why do we exist? The crazy, and perhaps not very satisfactory, answer is that organisms, and that includes us, exist simply to continue existing; and if they cannot continue existing, they produce replicas of themselves whose objective is also to continue existing. This has to be so, for if their objective were not to continue existing, they would not, for so long, have continued to exist. Behind everything we do, then there must be two basic motives: to survive and if we cannot survive, to reproduce.

There evolved two kinds of organisms, both with these two basic motives: the immobile plants and the mobile animals. The mobile animals seem to be neither better nor worse at surviving and reproducing than the immobile plants; they simply adopt different strategies for doing so. The kinds of machines that life forms most resemble are computers, and our familiarity with computers has enabled us to understand evolution better. Life forms, like computers, are programmed to behave in certain ways, but whereas computers have been programmed by humans, life forms have been programmed by chance variations in their gene pools. There are obvious similarities between instincts and programs. The computer analogy holds even for humans. Most of our bodily functions are controlled in a computer-like way and, as will be shown in the next chapter, even many of the brain's higher functions bear a close resemblance to computer activity.

Mobility

With mobility, animals turned into mobile machines, like motor cars, but unlike motor cars, they have a built-in driver, the brain, which makes decisions about where they should be driven. For most animals, mobility is very much bound up with feeding. Having exhausted one source of food they have to move on to another. Once animals became mobile they were able to catch and eat other animals. Catching and eating animals is much more efficient than eating plants, because animals contain much more concentrated food stores than plants do. Whereas herbivores have to keep moving and eating almost continuously, many carnivores can survive for long periods on just a single catch. Once animals began eating other animals they had to develop strategies for hunting, fighting and killing, and for fending off and escaping from animals that wanted to eat them. Moving is also very much bound up with reproduction. Animals need to seek out a mate and fight off rivals, and to feed and protect their young. Since humans are animals, all forms of human relating must have evolved out of these two basic activities of finding food and reproducing.

Sexual reproduction

There must be something extremely advantageous to sexual reproduction, as opposed to asexual reproduction, for it has evolved quite independently in animals and plants. It involves the mixing of the gene pools of two separate organisms, and this increases variability within the offspring, which in turn contributes to evolution. Most plants have both male organs for transmitting genes and female organs for receiving them. Most animals have a male form for transmitting genes and a female form for receiving them. Plants cannot select the recipients of their genes in the way that animals can. Many plants depend upon animals to disperse both their genes and their offspring. They lure insects to their flowers and reward them with nectar, a particularly concentrated and easily assimilable form of carbohydrate. By producing fruit, another source of carbohydrate, or barbed seeds, they induce animals to carry their potential offspring to distant parts.

Relating

With mobility came the ability to relate. This said, it has to be admitted that, even though they do not move, plants can relate. By way of their growing, plants actually do move, though relatively slowly, and in this growing they relate. This can be convincingly shown with time-lapse photography. They compete with other plants for light and water, climb up them, cling to them, feed off them, even kill them. They open and close their flowers by the differential rates of growth of their petals. They also relate without moving. By producing brightly colored and perfumed flowers they attract insects and some birds. They are able to defend themselves against animals by having hard or prickly outer layers that render them difficult to eat, having leaves that sting or that taste unpleasant, or producing substances that are poisonous to animals. Plants did not think up these various relating devices; those that had them had a better chance of survival than those that did not have them.

Insectivorous plants lure, trap, close in on and eventually eat insects. This looks more like the kind of relating that animals are capable of, yet it is entirely due to progressive changes in the anatomy and physiology of the plant. Certain plants that grew in acid soils, from which the absorption of minerals was not possible, gained advantage over other plants, by acquiring, through some genetic accident, sticky leaves to which flies got stuck. By a further genetic accident, these leaves became capable of absorbing minerals from the flies, and by a further accident still, the leaves came to be able to close over the flies and trap them. This brief diversion into the behavior of plants is intended to drive home the point that relating is no big deal, but simply an evolved device for ensuring our survival. Spiders, which also trap and eat flies, got to be the way they are by a sequence of genetic stages similar to that of plants. There came a time when one spider, again by some genetic accident, came to exude some silk-like material that, as the spider crawled about, got stuck on to plants. This formed a crude meshwork to which flies got stuck. Through successive evolutionary stages, spiders acquired innate patterns of moving that caused them to make proper webs; through further stages, they acquired innate behavioral patterns that enabled them to tie up and kill their prey. Thus, although the initial genetic breakthrough was a structural one–the exuding of the silk-like material–the later ones were behavioral. Because they were behavioral, they also required genetic changes to the brain in order that it could direct this behavior.

The role of the brain in relating

The brain plays a fundamental role in all animal relating because (1) it carries the plans for the directions that relating should take, and (2) it controls and monitors the relating behavior. It must always be remembered that as much as animals relate to other animals, they also are related to by other animals. A further function of the brain therefore is to monitor the relating of other animals and to determine the appropriate response to such relating. The question might be asked, to what extent does the human brain resemble that of other animals? The answer is, much more than we might think. There is no such thing in evolution as wiping the slate clean and starting afresh, of going back to the drawing board. Evolution works by slightly modifying that which has gone before. The human brain therefore must be a modified version of the brain of those animals from which we have evolved. According to MacLean (1973), what appears to have happened is that, with succeeding stages of evolution, extra layers, like the layers of an onion, have grown up around the original brain and provided us with additional capabilities. Although all the layers are still in place and functioning in their separate ways, there does appear to be a considerable degree of coordination among them. The earliest stage, which MacLean considered to be concerned with survival, he called the *reptilian brain*; the next, which he considered to be concerned with motives and emotions, he called the *palaeomammalian brain*; and the most recent, which he considered to be concerned with rational thought, he called the *neomammalian brain*. While MacLean's scheme met with considerable criticism (Reiner, 1990), this is now considered to be largely unjustified (Cory, 1988). A fuller account of the function of the brain in the relating process will be the subject of Chapter 2.

Human instincts

Freud revised his theory of instincts a number of times. Initially he considered there to be two classes of instinct. These he called the *ego instincts*, which are concerned with self-preservation, and the *sexual instinct*, which is concerned with reproduction. In 1911, he described what he called the *life instincts*, which appear to be mainly organized and regulated by MacLean's reptilian brain. They are concerned with the meeting of physiological needs such as hunger, thirst, defecation, urination and the release of sexual tension. He considered that the meeting of such needs is associated with pleasure, which in humans would indeed appear to be the case; but it surely cannot be that the earliest life forms experienced pleasure with the satisfaction of their physiological needs. Therefore, pleasure must have been introduced at some stage along the evolutionary chain and been retained because it reinforces the drive to satisfy these needs. Freud considered that an instinct is made up of four components: a *source*, namely, a deficiency such as lack of food; an *aim*, namely, a wish to eliminate the deficiency, thus removing the discomfort of hunger; an *object*, namely, that which is needed to eliminate the deficiency, which in this case is food; and an *impetus*, namely the intensity of the craving for the desired object.

Focusing this model specifically on the need for food, there must be a center within the brain that registers the lack of food and then generates a craving for it and stimulates activity directed toward making good this lack. If the lack is great, the craving will be intense, the activity directed toward making good the lack will be that much more frantic, and the pleasure when the food is found and consumed will be that much more rewarding. The center must have some means of registering when the lack has been made good; it must then turn off the craving and generate a sensation of satiety.

The mechanisms that operate these feedback loops, which we could call *primary*, must be relatively simple; but beyond them, there must be *secondary* neural mechanisms for serving them. The organism needs to know where to find the food and how to get to it. The memory must be called into play to select a possible source (the word "source" here is not used in the Freudian sense) and to inform the organism of the route to take to reach it. A journey must be selected and familiar landmarks checked out. If the source is another animal, strategies must be devised for catching and killing it. This may involve cooperation with other animals. Finally, the food must be eaten and digested.

At a *tertiary* level, the sense organs must be recruited for finding and following the route, finding and tasting the food and tracking down and catching the prey; and the muscle groups must be recruited for moving toward, finding, catching and eating the food. There has to be a whole hierarchy of commands that ensures that the organism works as one coordinated whole.

A similar set of neural mechanisms must be called into play for seeking out and attaining relating objectives. Examining these will bring us closer to understanding what might be involved in the processes of human relating.

The relating instincts

It is proposed that, akin to these life instincts, there must also be *relating instincts* that operate in a similar fashion. The movement of animals is not random; it is directed toward attaining certain *relating objectives* that, though perhaps rooted in the more fundamental objectives of survival and reproduction, are much more diverse. Animals then, and particularly humans, seek to attain what will be called *states of relatedness* (equivalent to Freudian objects), which place them, in certain advantageous respects, in relation to other animals/humans. The full range of these states of relatedness will be described later in the chapter, but first, the mechanisms for attaining them will be described. It is suggested that the organism has needs for these states of relatedness in much the same way as it has needs for food and that feedback loops similar to those described for satisfying hunger have to be set in motion.

Gilbert (1989) introduced the concept of *biosocial goals*, which are all to do with relating. He called them care-eliciting, care-giving, competition and cooperation. They provide a useful start, but they fall far short of a comprehensive, descriptive system. Later (1992) he argued that if organisms have biosocial goals, they must have *internal processing modules* for organizing information about these goals and what needs to be done to achieve them and to what extent they have been achieved. Of course, Gilbert was right. It must be assumed that there are centers for the regulation of relating instincts that are comparable to those for the regulation of Freud's life instincts (e.g., hunger and thirst).

Some biological needs, for instance, the need to stay at the right temperature, have to be regulated over long periods of time, with the brain acting as a kind of thermostat, turning on and off the feeling of being too cold or too hot and stimulating and inhibiting activity for getting warmed up or cooled down. The attainment of states of relatedness is usually like this. Once the state has been attained, the proposed brain center needs to keep monitoring it and raising an alarm and promoting corrective activity if there are signs of its being lost or depleted.

An example of a state of relatedness is *closeness*. For various reasons, animals, and particularly humans, seek closeness, but as with food, their closeness needs are finite. When they have a sufficient amount of closeness, they must reach a state of satiety, which in a sense is their neural reward for finding closeness; then their closeness need, like hunger, would cease. Let us assume that the closeness center registers a lack of closeness and generates a craving for it. The closeness equivalent of hunger would be a feeling of isolation or loneliness, a need to be with someone, a need for company or companionship. The need may be for a specific person or for just anyone. Once the need becomes apparent, behavior is set in play that has the objective of seeking and gaining closeness. As with seeking and finding food, the memory store must be tapped to locate possible sources of and routes to closeness; then strategies for approaching and negotiating these sources must be devised. If there is an obvious and readily attainable source, like calling on a neighbor or telephoning a friend, the strategy may be relatively straightforward. If there is not, the strategy could be much more complicated, like seeking out people who are potential friends and trying to make friends with them. As with food, when the closeness is attained, the closeness center would generate a sensation of satiety and turn off the craving for closeness.

Instinct-driven behavior is sometimes divided into two components called *appetitive* (e.g., feeling hungry, seeking and finding food) and *consummatory* (e.g., indulging in the pleasurable activity of eating the food). In the case of hunger, if the food supply is readily available, the consummatory phase could be quite short (i.e., the food is found and eaten). In the case of relating it could be brief, as when shaking hands, or it could be long. It could even extend over an entire lifetime. In the case of closeness, it would involve such experiences as indulging in all kinds of close activities, like going places and doing things together; sharing interests and opinions and exchanging ideas; making revelations to and wanting to know about each other; and being kind, sympathetic and understanding.

Perhaps more so than with food, animals can be exposed to what amounts to a surfeit of a state of relatedness. Taking closeness as an example, when unwelcome animals come close or even when welcome animals move too close or have stayed close for too long, neural alarm signals are set off and behavior is activated for either moving away or urging the other animal to move away. The condition is well recognized in humans and has been given the name *closeness fatigue*. It occurs in conditions of overcrowding. It occurs particularly when the closeness has been imposed by someone else, as when a man forces himself upon a woman or has overstayed his welcome. It has a claustrophobic or suffocating quality and induces such thoughts as "I need to be by myself". "Why can't he leave me alone?" "Why won't he go?" Closeness regulation can be an issue in the psychotherapy session and certainly features in the lives of psychotherapy clients.

Is the term "instinct" inappropriate for humans?

The term "instinct" is normally reserved for describing an innate, well-circumscribed, automatically performed, fixed set of behaviors, directed toward performing a specific task, like spinning a web or building a nest. The theory proposes that what we have in humans is a relatively small range of broadly defined, albeit innate tendencies (relating objectives), which have some of the characteristics of instincts, but which can be organized, expanded and modified in a broadly diverse manner, to incorporate an enormous variety of patterns of behavior. Relating objectives come closer to Freud's (1920) later concept of *drives*. The relating objectives must be under the control of neural mechanisms that make us aware of them, provoke us into behavior directed toward attaining them and generate emotional responses that cause us to feel good when we have succeeded in attaining them, alert us when we are in danger of not attaining them or losing them and make us feel bad when we have failed to attain them or have lost them.

The transition between these basic relating objectives and all the other, more detailed, behavior patterns that we accumulate will become clearer as the book goes on. Returning to the issue of closeness, what we start with is an innate general tendency to get close. What we develop from this is a whole range of behaviors that share the common objective of getting close, but are directed toward the different forms that closeness can assume in humans. Sexual closeness is such a fundamental objective–it has components such as desire, arousal, excitement, intercourse and orgasm, which come close to being classifiable as instincts–that perhaps it deserves to be treated separately. The bond that develops between infant and parent and parent and infant may be of a similar order of things. The acquisition of language is another specialized form of closeness that perhaps merits the name instinct (Pinker, 1995). We do not learn how to acquire language, we just acquire it. In fact, children who have no common language rapidly develop one of their own when left to themselves (Pinker, 1995).

But how do we acquire all the other manifestation of closeness? Evolution has provided the human brain with a degree of flexibility and adaptiveness that contrasts markedly with the rigidity and maladaptiveness of the brains of many lower animals. The brain is somehow able to work out that if we do this or if we do that, for example, talk to someone about ourselves or exchange ideas and experiences, it provides us with the same inner experience of closeness as we get from more elemental forms of closeness such as being in the presence of someone, touching and mutually gazing, and it rewards us accordingly, so we add a whole range of activities to our repertorire of closeness behaviors.

The role of the emotions in relating

It is difficult to say at what stage in the course of evolution emotions came into being as a means of reinforcing goal-directed behavior. It would be absurd to imagine that plants experiences emotion, and it seems unlikely that insects do. They seem to operate much more like complicated automata. Dogs certainly appear to be capable of experiencing pleasure and displeasure, and there is no doubt that primates do. Emotions are a powerful and extremely effective means of keeping us aware of whether or not we are on track in our goal-directed behavior. The feeling of pleasure has become a kin of self-donated reward for the attainment of a relating objective, and the feeling of displeasure has become a kind of self-imposed punishment for the loss of one. There are degrees of pleasure, ranging from contentment to elation, and of displeasure, ranging from sadness to dejection, which are indicative of the extent or expectedness of the attainment or loss of a particular objective. Other emotions can be fitted in around this dichotomy. Pleasurable anticipation and hope accompany the expectation of success, and anxiety and dread accompany the expectation of failure. When denied or deprived of a state of relatedness by the action of another, a person may experience anger as an expression of a determination to regain it or hatred as an expression of frustration at the unlikelihood of being able to regain it. At moments of change, when relating states are gained or lost, emotions are intense, but over longer periods, when they can be either satisfactory or unsatisfactory, they are more subdued.

These views are in keeping with the writing of Nesse (1990), an evolutionary psychiatrist who believes that emotions have been shaped by natural selection to regulate interpersonal behavior in the direction of increased fitness. Emotions, he says, inform an organism as to how well fitness-enhancing strategies are working; that is, unpleasant emotions signal that they are not going well and modification of strategies is needed, and pleasant emotions signal the opposite. An extremely important point to be made about emotions is that they are not experiences that we think ourselves into, we just find ourselves being happy, anxious, sad or whatever, and we take no part in the decision to experience them. The implication is that they must arise at a level lower than that of MacLean's (1973) neomammalian brain. LeDoux (1989) observed that "The core of the emotional system is a network that evaluates (computes) the biological significance of stimuli. . . . The computation of stimulus significance takes place prior to and independent of conscious awareness" (p. 267). The word "stimuli" here is used in the broadest sense, to include experiences.

The basic processes of relating

Taking again the example of the need for closeness, the infant is born with a range of mechanisms for attaining and maintaining closeness to its parents. It rapidly learns to recognize and respond to their smell, sound and appearance. It instinctively clings to them, smiles at them and gazes into their eyes. It has a range of different kinds of crying to which they are programmed to respond. When it becomes mobile, it follows them everywhere, and when it learns to talk, it talks to them incessantly. These mechanisms serve it well in the first months and years of life, but as the years go by, the child, the adolescent and the adult have to acquire strategies for gaining and maintaining closeness not just to parents but to others in general.

If it is to actively seek closeness, it has to learn to become comfortable in the condition of closeness and to find it a pleasurable experience. Not all children, and certainly not all adults, become comfortable in such a condition, and many do not find it pleasurable. Some become shy and withdrawn and avoid contact with others. The child has to learn how to become appealing to others and to learn how to gain and maintain their friendship. It has to practice getting close and staying close to a range of people. They give the individual *competence* in the sphere of closeness. Competence in any particular form of relating enables the individual to attain the particular state of relatedness whenever s/he needs to. Staying with the food analogy, a carnivore has eating competence when it is capable of catching and killing its prey. With competence comes *confidence*. The individual comes to feel confident that s/he can get closeness if and when s/he needs it.

The interplay of internal and external relating

Just as with food, the individual has to accumulate *inner stores* of particular states of relatedness that, in a sense, can be drawn upon when other people are not around. These inner stores are kinds of memories, which are sometimes called *internal representations* of the self and others. Everything experienced as happening in the outside world becomes represented in the inner, or psychic, world. Inside the psyche there are representations (or memories) of all kinds of people that the self has had involvements with in the outside world, and in the inner world the self continues to relate to these people. This is called *internal relating*. A particularly vivid form of internal relating occurs in dreams.

Continuing the food analogy, besides having inner stores of particular states of relatedness, the individual also needs to have *external sources*. Such sources are people or situations from which it is possible for her/him to derive the state of relatedness should s/he feel the need of it. In the sphere of relating, the term *opportunities* is appropriate. In the case of closeness these could extend over communities and social groups into which s/he feels embedded, the workplace, colleagues and work mates, the family and individual family members, friends and acquaintances and intimates with whom s/he has a special relationship. In many instances, these external sources are the external equivalent of internal representations. Sometimes, however, the internal representations remain long after the external sources have ceased to exist. In their dreams, people are able to have relationship with parents who have died or lovers who have left them.

As with food, some internal monitoring mechanism has the responsibility for deciding whether the individual has enough of any particular state of relatedness and of generating restless unease, like hunger, if a deficit is registered. Certain amounts of a particular state of relatedness are derived from all the different sources. This is a notion similar to Weiss' (1969) fund of sociability. Some sources provide small amounts, other sources provide huge amounts. Also as with food, there appear to be short-term stores and long-term stores. The presence of long-term stores does not preclude the individual from experiencing the urge to replenish her/his short-term stores, that is, from becoming needful of seeking new external sources, In the same way, a fat person who has perfectly adequate long-term, internal stores of food will frequently become hungry in order to satisfy some short-term craving. It seems likely that a recent loss of a particular state of relatedness will trigger a sudden urge to put things right either by trying to regain the lost state or by seeking out another source.

The distinction between positive and negative relating

The distinction between *positive* and *negative* relating is extremely important. Essentially, positive relating is adaptive and negative relating is maladaptive. The person who has competence and confidence in a particular sphere of relating is more inclined to relate positively within that sphere of relating; the person who lacks competence and confidence is more inclined to relate negatively, but the issue is more complicated than this. Related to lack of competence and lack of confidence is *fearfulness*. A person will acquire fearfulness of a particular state of relatedness if s/he has had bad experiences of it. Someone who is incompetent, unconfident and fearful in a particular sphere of relating may simply *avoid* that form of relating completely. Even though all states of relatedness are advantageous, desirable and pleasurable, the avoidant relater will persistently deny her/himself that particular state. In the sphere of closeness, the avoidant relater will persistently avoid becoming close to people. A position less extreme than avoidant relating is *insecure* relating. The person who relates in an insecure way is capable of attaining a particular state of relatedness but is not confident of being able to hold on to it. Insecure relating is not always the fault of the relater; it is sometimes the fault of the person being related to. In the sphere of closeness, the insecure relater will cling anxiously to the person s/he is close to. Such clinging may be due to either the person's lack of competence as a close relater or to the unreliability of this other person.

A different category of negative relating, though one also usually due to lack of competence or lack of confidence, is what may be called *desperate, inconsiderate, disrespectful* or *egocentric* relating. The person who relates in this way is so needful of a particular state of relatedness that s/he has no regard for the effect that her/his relating behavior is having, or will have, upon the person s/he is relating to. Because of this, s/he may *impose* a particular form of relating on this other person by persistence or force. In the sphere of closeness, the disrespectful relater may try to stay close to the other even though s/he is clearly not welcome, or may make it difficult or even impossible for the other to break away.

A different category still, which may also result from lack of confidence or lack of competence, is what might be called the *exaggerated normal response*. From an evolutionary point of view, there are advantages to certain (probably innate) responses, but some people adopt these responses so readily, or to such an extent, that they become disadvantageous to them. In the non-relating sphere, fear of heights is an example. In the relating sphere, paranoia and jealousy are examples. There are times when it is clearly justifiable and advantageous to be suspicious or jealous of others. These responses become maladaptive when the danger to which they are directed is non-existent or minimal.

There is a version of each of these five forms of negative relating for each category of relating (see later in the chapter). One of the consequences of negative relating is *rigidity*. If a person is excessively avoidant of one particular form of relating or is compelled, through lack of competence, to relate excessively in one particular way, this restricts her/his repertoire of relating and in turn imposes restraints upon the relating of others toward her/him.

Relating and being related to

In order to attain a particular state of relatedness, a person has to seek out someone with whom to relate. That person, however, is also being sought out by other people as someone to relate to. Thus, people are being related to *by* others as much as they are relating *to* others, and the experience of being related to *by* others is just as important as the experience of relating *to* others. A further twist to the picture is that people are just as likely to attain a particular state of relatedness from the relating of other people to them as they are from relating to other people. In the case of closeness, for example, a person can be as much the recipient of closeness as the giver of closeness, but whether it is received or given, it is still closeness.

Two sets of terms for defining the direction of relating are *active* and *passive* relating, and *donative* and *receptive* relating. Active relating is making a direct move or gesture in a particular direction, and passive relating is being related to in that way. Active relating may be positive or negative. The active relater may make an initial *offer* to the other to relate in a particular way, and a passive relater may make an initial *invitation* to the other to relate to her/him in a particular way. A further term is *reactive* relating, which is responding to the active move or gesture. It is sometimes important to know whether a particular relating act is active or passive. As a form of active relating, a person may make a direct bid for closeness. As a form of reactive relating, a person may make a bid for closeness as a response to the other showing signs of moving away. Donative relating is a particularly generous (i.e., positive) form of relating: It is perceiving that a person would like or benefit from a particular state of relatedness (e.g., being consoled) and willingly providing it. Receptive relating is accepting that which is being provided.

Relating and being related to occur both in the external world and within the psyche. It has already been mentioned that the person relates to the internal representations of others. It is also the case that these internal representations of others relate to her/him. In a general way, or in relation to specific people, s/he may feel liked or disliked, appreciated or unappreciated, approved of or disapproved of. The conscience may be an amalgam of these internalized others, though sometime it is experienced as the self relating to the self. God is both externalized and internalized, and people relate to Him and He relates to them.

Interrelating

Interrelating is the process by which two people relate to each other. It will be fully described in Chapter 7. It may take place over any time period, from an interaction lasting a few seconds to a relationship lasting an entire lifetime. It may take place predominantly in one direction (e.g., one participant always leading and the other always following) or it may take place in two directions (e.g., sometimes one leads and sometimes the other leads). In the most satisfactory forms of interrelating, the two participants meet their relating objectives to an equal extent. In the least satisfactory forms, one participant meets her/his relating objectives at the expense of the other. Interrelating is initiated by the *relating encounter*, which mostly takes place quite automatically, in which two potential relaters act in such a way as to make their relating needs apparent and try to determine whether "*a deal can be struck*" to their mutual advantage. It is also in the relating encounter that one participant may decide that s/he can (disrespectfully) impose a particular form of relating upon the other, which may be more to her/his advantage than to the other's. Between these two extremes a number of compromise arrangements are possible. For example, one person may decide to allow the other to relate to her/him in a particular way, even though this is not the way s/he would wish to be related to, because s/he perceives that it is something the other badly needs. Beyond the relating encounter is the *period of relating*, which may be long or short and during which time the relating positions of the participants may be negotiated and re-negotiated many times over.

Schemata for classifying relating objectives

Human relating objectives have not arisen out of thin air. In fact, although this may seem strange, at the most basic level, the relating objectives of humans are exactly the same as the relating objectives of practically all other animals. This sets humans fairly and squarely within the animal kingdom and creates a continuity, both historically and across species, between humans and all other animals. More important than this, it provides a rational explanation for why we do the things we do, for we do these things for the same reasons that other animals do them, because they carry advantages for our survival and for our reproductive capabilities. Closeness, the objective used as an example in this chapter, is important for practically all animals because organisms gain, to a greater or lesser extent, from staying in close proximity to one another.

The interpersonal circle

The most widely adopted system for the classification of relating behavior has grown out of that school of psychology called *interpersonal psychology*. Ironically, the usually acknowledged originator of this school is not a psychologist, but a psychiatrist, Harry Stack Sullivan. His book, *The Interpersonal Theory of Psychiatry* (1953), is frequently quoted, but the system, which is called the *interpersonal circle*, is not included in this book and did not, in fact, come into existence until after Sullivan's death in 1949. The inspiration for the circle may have come from an open letter from Freud to Einstein, entitled *Why War?* which was published in 1950 (Birtchnell, 1993/1996). In this, Freud drew attention to a certain G.G. Lichtenberg, who had invented what he called *a compass of motives*. This proposed that human motives might be arranged like the thirty-two winds. The first account of the circle was published by Freedman, Leary, Ossorio and Coffee in 1951, and it was said to contain "all the interpersonal mechanisms considered to be required for systematising interpersonal behavior". It was more fully developed by Leary in his (1957) book called *Interpersonal Diagnosis of Personality*, in which Sullivan's contribution was acknowledged. The circle is constructed around two dimensions. Because the dimensions are independent of each other they are called orthogonal and can be represented graphically as two intersecting lines, drawn at right angles to each other to make the diameters of a circle. The horizontal one is called love versus hate and the vertical one, dominate versus submit. A sixteen-segment circle is formed by inserting three intervening segments in each of the quadrants created by the two intersecting diameters.

Since its first publication, the circle has undergone a number of modifications (e.g., Lorr & McNair, 1963, 1965; Benjamin, 1974; Wiggins, 1979; Kiesler, 1983; Strong et al., 1988), but its basic structure and the principles

upon which it rests have remained the same (Birtchnell, 1990). Psychotherapeutic strategies based upon the circle depend largely upon the principle
of *complementarity*, which was first outlined by Leary (1957) and later
developed by Carson (1969). The principle proposes that people express their
interpersonal styles in the form of reflexes, which have the effect of inviting or
initiating complementary responses in others, which has the effect of
reinforcing the original reflex action. This will be discussed further in relation
to interpersonal psychotherapy (later in this chapter) and interrelating
(Chapter 7).

The interpersonal octagon

The theory upon which this book is based resembles classical interpersonal
theory, but differs from it in a number of important respects (Birtchnell,
1993/1996, 1994). Classical interpersonal theory is not set within an evolutionary context and does not establish continuities with the relating of
animals. It is not couched in terms of relating objectives that carry advantages for the organism. Instead, Leary (1957) viewed relating strategies as a
means of allaying anxiety. It is not concerned with sources, stores or the
acquisition of competencies, or with the possible mental mechanisms by
which the attainment of relational needs is regulated. It does not adequately
distinguish between relating and being related to. It makes no rational distinction between positive and negative relating; instead, Leary (1957) considered all maladaptive relating to be simply an extreme version of adaptive
relating. While, within the present theory, the exaggerated normal response is
included as a possible category of negative relating, it is only one of a number
of categories, and it does not account for most examples of negative relating.

The present theory is concerned with axes rather than dimensions. Dimensions carry the implication of bipolarity, and axes do not. This is a complex
issue that cannot adequately be discussed here. Suffice it to say that naming
the horizontal axis "love versus hate" creates an unnecessary and unhelpful
bipolarity, because love is a positive attribute and hate is a negative one. The
two axes in the present theory, like the dimensions of classical interpersonal
theory, are orthogonal, but the names of the axes are not the same as the
names of the Leary dimensions. They are neutral words that can be expressed
either positively or negatively, and they are generic words that were selected in
order that they should cover the entire range of relating attributes that can be
subsumed by them. In the interpersonal circle the names of the dimensions
are anything but neutral and are far too specific. A central principle of the
present theory, in keeping with its basis in evolution, is that no position can
be regarded as either better or worse than any other. If we have arrived at
these objectives through the process of evolution, then each must carry
similar advantages for the individual.

The horizontal axis, called the *proximity axis*, is concerned with the extent to which an individual seeks to become either closely involved with others or separate from them. Closeness, which has been used throughout this chapter as an example of a relating objective, is located at the left extremity of the axis. The opposite objective, called *distance*, is located at the right extremity. The characteristics of closeness have been alluded to in various places in the chapter. Distance is concerned with escape from danger, exploration, creating and maintaining secure boundaries and a separate identity, the establishment and maintenance of personal space and privacy, having a mind of and place of one's own and being original and creative. The proximity axis will be the subject of Chapters 3 and 4.

The vertical axis, called the *power axis*, is concerned with the extent to which the individual may seek to become either the one who exercises power within a relationship or the one upon whom such power is exercised. The upper extremity of this axis is called *upperness* and the lower extremity is called *lowerness*. In animals, the vertical axis is concerned with issues of domination and submission, the names ascribed to it by classical interpersonal psychology. In humans, it is much more to do with interdependence. People who have power use their power for the benefit of others. Upper people assume responsibility for, set example for, lead, guide, teach, advise, support, protect, encourage, help and care for others; and lower people look up to, admire, trust, respect, obey, rely and depend upon, seek help and guidance from and feel comforted by others. Lowerness is the predominant position of the client in psychotherapy. The vertical axis will be the subject of Chapters 5 and 6.

The system allows for intermediate positions, which are called upper distant, upper close, lower distant and lower close, and the characteristics of the intermediate positions are a blending of the characteristics of the positions on either side of them. Upper distant is organizing, directing and controlling, and upper close is providing care, encouragement and protection. Lower distant is respecting, obeying and accepting direction, and lower close is depending upon and accepting care and approval. The four main positions and the four intermediate positions together form an octagon (Figure 1), which is called the *interpersonal octagon* in order to distinguish it from the interpersonal circle. There are both positive and negative forms of relating within each position (Birtchnell, 1993/1996, 1994). They are summarized in Figure 2 and will be described in Chapters 3 and 5.

Initially, because the terms of both the horizontal and the vertical axes refer to positions in space, the theory was called *spatial theory*, but this is not to say that it is concerned, in any concrete sense, with issues of space. The terms are used almost entirely in a metaphorical sense. It does appear to be the case, however, that people do conceptualize their relations with others within a spatial imagery, and perhaps even visualize such reactions in this simple and primitive way. We speak of a person as being "close" when we mean concerned and involved and of being "distant" when we mean

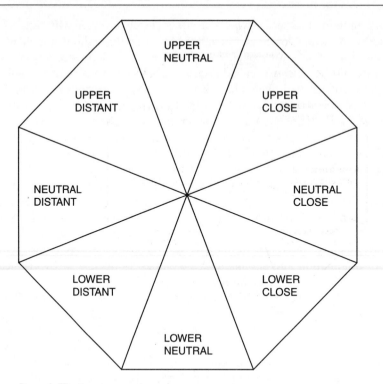

Figure 1 The interpersonal octagon.

Source: John Birtchnell, *How Humans Relate: A New Interpersonal Theory* (Westport, CT: Praeger Publishers, 1993). Copyright © 1993 by John Birtchnell. Reproduced with permission of Greenwood Publishing Group, Inc., Westport, CT.

unconcerned and uninvolved. We also urge people not to get too close and to keep their distance. We speak of looking up to someone when we mean being admiring of and respectful toward and of looking down upon someone when we mean disapproving of and feeling sorry for. We also invite people to come down to our level or to help us up. Since the term "spatial" does not sound as though it refers to relating, in this book the theory has been renamed *relating theory*.

Relating and interrelating in psychotherapy

In psychotherapy, therapists and clients meet regularly and talk together. Different therapists relate to their clients in different ways, and different clients relate to their therapists in different ways. Because of the theoretical orientation of this book, particular emphasis will be placed upon the more interpersonal forms of psychotherapy; but in order to take account of the different ways that therapists relate, reference will be made to a wide range of

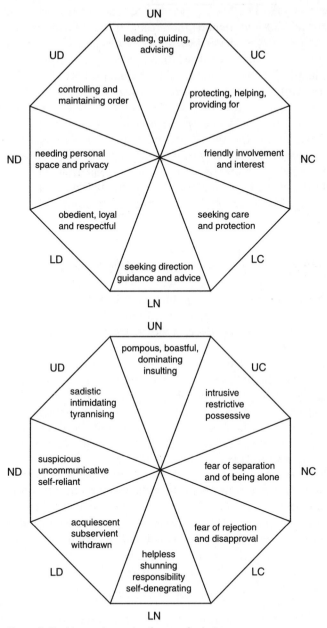

Figure 2 Positive and negative forms of relating.

The upper diagram gives examples of positive forms of relating for each of the octants; the lower diagram gives examples of negative forms of relating. The pairs of initial letters are abbreviations for the full names of the octants given in Figure 1.

Source: John Birtchnell, The interpersonal octagon: An alternative to the interpersonal circle. *Human Relations,* 47, pp. 518, 524. Copyright © The Tavistock Institute, 1994. Reproduced with permission.

psychotherapeutic styles. The book is written around three basic assumptions: (1) the interrelationship between therapist and client forms an important feature of the psychotherapeutic process; (2) the negative relating of the client toward others and of others toward the client are the predominant sources of the client's difficulties; and (3) the principal objectives of therapy are to enable the client (a) to become more clearly aware of the nature of the relating behavior of her/himself toward others and of others toward her/himself and (b) to modify such behaviors as are causing her/him difficulties. From an early stage in therapy, the client's relating deficiencies will become apparent to the therapist. In one way or another, depending upon the therapist's style of working, the endeavors of therapist and client will be directed toward assisting the client to make good these deficiencies. In terms of the present theory, this will involve improving the client's relating competencies, in order that her/his negative relating tendencies will be minimized and her/his positive relating tendencies will be maximized.

From an early stage in therapy, it will also become apparent that the client's difficulties are, in part at least, a consequence of the way that certain significant others either have related to her/him in the past or are relating to her/him in the present. Such relating may have influenced, or may presently be influencing, the client's relating tendencies. A certain other, for example, may have been, or may presently be, so dictatorial that the client is unduly meek and apologetic. Behavioral and cognitive therapists pay minimal attention to the effect of the present or past relating of others, but an important feature of the form of interpersonal therapy described here, and of a number of other forms of psychotherapy, is the opportunity it affords the client, first, to acknowledge that s/he has been, or continues to be, the recipient of such behavior; second, to express her/his reaction to this; and, third, to find ways to come to terms with it. If it is an experience from the past, many months of therapy may be required to free the client from its effects. If it is something that is presently happening, attention will need to be directed either toward influencing the other to change this behavior or to enabling the client to cope with it or escape from it.

In terms of the present theory, and certainly also in terms of psychoanalytic theory, what happens between client and therapist is considered almost as important as the relationship issues talked about by therapist and client. In order to acquire the competence to relate positively, people need to have been exposed to the positive relating of others, to discover how satisfying this can be and to be encouraged to relate positively themselves. Although it is acknowledged that therapists may sometimes relate to their clients in negative ways, it is likely that they relate positively for much of the time. They thus provide the exposure to positive relating that many of their clients have lacked.

When people relate negatively they tend to evoke negative responses in those to whom they relate. For example, a person who clings excessively will induce the other to pull away. The effect of this response is to reinforce the original negative relating. Negatively relating clients have gone through this cycle of reinforcement many times. By declining to respond negatively to the client's negative relating and instead responding positively, the therapist can, over time, inhibit the client's negative relating and reinforce her/his positive relating.

Existing forms of interpersonal psychotherapy

Although all those who call themselves interpersonal psychotherapists would claim to have been influenced by the writing of Sullivan, the range of therapies now included under this heading is confusingly diverse (Anchin & Kiesler, 1982). The approach most directly linked with Sullivan is one that remains firmly based in the psychoanalytic tradition. Mitchell (1986) explained that Sullivan was influenced by those American pragmatic philosophers who had turned their back upon the intangible abstractions of European metaphysics. Consequently he became disenchanted by Freud's preoccupation with unseen, intrapsychic processes and developed a form of psychoanalysis that placed greater emphasis upon the client's observable relationships.

For Sullivan, psychotherapy consisted of an individual employing an expert to assist in understanding and correcting problematic interpersonal patterns. He envisaged the therapeutic alliance as therapist and client working collaboratively together. Unlike Freud, he favored the give and take of human dialogue, and he insisted upon the use of common language. Evans (1996) considered Sullivan to be the first psychodynamic psychotherapist to declare specifically interpersonal learning as the goal of treatment. Sullivan's approach incorporated elements of what today might be called social learning, behavioral and cognitive therapy.

He used open-ended questions to lead the clients to reveal their perceptions of themselves and others, to understand how they came to these perceptions and to safely expose the inappropriate and ineffective aspects of these perceptions. For him, psychotherapy involved correcting rigidities in the self system, by making sense of actual interpersonal experience and subtly teaching more effective forms of relating. He believed in tailoring the intervention to fit the problem (Evans, 1996).

That form of interpersonal psychotherapy developed over a 25-year period by Klerman and associates (1984) carries the pragmatic approach even further. It comprises sixteen 50-minute weekly sessions and is aimed specifically at the removal of depressive symptoms. Therapists adhere closely to the directives laid down in a treatment manual and are strictly supervised. Throughout therapy they are required to stress to the clients the connection between their depressive symptoms and their current interpersonal relationships, and they aim to remove the symptoms by improving these relationships. They focus upon one or more of four designated problem areas: grief, interpersonal disputes, role transitions and interpersonal deficits. Therapists are instructed not to frame the client's current situation as a manifestation of internal conflict or as a recurrence of prior intrafamilial maladaptive patterns and are advised to avoid any considerations of transference or countertransference (see Chapter 4).

Kiesler (1986) described a form of interpersonal psychotherapy much more closely related to classical interpersonal psychology. In this the therapist deliberately introduces an *anticomplementary* response as a means of breaking the cycle of reinforcement. Benjamin (1987a) described a similar approach involving the prescription of what she called *antithetical* and *antidotal* responses, which are aimed at provoking behavior that is opposite to that being exhibited. Although he did not have access to the two dimensions of classical interpersonal theory, Sullivan (1954) adopted methods that could render inoperative clients' projections and expectations, but he was less confrontational than Kiesler. By subtly challenging the client's expectational set he enabled the client to reappraise her/his present relating behavior and develop behavior that was more effective. Havens (1986), discussing Sullivan's therapeutic technique, coined the term *counterassumptive* to refer to statements made by the therapist to unsettle the assumptions that clients appeared to hold about themselves and others.

Benjamin's (1987b) approach came much closer to Sullivan's than did Kiesler's. She acknowledged that treatment was a slow process involving collaboration between therapist and client. The client, she believed, needs to recognize her/his maladaptive interactive patterns and discover how s/he learned them. She considered that the therapist should help the client decide whether s/he wants to give up her/his old patterns and support her/him during the long and painful process of change.

Psychotherapy based upon relating theory

In Chapters 4 and 6 the therapeutic considerations and strategies appropriate to horizontal and vertical relating respectively are described. Here it is necessary only to discuss in general terms the way that relating concepts can usefully influence the thoughts and actions of therapist and client. First it should be stressed that relating terms are simply *directional*. As such they may be applied to acts of relating of any person, over any time period, extending from a momentary gesture to a lifetime disposition.

The discourse that takes place between therapist and client inevitably involves clients recounting how they have related to and do relate to others and how others have related to and do relate to them, at various times and in various situations. Such relating may seem to the therapist to have been appropriate or inappropriate, competent or incompetent, constructive or destructive, and the therapist may respond to what has been said in ways that may imply shock, horror, sympathy, delight and so forth. The therapist who is familiar with relating concepts will be thinking in terms of such concepts and will automatically be allocating attitudes and actions to various positions within the octagon, though in making responses to clients' accounts s/he may not adopt such relating terminology.

A person who is competent in the entire range of relating styles (i.e., all eight positions of the octagon) is capable of adopting the style appropriate to the situation s/he happens to be in. Sometimes it is appropriate to be close, sometimes distant, sometimes upper and sometimes lower. The person who can adapt in this way is described as being *versatile*. In listening to a client's account the therapist is able to observe how versatile the client and those who relate to her/him are capable of being, for it is a feature of the relating approach to therapy that clients' difficulties are not necessarily considered to be consequences of their own relating inadequacies. A person may be observed to avoid or to be insecure in certain styles of relating or to relate in certain directions in a disrespectful way; or s/he may be observed to be the victim of the avoidant, insecure or disrespectful relating of another or others. The therapy will involve drawing attention to the relating inadequacies of clients or others and helping clients either to improve their own relating incompetencies or to respond adaptively to the relating incompetencies of others.

People acquire competence in each of the four ways of relating by repeatedly (1) being exposed to positive experiences of them by parents and other important figures, (2) being encouraged to try each of them in a variety of situations, (3) being praised and congratulated by parents and others whenever one of them is successfully accomplished, (4) practicing each of them under a range of circumstances, (5) being consoled and reassured by supportive parents and others when an attempt at any one of them has not been successful and being encouraged to try again, (6) coming to feel safe in each one of them, (7) coming to feel confident and having a sense of mastery in each one of them, (8) indulging freely in each one of them, (9) experiencing the pleasures associated with the successful accomplishment of and free indulgence in each of them and (10) reaching a stage when they are performed quite naturally, automatically and appropriately without any thought or effort. When a client appears to be deficient in any one of them, this deficiency is made good by therapist and client working together through these ten stages.

A theme that underlies many forms of classical interpersonal theory is that because some people relate excessively in one particular direction, therapy should be directed toward reducing this excess by the therapist making anti-complementary responses to the behavioral excesses. Relating theory would acknowledge that some people do appear to relate excessively in one direction but would explain this in terms of a lack of versatility. Because they lack the competence to relate in certain directions, clients restrict their behavior to those directions in which they are competent. Therapy would be directed toward exploring the origins of such lack of competence and attempting to build up this competence. An important difference between relating theory and classical interpersonal theory is that, in relating theory, a clear distinction is drawn between positive and negative relating. There are positive and negative forms of each of the four main relating positions, and therapy is directed toward encouraging and reinforcing positive forms and discouraging and eliminating negative forms.

It should be mentioned parenthetically here that there may be such a thing as a *disposition* to relate in a particular direction, which could be both positive and negative. Allied to this is the idea that the distinction between positive and negative relating in a particular direction is not always as clear-cut as the theory might suggest. Although the point stands that excessive relating in a particular direction is usually a sign of a lack of versatility, there may also be a dispositional element involved. It might also be said that people are often able to turn a tendency to relate in a particular way to good use. For example, people who are distant, for whatever reason, are able to work for long periods on their own. The therapist might respect this and even encourage clients to do it.

Incompetent relating is made up of various forms of negative relating, and the assumption is that such incompetent relating is a consequence of exposure to the relating incompetencies of others, in either the early environment or the current environment. For example, a person may grow up afraid of getting close to others because, in childhood, a particular parent was always being suffocating and intrusive. (This would be an example of negative, upper closeness.) The therapist tries to make the nature of this experience clearer to the client and to compensate for it by exposing the client to a more respectful form of closeness.

During the course of a normal conversation, the relating of two versatile people will shift around the octagon, each one sometimes being close and sometimes being distant, sometimes being upper and sometimes being lower. Within a therapy session such shifting around is limited by (1) the structure of the situation, the therapist normally tending to be upper close and the client normally tending to be lower close, and (2) the restricted range of relating competencies of the client. Providing that the roles of therapist and client are not too rigidly imposed, the therapy session can afford the therapist the opportunity to both observe and experience (by being related to) the client's repertoire of relating behaviors and subsequently to devise strategies for modifying and extending it.

A client may, for example, try to reverse the normal interaction of upper close therapist to lower close client and try to ease or urge the therapist toward a lower close position by repeatedly enquiring after her/his welfare and making encouraging, reassuring or consoling remarks. The therapist may tactfully point out what the client is doing and (unlike in the classical interpersonal approach) enquire why s/he has such a need and where the need may have come from. It is possible, for example, that the client had been coerced into behaving in such a way by a parent who had always wanted to be parented. The therapist might then seek a way of freeing the client from this compulsion and enable her/him sometimes to allow her/himself to be parented.

Summary

The book is based upon the assumption that the behavior of all living organisms is purposeful because they have evolved to be purposeful. By far the greater part of the purposeful behavior of humans is relating. Since relating is purposeful, there must be relating objectives, which have been defined as closeness, distance, upperness and lowerness. People need to become competent in relating in each of these directions. Competent relating is called positive, and relating that falls short of competent is called negative. Besides relating to others, people are related to by others, who are seeking to attain their own relating objectives. When people relate to each other it is called interrelating. The two broad aims of psychotherapy are to help people shift from the more incompetent forms of negative relating to the more competent forms of positive relating and to resist yielding to the less competent negative relating of others.

Chapter 2

The inner brain and the outer brain

While describing the mental processes involved in social exchange theory (Thibaut & Kelley, 1959), a theory that shares certain features with the present theory of relating (see Chapter 7), Frude (1991) observed that the choice between alternative actions depends upon estimates of the probabilities of possible outcomes and that people often are unaware of the elements involved in making their decisions. They sum up complex situations "implicitly" rather than by systematically working through a series of calculations, just as when catching a ball they do not explicitly work out the complex mathematics of the trajectory. When Frude says that people are "unaware of the elements involved", he really means that these elements are not brought into consciousness when the decision about what to do and how to act is made; but since the decision does get made, some part of the brain must have been aware of them, and the decision cannot have been made without taking them into account. What exactly do Frude's terms "implicitly" and "explicitly" mean? Whether Frude realizes it or not, they must be alluding to the level of the brain at which the summing up of the complex situations is made; implicit being at a lower (non-conscious) level and explicit being at a higher (conscious) level.

As Mary Drower, a character in Agatha Christie's (1936) *The A.B.C. Murders*, said, "Your mind gets made up for you sometimes without your knowing how it happened" (p. 103); so there has, for some time, been an understanding by some people that there is a part of the brain that has a way of working things out without any conscious involvement. Whyte (1978) observed that, by the middle of the nineteenth century, psychologists were beginning to think in terms of mental processes that occurred outside of our awareness and cited Maudsley (1867) as saying that the most important part of mental action, the essential process on which thinking depends, is unconscious mental activity. One might question the word "thinking" here, for there is the well-known phrase *to do it without thinking*, which implies that some process other than thinking is involved when the decision to act in a particular way is made.

We may find it hard to accept that decisions get made by something inside us, but this should not surprise us when we consider the many processes that go on within our bodies that we are not aware of. Food gets digested, energy stores get laid down and drawn upon, invading organisms get attacked and put out of action, wounds heal, and waste products get eliminated. The endocrine system and the autonomic nervous system function without our being aware of them.

In Chapter 1, it is observed that wrapped around the palaeomammalian brain is a more recent development (in terms of evolution) called the neo-mammalian brain (MacLean, 1973). Its salient functions are self-awareness, the use of words, the capacity to observe and comment on our behavior and the ability to think things out by conscious steps. If MacLean is right, there must have been a stage in the course of evolution when there was no neomammalian brain and animals managed without one. Even now, the palaeomammalian brain probably controls most of what most animals do.

Consciously thinking out the steps in a decision-making process and using words with which to do so is a slow and laborious process. Without the intermediaries of consciousness and words, the palaeomammalian brain functions more quickly, and in the wild, where speed of action is essential, this is an advantage. Many movements, or sequences of movements, are carried out more efficiently without conscious intervention. Hence the joke that the centipede would never move at all if it had to think out which step each leg had to take.

What then is the use of the neomammalian brain? With consciousness, or self-awareness, we take an objective view of what we are doing and watch ourselves in action. With words, we give names to the components of the decision-making process and, with suitable grammar, we construct sentences that describe sequences of events. With the neomammalian brain we look back at those things we have done automatically and try to make sense of them.

The palaeomammalian brain is good at following well-established routines, but it runs into difficulties when it encounters unfamiliar situations. Then, it can only pursue the routines that normally would work. Making comparisons to computers enables us to understand more clearly how brains might work and clarifies for us the difference between the functions of the palaeomammalian brain and the neomammalian brain. The palaeomammalian brain, being quick and efficient, but totally unoriginal, works like a computer. In earlier evolved animals, this probably is the sum total of the brain's activities. In later evolved ones capable of adapting to changing circumstances and modifying their behavior to account for new information, something akin to rewriting old computer programs must take place. This is what the neomammalian brain appears to do. It notices when the standard routines of the palaeomammalian brain are no longer helpful to us and "writes new programs" that enable it to update these routines.

Automatic responses and actions

Certain movements, like the blinking of the eyes, can be performed either by conscious decision or automatically. The automatic movement is referred to as *reflex action*. It is brought into play when speed of response is essential. When a plate feels slightly hot, we have the option of deciding whether or not to move our hand away, but when it is extremely hot, we find our hand has moved away without our making a conscious decision. In fact, it was observed by Gray, at the Institute of Psychiatry, that the hand has moved away fractionally before the sensation of pain is registered in consciousness (as reported on a television program). Taking a more complicated situation, when an object is moving slowly toward us, we have the option of deciding whether to move out of its way, but when it comes at us quickly and unexpectedly, we find our whole body has jumped out of the way, without our thinking about it.

Such automatic responses are probably innate, but other rapid patterns of behaviour are initially worked out at a conscious level and later, after repeated practice, become automatic. A good example are the complex routines of acrobats, gymnasts and high-board divers. They are carried out at such speed that there is no time to consciously think out each separate step. Craftsmen and professional musicians perform best when they are so relaxed that they pay no attention to what they are doing. In the course of their training, they had, repeatedly and tediously, to learn the complicated steps that have become second nature to them.

Automatic responses do not have to be quick. We are not normally aware that, when we walk into a dark but familiar room, one of our arms has reached out to exactly the right spot on the wall to switch on the electric light. If the switch is moved, even by ourselves, every time we walk into the room for days or weeks afterwards our arm reaches out to the wrong spot on the wall. Most actions or sequences of actions that are carried out repeatedly and routinely become automatic in this way; sometimes this is referred to as *going on automatic pilot*. People in factories or typists who do repetitive and complicated tasks work while listening to music or talking to their neighbors. The automobile driver takes note of the changing traffic conditions ahead of and behind her/him and makes decisions and takes action to adjust to them. S/he does all this while listening to music and talking to a passenger. It is not uncommon for a driver on a familiar journey to cover long distances, making all the right decisions and taking all the right actions, without being aware of the places s/he has driven through.

The inner and the outer brain

The kinds of automatic behavior described here might not be considered by MacLean to fall within the range of activity ascribed to the palaeomammalian brain. Because further reference will be made to mental mechanisms assumed to take place at different levels of the brain and because these will be equally difficult to fit into MacLean's anatomical divisions, it might be wiser, rather than taking further liberties with MacLean's nomenclature, to simply refer to two layers of the brain, called the *inner brain* and the *outer brain*. In the earlier book (Birtchnell, 1993/1996), the terms *subcortex* and *cortex* were used for this distinction. Further reason for breaking away from MacLean's terminology is the fact that, in the sections that follow, that which will be called the inner brain is capable of being extremely sophisticated, which does not fit well with the idea that it represents a primitive region of the brain.

The distinction between the inner and the outer brain seems to fall midway between the anatomical distinction between the palaeomammalian brain and the neomammalian brain and the psychoanalytic distinction between the unconscious and the conscious. Unlike the palaeomammalian and the neomammalian brain, the inner and the outer brain are not to date demonstrable regions of the brain, nor are they, like the unconscious and the conscious, strictly metaphorical concepts. The distinction draws upon both the anatomical and the metaphorical and represents a compromise that has advantages over both. It is more anatomical than the psychoanalytic system and more metaphorical than the MacLean system. Although no attempt has been made to locate the inner brain, it may, in time, be possible to do so, for its functions are probably carried out by such structures as the thalamus, hypothalamus, hippocampus and amygdala (LeDoux, 1989). The same applies to the outer brain, the functions of which are probably carried out by the frontal cortex (Pinker, 1997).

In psychoanalysis, the conscious and the unconscious are called components of the mind. Here the components are called components of the brain. The word "brain" is used partly because it is considered that somewhere there must be anatomical structures that perform the functions ascribed to these places; partly to emphasize that the brain is an organ, like all other organs, that has structures that perform functions; and partly to maintain a continuity between the brain of humans and the brain of other animals. The proposals made here, concerning the possible functions of the inner and the outer brain, are based not upon neurological research but upon observing human behavior and trying to set down a theoretical framework within which to explain it.

A point that cannot be emphasized too strongly is that the inner brain must be responsible for far more of our mental activity than we are normally prepared to admit. Since we have no conscious awareness of what goes on within it, this is a sobering thought. Groddeck (1923) is one of the few writers to have expressed things in this way. He held the view that we are animated by "some wondrous force" that directs both what we do and what happens to us. This force he called the "Es" or the "It", and he proposed the principle that we are lived by the "It". That which we would normally refer to as "we" is a self-awareness, which feels as though it is located in that which will be called the outer brain. "It" looks on while the inner brain gets on with what must be done.

Some people feel easier than others about giving the inner brain free rein. Harold Pinter has said that it feels as though his plays write themselves, and he is happy to let this happen. Artists like Picasso and Matisse were known to work quickly and unthinkingly, allowing their pictures to materialize before them. Even though their pictures are not strictly representational, they some-how feel right; in fact, they feel more right than if they had been represen-tational. In such activity, the outer brain seems to be totally outclassed by the more spontaneous inner brain. The outer brain depicts only what it logically knows to be so, whereas the inner brain depicts what feels right to it. Some composers have felt as though their hands have been guided by an external force, which some have called God.

In much everyday activity, perhaps because we have been through it so many times before, we cruise along on automatic pilot, walking familiar routes, working through familiar sequences of actions, saying familiar things and thinking familiar thoughts. Often, when people speak to us, we find that the inner brain has answered for us, and usually quite appropriately. It seems possible to conduct entire conversations on automatic pilot, though when we do this, the outer brain is not entirely idle. It seems to have foreknowledge of what we are about to say and has the power to stop us in our tracks or to modify the way we speak, if it thinks our speech is not going to be to our advantage.

The relationship between the inner and the outer brain

The idea of the inner and the outer brain grew out of a need to understand the monitoring of relating objectives. Simpler animals attain their objectives through precise, but rigid, behavioral sequences. Humans have less precise relating objectives, and by means of the outer brain they generate routes by which these objectives can be attained. During the early years, the outer brain works hard, mapping out routes, which in later years get passed down to the inner brain for automatic control. The young brain is well adapted to this task, for children learn quickly and effortlessly. They learn languages at astonishing speed (Pinker, 1995), but once the languages are learned they get taken over by the inner brain. In new situations, humans tire easily because every new step has to be laboriously worked out and assimilated. With advancing years, the outer brain loses its capacity for adaptation; as the saying goes, it is hard for an old dog to learn new tricks.

This having been said, it may seem contradictory to suggest that only the inner brain is fully aware of our relating objectives, because only it can moni-tor our successes and failures in meeting them. It generates "reward" emo-tions when we are on course and "punishing" emotions when we are off course. Somehow, the inner brain conveys to the outer brain where we are supposed to be going, so that the outer brain can work out routes for getting there.

Deviating for a moment to non-relating objectives, when we touch something hot, it is the inner brain that has moved our hand away even before we have experienced the sensation of hotness. Besides this, there are autonomic responses to hotness, like sweating, which cools us down, without any conscious intervention. The outer brain has other ways of regulating temperature that are not available to the inner brain. These include deciding to dress in warmer or cooler clothes, or to turn on the central heating or the air conditioning. The inner brain is capable of comprehending and assuming these activities, for sometimes we will automatically take off or put on a jumper or switch on the central heating or the air conditioning.

Although the outer brain is aware of the existence of the inner brain, the inner brain often behaves as though it is unaware of the existence of the outer brain. Because the inner and the outer brains appear to have evolved independently, it is as though they sometimes vie with each other to do the same thing. One of the functions of the outer brain appears to be to observe and correct some of the errors that the inner brain makes. When external circumstances change, so that a discrepancy arises between outer reality and the internal representation of it, it is the outer brain that perceives this discrepancy and instigates changes for rectifying it in our internal (inner brain) representations.

The inner brain is fast, and the outer brain is slow

The inner brain works best in situations where immediate decisions and immediate actions are needed. When a vehicle is approaching swiftly, the inner brain immediately perceives the danger and causes the person to jump out of the way. When s/he is safely out of danger, the outer brain reflects upon what exactly happened and realizes what a near thing it was. When learned actions, learned skills, even learned languages, are passed down for the inner brain to take over, time is saved. The individual no longer has to think about what to do. The action is immediate. The inner brain sometimes has to sum up complex situations and decide upon courses of action, but the point to be stressed is that it does these things extremely quickly–in a flash, in fact. Even though the inner brain takes over many language functions, many of its decisions seem to be made without the intervention of language. It seems able to short-circuit language.

The show of emotion is the most obvious demonstration of the inner brain in action and of the speed with which it acts. The moment some success becomes apparent, joy is experienced; the moment some setback becomes apparent, despair is experienced; the moment something frightening becomes apparent, fear is experienced; and the moment something sexually exciting becomes apparent, sexual excitement is experienced. The person does not think her/himself into experiencing these emotions; s/he just finds her/himself experiencing them. There is no linguistic sequence such as, "I really wanted to pass that examination and now I have. That's good, so I shall feel happy".

After the spontaneous act has taken place or the emotion has been experienced, the outer brain comes lumbering on behind, late on the scene. So what does it do that the inner brain cannot do? What it does is of immense importance, but it does not need to be fast to do it. In fact, what it does, it needs to do slowly. It can take apart past actions bit by bit and try to make sense of them. It can mull things over and speculate about the future. It can think out new ways of doing things and ways of circumventing difficulties.

What we like and what we think we ought to like

Only the inner brain can tell us what we like. In terms of relating, we like anything that brings us closer to a desired state of relatedness, and the inner brain is specialized in being able to determine this. Once it has done so, it generates an emotional response of pleasure or displeasure that communicates to us whether we have "scored a hit or a miss." The inner brain can surprise us by being indifferent to or displeased by something we (i.e., the outer brain) thought we liked, or being pleased by something we (i.e., the outer brain) thought we were indifferent to or did not like. Because it is the inner brain that controls our emotional responses, it must always be right. Sometimes the outer brain tries to make out that we like something that the inner brain knows that we do not like, but it always fails.

The head versus the heart

When we draw a distinction between the heart and the head, we are drawing a distinction between decisions arising from the inner brain and those arising from the outer brain. The heart urges us to go the way of our passions, but the head tells us to be sensible. Sometimes following our passions can prove right, like marrying someone who thrills and excites us; but sometimes it can prove wrong, as when the person who thrills and excites us turns out to be hopelessly impractical. The distinction between responding to the heart and responding to the head is similar to that between intuition and thinking. One of the functions of the outer brain seems to be exercising restraint upon the more impulsive inner brain. The well-balanced person will draw equally upon the inner and the outer brain, but there are those who go to extremes, drawing predominantly upon either the inner brain, like Jung's (1921) *intuitive type*, or the outer brain, like his *thinking type*.

The inner brain

The inner brain could be described as the human core. Only the inner brain knows where we are going. Without the inner brain we would have no sense of direction. While the inner brain could function without the outer brain, the outer brain could not function without the inner brain. An analogy might be drawn between the horse (the inner brain) and the rider (the outer brain), but in this instance, it is the horse that knows the way. That which we call "we," that part of us that is self-conscious, can only watch the inner brain in action and learn about it. It can, however, exert some control over it.

The inner brain and particular capabilities

Certain people with degrees of mental handicap are capable of the most extraordinary feats of memory or calculation. They are called *autistic savants*. One, after only a brief sighting, could draw the complex architectural details of a public building; another, after only a single hearing, could play a long piece of classical music; a third could multiply very large numbers, instantly and correctly; and a fourth, again instantly and correctly, could name the day of the week of any date in history. These people never learned these skills; they just discovered that they had them. They cannot say how they do these things, but the speed with which they do them suggests that they are the work of the inner brain, which illustrates the astonishing potential of the inner brain. Does it, like a computer, simply take the normal steps of calculating much more quickly, or has it got a way of by-passing these normal steps? That which is sometimes called intuition has much in common with the incredible feats of idiots savants. When people come to a conclusion intuitively they appear to have raced through, or even bypassed, the normal stages of deduction (see Claxton, 1998).

The inner brain knows what it wants

The inner brain has a much clearer idea of what it wants and where it is going than the outer brain has. The inner brain works out all the priorities and makes all the decisions about how we should act, long before the outer brain is aware of what is happening. A normally restrained woman was talking to her husband in the bathroom and noticed him washing sand from between his toes. In the ensuing conversation it emerged that he had spent the day on the beach with another woman. In an instant, she had beaten him across the head and sent him tumbling down the stairs. She was quite taken aback by what she had done and realized that she could have killed him. Her action was an inner brain response. Her horror at what she had done and the realization of what she might have done was an outer brain response.

The self is very much concerned with the uniqueness of the individual, and that is about personal tastes and personal values. The inner brain knows what it wants and what it likes because the relating objectives are located within it, and its main function is to precisely monitor whether what we are experiencing corresponds with one of the four sought-after states of relatedness (Chapter 1). It has found its own sources of and routes to these states of relatedness; and by accumulating a whole range of sources and routes, the innate, general tendencies within the inner brain become personalized.

The inner brain is entirely responsible for determining when we will and will not become emotional and which form of emotion, and how much, we feel. When we experience something which the inner brain decides is pleasant, we find ourselves feeling pleasure. When we experience something it decides is unpleasant, we find ourselves feeling displeasure. Sometimes, particular emotional responses give rise to facial or bodily gestures. These gestures just happen; we have no control over them, and we cannot consciously make them. This is referred to as *body language*. Such body language reveals our true feelings and, because we cannot conceal them, this sometimes gives us away. Sexual arousal also arises within the inner brain. We cannot make ourselves be sexually aroused by someone who does not turn us on, and it is the inner brain that determines whether or not a particular person does turn us on. As Freud once said, "The penis does not lie." All these things add up to one simple principle: The inner brain knows what it wants and knows when it has got what it wants. It also knows what it does not want and when it has got what it does not want.

The discriminatory capacity of the inner brain

The inner brain has to be capable of drawing subtle distinctions and making complex decisions. Take, for example, its management of the need for closeness. It has to have a clear understanding of what is and is not closeness and of whether some other person is or is not being close. It needs this understanding in order to generate the sensation of pleasure if closeness is attained or displeasure if it is lost. Thus, it has to be capable of interpreting the significance of certain actions and the meaning of certain remarks. It has to be able to determine when someone is being genuine and to pick up some small, subtle cue that might indicate that that person intends to be close (giving rise to pleasure) or to pull away (giving rise to displeasure). It seems to be more difficult to deceive the inner brain than to deceive the outer brain. When a young wife is feeling depressed, her outer brain may be telling her that her husband cares for her because he works long hours to earn money to provide for her and that she wants for nothing, but her inner brain is registering that there is no love coming through from him to her and consequently it is causing her to feel depressed.

The inner brain and concept formation

A concept catches the very essence of a range of different ideas or experiences. Somehow, the inner brain must be capable of grasping that which many related ideas have in common and generating a concept that holds them all together. This already has been referred to in terms of relating, that is, the inner brain needs to be able to recognize what is and what is not closeness, but it also needs to formulate concepts that are linked with closeness like compatibility, sympathy or jealousy. Since it is the outer brain that has to make sense of new situations, these concepts must first be learned by the outer brain and passed down to the inner brain; or is concept formation another of those high-speed, intuitive skills that the inner brain possesses?

Making meaningful connections

Another remarkable feature of the inner brain is its capacity for spontaneously linking together related ideas and bringing them into consciousness. The process described here happens without the person making any conscious decision. By this process, a memory that is meaningfully connected with an idea with which the person is presently preoccupied simply enters consciousness. This process occurs many times a day, and most people pay little attention to it. The more one becomes aware of it as a possibility, the more one begins to notice it and the more amazing it seems. The connections can be recollections of relevant people or experiences, phrases and quotations and, perhaps most striking of all, the words of a popular song, which are always astonishingly appropriate. They can be concepts, analogies or metaphors. This is not quite the same as what is normally meant by *free association*, the strategy, sometimes adopted by psychoanalysts, of inviting the client to make a conscious decision to draw upon this capacity, to see what connections the inner brain makes with an idea that is causing problems. The inner brain must have a "filing system" from which it selects connections that correspond amazingly well with the person's present preoccupations. The connections need to be precise, for if they were not, the outer brain would become so cluttered up with them that they would impair our ability to think constructively. In some states of mania the precision of the selecting process becomes so relaxed that this impairment happens.

The inner brain and memory

The inner brain then is capable of bringing memories into consciousness, unaided by the outer brain, if prompted by current circumstances that are in some way linked with them. The outer brain has largely to rely upon the inner brain for the recollection of words. Say the outer brain wishes to remember a word that has a particular meaning. It passes on to the inner brain as much information as it can about the meaning, and then it waits. After a short delay, the word pops into consciousness. The outer brain has no idea what steps the inner brain took to find the sought-after word. This process is not so amazing now that we have computers that can perform similar tasks. We now know that, in a computer, vast amounts of data can be stored in a very small space and that selected items of data can be accessed with astonishing speed. Nevertheless, it is impressive that the inner brain can perform tasks of this kind at the bidding of the outer brain. Although the inner and the outer brain are separate structures, for this kind of intercommunication to take place, a degree of integration must have evolved between them.

The outer brain must have a memory of sorts. It needs to remember that particular places, persons or ideas exist to be able to ask the inner brain to come up with the name of a certain place, person or idea. Since a name sometimes takes several days to come up, the outer brain needs to be able to remember that it is waiting for a name.

Memories can sometimes reveal what the inner brain truly likes and dislikes. When a certain memory comes to mind, we find ourselves unexpectedly feeling happy. At the time of the original experience we did not realize how much we liked it. Feeling happy when we remember a certain person may be our first realization that we really like, or love, that person.

The alerting function of the inner brain

When a person has an emotional experience, the characteristics of it are linked with the emotion, so that when these characteristics are re-encountered, the emotion of the experience is released. This alerts us that something good or bad may be about to happen. If a person skids on a stretch of road, s/he will start to feel anxious the next time s/he approaches that stretch of the road. Because this alerting function is something that has evolved, it is very much a hit-or-miss affair. If, for example, s/he were wearing a particular jacket at the time of the skid, s/he may start to feel anxious when next s/he puts on the jacket. Since the jacket in no way contributed to the skid, it is not a source of danger to her/him. A woman was raped by a man with a gap between his front teeth. For the rest of her life, she was frightened of men with gaps between their front teeth. Men with such gaps are no more likely to commit rape than men without them. The fear therefore served no useful purpose. Emotions of this kind commonly arise in psychotherapy. When the outer brain discovers that they are of no value to the person, it will try to extinguish them.

Dreams

Dreams are predominantly an inner brain activity, for we (that is, our outer brains) do not control what we dream. An important feature of dreams is that they reveal to us what the inner brain considers to be important. Sometimes we find we have dreamed about what we thought was a trivial event. It obviously was not trivial to the inner brain, and sometimes we realize when we think about it why it meant so much to the inner brain. Dreams reveal the remarkable ingenuity and inventiveness of the inner brain. They draw upon the inner brain's vast store of memories, and sometimes they involve memories from many years ago. They draw upon the inner brain's capacity for making meaningful connections. They are largely organized around the inner brain's capacity for extracting and constructing concepts, and mainly they comprise concrete representations of these abstract concepts. For example, if a person is preoccupied with the idea of not being accepted, s/he will have dreams in which s/he is not accepted and will feel the pain of this. Most of all, dreams draw upon the inner brain's astonishing capacity to create new scenes and scenarios that represent aspirations, fears and difficulties, sometimes metaphorically or symbolically. Dreams often involve what Freud (1902) called *condensation*, a process by which two or more images or ideas combine to form a composite image or idea. Sometimes images or ideas from different time periods are combined in this way.

Dreams can be prompted by extraneous sounds, but these sounds get incorporated into images that link up with a current preoccupation. The sound of someone using a vacuum cleaner might get incorporated into a dream about a machine sawing a sheep's head off, which may be a dream about castration. Dreams prompted by current experiences and preoccupations become linked with significant past experiences. Dreams mostly involve people, usually but not always people who are known to us. What happens in dreams seems to be that thoughts about, and reactions to, people that we have had to set aside during our waking hours in order to attend to more pressing matters get brought back and re-examined. The appropriate emotion is also re-experienced.

Although the inner brain is the prime mover in dreams, the outer brain also plays a part. In a dream, just as in our waking hours, the outer brain watches and reacts to what is being played out. However absurd the dream may be, the outer brain never realizes it is a dream. As Freud (1902) pointed out, much of the material that gets brought into dreams is of a threatening or disturbing nature. The outer brain, performing its function of *censor*, reacts to this with alarm. A struggle might ensue between the inner brain, wanting the material brought out, and the outer brain, wanting to keep it buried. As a consequence, ambiguity and camouflage are brought into dreams. Another consequence is what Freud (1902) called *displacement*. In this, an apparently innocent image comes to represent a more disturbing one, or a nonthreatening person becomes a stand-in for a threatening one. Because of this, Freud (1902) wrote of the *manifest content*, the final product after modifications and disguises have been introduced, and the *latent content*, what the inner brain is trying to get revealed.

Unlike in waking life, there is no continuity in dreams; we never take up one night where we left off the previous night. A serious problem in working with dreams is the difficulty we have remembering them. Even though experiments involving waking people during periods of sleep have demonstrated that everybody dreams, some people maintain that they never recall their dreams. This may be so because, as dreams have no exact equivalent in outer reality, we have few prompts to connect us with them. We remember a dream most easily shortly after waking or when something happens during the day that reminds us of one.

An interesting woman reported by Spinelli (1994) complained that she could not dream. Each time she started to dream she saw the image of part of a chess board that would "startle her out of her sleep". Whenever she saw the image she became anxious. Over a number of weekly sessions, she was encouraged to free associate on the image, but nothing came. Finally, she was told to sit in silence and dwell upon the image. Soon she became shocked and began to cry. She realized that the image was really the linoleum on the floor of the basement in her family home. She then made the connection that once, in this place, she had been forced to fellate a friend of her brother.

The outer brain

The outer brain is a remarkable development. It is through the outer brain that we are able to observe ourselves in action, to be conscious of ourselves, to be objective about ourselves. If the inner brain is the human core, buried deep within the person, the outer brain is the leading edge, the interface between the person and the environment, that has to face and adapt to new situations, modify our behavior to take account of changing circumstances and update the understandings and strategies of the inner brain. The inner brain makes clear what it wants. The outer brain has to find ways of getting what the inner brain wants. It can take a longer-term view. It also has a sense of morality. While it has been possible to create computers that emulate the inner brain, it has not been possible to give computers the equivalent of the outer brain. The outer brain is more like the computer operator. Without the outer brain, psychotherapy would not be possible.

The self

Although the inner brain has been described as the human core, the outer brain is that which we experience as the self. Because, in terms of evolution, the outer brain is one stage on from the inner brain, it is able to observe the relating behavior that the inner brain has steered us into, just as it is able to experience the emotional rewards and punishments that the inner brain has dealt out to us. It has to make sense of, and justify, these actions and emotions, just as when a person has to justify an action that s/he carries out by posthypnotic suggestion. If, in its objective judgment, the outer brain decides that certain behaviors are no longer in the best interest of the individual, it must be capable of interfering with them, revising them or totally eliminating them by means of procedures that are equivalent to the rewriting of a computer program. This kind of conscious modification of the inner brain's automatic behavior must be one of the components of psychotherapy.

Self-consciousness

Because the outer brain is so bound up with the state of consciousness, the conclusion must be drawn that this is where the *sense of self* is located. It seems unlikely that most animals are aware of themselves in the way that humans are. They probably do not have that which we call *self-consciousness*. The outer brain provides us with the capacity to be conscious of and think about ourselves and to make observations about ourselves and to pass judgments upon ourselves. Although all of that which the inner brain causes us to do is part of that which we and others experience as our selves, the outer brain seems to have to carry the responsibility for presenting ourselves to the world.

Self-judgment and self-control

If it is the outer brain that observes and thinks about ourselves, it must also be the outer brain that passes judgment upon ourselves. It must therefore be the seat of the conscience or, in psychoanalytic parlance, the *superego* (Freud, 1923). More will be said about the controlling function of the outer brain in the following section on psychoanalysis, and more will be said about the conscience or superego in Chapter 5. If humans are the only animals with a conscience, this is further reason for believing that conscience is an outer brain activity; but one complication to this is the capacity of the conscience to make us feel good or bad about ourselves, which is an emotional (inner brain generated) experience. The emotions involved can be positive, such as pride or self-satisfaction, or negative, such as guilt or shame. Since the emotions are generated within the inner brain, they cannot be part of the judging process. Can they be the inner brain's response to the outer brain's judgments? If so, then the inner brain must be aware of at least some of the outer brain's activity.

The outer brain's capacity for deception

Certain authors have considered the unconscious to be naive or dumb (Loftus & Klinger, 1992). The inner brain is certainly not dumb, but because it acts automatically and sometimes inappropriately it might be considered naive. It is this way because it is incapable of being otherwise. It always tells the truth because deception is not part of its repertoire. Our capacity to lie and deceive is probably of recent origin; therefore, it must be a function of the outer brain. The outer brain can decide whether it is in our best interest to lie or to tell the truth. That which the inner brain would have us openly express, the outer brain may decide to conceal. Beyond this, the outer brain may decide to present a false picture in order to deceive. It may try to fake a facial or bodily gesture, to force a smile, but forced gestures and forced smiles always look false because the outer brain does not have access to the neural pathways that the inner brain has.

How do we deceive ourselves?

Since the outer brain is concerned with both the self and deception, it must be concerned with that which we call *self-deception*. There is no doubt that there is such a thing as self-deception, but how does it happen? It is easier to explain how we can lie to others than how we can lie to ourselves. In order to do so, it is necessary to postulate the existence of compartments within the outer brain. In psychoanalysis there is the term *compartmentalization*, which means that one part of the psyche is unaware of ideas that are contained in another. This is not such a strange idea, considering that we can talk to ourselves and hear hallucinatory voices that both talk to us and make comments about us. The idea of one compartment deceiving another is not so different from that of our being able to pass judgment upon ourselves. This would require the existence of an additional (superior) layer to the outer brain, which may be similar to the psychoanalytic concept of the superego.

The controlling nature of the outer brain

It is hard to escape the conclusion that one of the outer brain's functions is control. It seems able to exert control over the inner brain in a number of ways. While the inner brain may press for certain things to get said or done, the outer brain seems able to intervene and prevent them being said or done, if it decides that this is in the person's best interest. It is hard to imagine what the additional information might be that prompts the outer brain to intervene in this way, but information there must be. It would appear that the outer brain is more restrained, shrewd, cunning, devious, prudent, tactful and diplomatic than the inner brain. Whatever it is that these restraints amount to would appear to be interfered with by alcohol. When a person is drunk, the inner brain seems better able to get its way. This also would apply to someone who has suffered frontal lobe damage, which provides a clue to the location of the outer brain.

The outer brain also seems to be able to exert control over what memories the person has access to. Although the outer brain is dependent upon the inner brain for the retrieval of memories, once the memories have come through, the outer brain can somehow prevent their passing into full consciousness. When we dream, it seems that the outer brain's control over our access to memories is relaxed.

Finally, as is evident from the previous section, the outer brain seems capable of splitting in two, in order that one half can exert control over another. This kind of control is mainly in the domain of approval or acceptability. An autonomous individual is capable of passing judgment upon her/himself. This must involve the setting aside of one part of the self that can objectively view the other part. We are also judged by internalized others, an issue that will be covered in Chapter 5.

The outer brain's role in devising relating strategies

During childhood, the inner brain has certain general relating objectives, which have to be shaped by the outer brain into refined and specific relating strategies. Once these have been worked out, they can be passed on to, and taken over and executed, in its automatic way, by the inner brain. This is what is meant by acquiring relating competence (Chapter 1). Taking closeness as an example, the inner brain simply puts out the message: get closeness. It does not know how closeness is got; it simply knows that closeness is what has to be got. The outer brain has the task of discovering ways and learning skills for getting it. In the background, the inner brain continues to confirm whether this or that experience is or is not close and providing the appropriate emotional feedback in terms of rewards for getting it and punishments for losing it. The outer brain, for example, learns ways of making and keeping friends, learns what to say and what to avoid saying, how to say things and how not to say things, how to make people feel good by paying them compliments, and how to make them feel bad by being offensive, how to appear interesting and appealing to other people and how not to be boring and repellent to other people.

Comparing the inner/outer brain concept with other concepts

Two sets of concepts have clear connections with the inner-outer brain concept: the psychoanalytic and the cognitive. They will briefly be described here.

Psychoanalytic concepts

Freud (1915a) was responsible for formulating the psychoanalytic concepts of the *unconscious* and the *conscious*. He wrote of the unconscious as though it were a place, though he was careful not to locate it in any particular part of the brain. In fact, he saw it more as a metaphorical than as an actual place. He was less inclined to think of the conscious as though it were a place; more simply, he viewed it as that which was not the unconscious. Sullivan (1964), the father of interpersonal psychology and interpersonal psychotherapy, was opposed to the idea of the unconscious as a place in the mind with knowable contents, though his own concept of *covert processes* did not provide an adequate substitute. The inner and outer brain are conceived of more as actual than as metaphorical places, though, like the unconscious and the conscious, they do not as yet have a precise location. As an indication of how important he considered the unconscious to be, Freud likened it to the sub-merged nine tenths of an iceberg, which is in keeping with the present theory. This is not to suggest that the inner brain is ten times larger than the outer brain, or even that it is ten times as important, but it is certainly the more fundamental structure. In what is also in keeping with the present theory, Freud considered the unconscious to be the source of the instincts, though he did not have in mind the relating instincts; and from an early stage, he wrote of the drives rather than the instincts (Freud, 1920). Comparison of the inner brain and the unconscious will be pursued further in Chapter 10.

Freud used the word *unconscious* to mean two separate things: (1) a place in the mind and (2) that which is not conscious. The implication is that when we are not conscious of something, it is in this other place. He considered that certain disturbing thoughts and memories get relegated to, and kept within, the unconscious by the process of *repression* (Freud, 1915b). This raises the question, does the conscious mind relegate these thoughts and memories to the unconscious or, as Loftus and Klinger (1992) suggest, does the unconscious decide to protect the conscious from them? Insofar as we do not consciously decide to repress material, the latter would seem to be the correct explanation; yet why would the unconscious wish to behave in this way, par-ticularly as the inner brain is scarcely aware of the existence of the outer brain? In terms of the inner and the outer brain, the inner brain is direct and honest, and it is the outer brain that decides what is and is not in our best interest and that chooses to deceive.

A number of writers have had difficulty with the concept of repression. Power and Brewin (1991) wrote, "We would question however whether there is room in a model of the unconscious for repressed material that was previ-ously conscious" (p. 307). Cannon (1991) wrote, "Only a subject who both knows and does not know his or her own tendencies and desires could recog-nise what had previously been hidden" (pp. 36–37). And Spinelli (1994) wrote, "an alternative theory to that of the psycho-analytic unconscious stresses the idea of *consciously unreflected dissociation* rather than repres-sion". Just as, when we concentrate upon one source of sound, there are other sounds that we choose not to hear and just as when we are concentrating upon one line of thought, there are other lines of thought that we choose to disregard, it is not unreasonable to suppose that there are certain ideas that we can *put to the back of our minds* and not think about, even though we know they are there. We connect up with them when we make *Freudian slips*.

This has much in common with Sullivan's (1953) concept of *selective inattention.*

These objections do not seem insuperable. What, after all, we are talking about here is access to memories. Surely, if the outer brain is capable of recruiting the inner brain to retrieve memories, it should be capable of stopping those memories coming into itself (*i.e.*, into consciousness). It seems likely that the outer brain has a gatekeeper function, similar to the psychoanalytic concept of the *censor* (Freud, 1902), but what would the value of such a function be? The memories may be those to which the inner brain has reacted with anxiety, because they carried some threat to the individual; or they may be memories judged by the outer brain, in its capacity as overseer or conscience, as shameful or immoral and which the outer brain may wish to be dissociated from.

Another psychoanalytic distinction is drawn between the *id* and the *ego* (Freud, 1923). The id has much in common with the inner brain, as has the ego with the outer brain. Freud maintained that at birth there was only the id and that the ego gradually became differentiated from it. The id is considered to be the source of selfish urges, and one of the functions of the ego is to delay the satisfaction of such urges until the environmental circumstances are the most favorable. If the outer brain is virtually the same as the ego, then it must be responsible for those processes, like denial, suppression and projection, which Anna Freud (1937) has called the *mechanisms of defense.*

The id is assumed to be associated with what is called *primary process* thinking and the ego with *secondary process* thinking (Freud, 1911). Freud considered the id to be more primitive and therefore to have been established earlier, both in evolutionary and developmental time. It is concerned with preverbal and prelogical mental activity like visual imagery, analogy and irrationality, and it features prominently in dreams, which are predominantly an inner brain activity. In keeping with its inner brain equivalence, it is faster. The ego is concerned with language, logic and rational thought, and, in keeping with its outer brain equivalence, it is slower.

Cognitive concepts

Some cognitive psychologists (e.g., Power & Brewin, 1991) maintain that both psychoanalysis and cognitive science recognize that behavior can become automatized through repetition and that the control of such behavior is devolved into autonomous or semiautonomous unconscious structures. Lewicki and colleagues (1992) believed that most of the mental work in learning takes place at what they called the *nonconscious* level. They considered that much of what we learn about the world is too complex to be discerned at the conscious level, but that it can be picked up relatively quickly at the nonconscious level. They conceded, however, that procedures used for conscious learning are more adaptable to different situations. Spinelli (1994) cited a number of studies that demonstrate that non-conscious mental processing must occur. For example, images flashed too quickly for the conscious mind to register could later be picked out from a series of images presented randomly, and the conscious mind had no idea why they were being selected. LeDoux (1989) wrote, "It is now widely accepted that mental information processing takes place largely outside of conscious awareness, with only the end products reaching consciousness and being represented as conscious content" (p. 271).

Claxton (1998) distinguished between what he called *explicit, articulate thinking*, or *figuring it out*, and the *implicit approach*, or *intuition*. He contrasted rational problem solving, which involves simplifying a situation by starting from plausible premises, with open-mindedly attending to what happens as you interact with the system. The former requires decomposing the problem into describable components by the use of words. The latter requires playing around with the problem and waiting for the answer to *just pop up*. He considered the figuring out process to be a conscious one and the intuitive process to be an unconscious one. He observed that, until recently, the view was held that whatever is nonconscious is unintelligent, but he believed that cognitive science is well on the way to accepting the idea of the *intelligent unconscious*.

Jacoby and colleagues (1992) wrote of *automatic* processes and *intentional* processes, which correspond well with the processes of the inner and the outer brain. At the automatic level, many of the neural processes that congnitive psychologists describe, such as *mental algorithms* and *rules of inference* for solving recurrent adaptive problems (Cosmides, 1989) and *internal processing modules* (Gilbert, 1992), could appropriately be attributed to inner brain functioning. Cognitive theorists have given us the terms "automatic" and "intuitive", which usefully complement the now rather dated psychoanalytic term "the "unconscious".

The inner and the outer brain in psychotherapy

Psychotherapy is a technique that has to be learned. The learning process, like all learning process, takes place mainly at the level of the outer brain, but over time, many of the attitudes and behaviors that are learned get taken over by the inner brain. Therapists in training and inexperienced therapists conduct a lot of their work at the level of the outer brain, but experienced therapists are more inclined to sit back and let the therapy happen, that is, they function to a much greater extent at an inner brain level. Good therapists, like good exponents of any craft, do their best work when they are relaxed and doing what comes naturally. In this state, they are attentive and receptive. Quite spontaneously, they do and say the right things.

There must be times when therapists superimpose upon this "automatic pilot" mode a more objective mode, in which they make conscious decisions about what should be done or said next. While there is an inner brain-driven dialogue between myself and the client, there is often a parallel outer brain-driven dialogue between myself and me, in which I am asking myself, "What is going on here? Why is s/he telling me this? Where is s/he taking me? Should I not be saying something here? What should I say? How should I put it? When should I say it? How will s/he take it? Will it move us on or set us back?"

There are times when the therapist observes and judges, at an outer brain level, those things that s/he is doing and saying at an inner brain level. I sometimes have the experience of watching (at an outer brain level) my inner brain at work. By simply placing myself in a receptive mode and allowing myself to respond automatically to what the client is saying, I perceive myself making remarks that I (at an outer brain level) had no part in. It is reassuring that they are astonishingly appropriate. I even find myself thinking, "That was a good thing to say", as though I am observing and judging another person at work.

Therapists should become skilled at telling whether it is the client's inner brain or her/his outer brain that is doing the talking and find ways of breaking through the client's outer brain controls to get to the inner brain and communicate directly with it. They should become skilled at understanding what the inner and outer brain respectively are trying to say and do and perceiving conflicts between the inner and the outer brain. Some clients keep the dialogue between themselves and the therapist at an outer brain level, by remaining restrained and unemotional and taking the therapist, by logical steps, through their perceived difficulties. They give objective accounts of events, circumstances and relationships and make observations about them. This is called *intellectualizing*. When the client becomes more relaxed and spontaneous, her/his remarks will come directly out of the inner brain, and s/he will be more spontaneous, irrational and emotional. If the client does not get her/himself into inner brain mode, the therapist has a responsibility of helping to get her/him there, by being simple, direct and personal.

Understanding what the inner brain is up to

It is because the inner brain operates independently, working according to its own priorities, making its own decisions, that people become so confused about themselves. Most people are unaware that they, that is, their outer brains, are not the prime movers and believe that they, that is, their outer brains, know what they want, plan where they are going, make choices and know why they feel what they feel. Coming to understand themselves is mainly coming to understand their inner brains. Neither they nor their therapists need be aware that this is what is happening in therapy, though being aware of it makes the task easier.

Improving relations between the inner and the outer brain

The client's decision to seek therapy is more likely to have been made at an outer brain level, though it may have been prompted by stirrings from the inner brain. The client may perceive that something is not right but may not understand what that something might be. S/he may feel anxious or depressed but may not understand why. The inner brain is sending out alarm signals because certain states of relatedness are under threat or being lost or denied, but it cannot convey these details to the outer brain.

The idea of an inner and an outer brain is a strange one, even for the psychotherapist. It is not normally necessary to explain their existence or how they work to clients, though at times it helps to describe problems to clients in these terms. After I have explained them, some clients have started using the terms quite correctly to say things about themselves. A client recently said that her inner brain was stopping her doing something that her outer brain wanted to do.

Clients benefit from gaining greater access to their inner brains and from becoming more familiar with and more trusting of them. To this end, the therapist should try to make it easier for ideas from the inner brain to come through more clearly, without too many interventions from the outer brain. Sometimes by responding to what sound like inner brain remarks, that is, remarks that are simple, direct, uncontrolled, quickly spoken and accompanied by emotion, and by speaking back in the same simple, direct, uncontrolled and emotional way, the therapist may be able to set up a dialogue between her/his own inner brain and that of the client and to eliminate much of the outer brain's slower and more laborious intellectualizing.

One of the therapist's tasks is to improve the working relations between the inner and the outer brain. Since it is not possible to get the inner brain to become more aware of, or more tolerant of, the outer brain, all of this work has to be done at the outer brain level. The client's outer brain has somehow got to understand better what her/his inner brain is trying to do and trying to communicate. This should help the outer brain to gain more trust of the inner brain and to allow the inner brain more freedom to act on its own.

The outer brain may come to perceive that some of the inner brain's apparent concerns or apprehensions are no longer appropriate in the light of changes that have taken place in the client's circumstances, or that perhaps they never were appropriate. It may be that the inner brain has been reaching its conclusion on the basis of assumptions that were correct at some earlier period in the client's life but are not correct any more. The outer brain has to comprehend how these misperceptions might have come about and try to convey to the inner brain that the danger is no longer present or that it never was as great as it might have seemed. The inner brain may, long ago, have decided that, because a particular significant other in the client's past could not be trusted, everyone cannot be trusted; or that, because a dog, on one significant occasion, did something frightening, all dogs are always frightening.

Conflict between the inner and the outer brain

The outer brain is able to put forward perfectly sound reasons why a particular experience should please us. We subject ourselves to the experience only to find that it does not please us; more precisely, it does not please the inner brain. The outer brain has assumed that we (*i.e.*, the inner brain) would like the experience, but the outer brain has assumed wrongly. This has important implications for psychotherapy. People often become unhappy because they do the things they think (at an outer brain level) they ought to like and find that (at an inner brain level) they do not like them. They cannot live their lives doing the things they think they ought to like. This was called by Horney (1945) *the tyranny of the shoulds*. They have to let the inner brain decide. They have to trust their intuition.

A typical inner/outer brain conflict occurs when a woman has given up fulltime, paid employment to have a child. When the child is born, she is left at home all day while her husband goes to work as usual. Her inner brain protests by making her depressed, because, as far as it is concerned, she no longer enjoys the pleasurable interaction with her workmates, the interest and satisfactions of her work, the appreciation and praise of her employer and the independence of having her own pay-packet. Her outer brain is puzzled because logically she should be happy. She knew what she was doing when she consciously decided to give up work in order to have the child. The child is healthy, happy and thriving, and everybody loves it, but her inner brain has decided that this is not sufficient to compensate for all that she has lost.

When there is a trial of strength between the inner and the outer brain, the inner brain (because it alone knows where the person is heading and because it controls the emotions) will always win. The inner brain will not be shut up. However much the outer brain may try to override it, it will always win through. People who aspire to function at a rational, outer brain level will come to grief if they do not pay attention to the insistences of the inner brain.

Despite all this, a great deal that happens in psychotherapy has to do with the outer brain exerting an influence upon the inner brain. In this, the inner and the outer brain are not in conflict. It is more that the outer brain reaches certain conclusions about how things are and manages to convince the inner brain of this. If, for example, a cognitive therapist can convince a client that a spider is not dangerous, the client will stop being afraid of it.

Therapist's interventions

The therapist's job is to try to help the client's outer brain to understand more clearly what the inner brain is trying to say or do. It may sometimes feel to the therapist as though there are two people sitting in front of her/him, one the inner brain and one the outer brain, and that s/he is conducting a conversation with each of them separately. Sometimes, it is as though the inner brain is trying to say something when the outer brain butts in and stops it. S/he can, without too much difficulty, introduce the outer brain to the inner brain, but s/he cannot introduce the inner brain to the outer brain.

Therapists vary in the extent to which they offer to the client what are called *interpretations*. These are the therapist's understanding of what appears to be going on in the client's life. They may include the therapist's understanding of what the inner brain and the outer brain are trying to do. What complicates matters is that the part of the outer brain that controls and censors the inner brain may be aware of what the inner brain is trying to do and is trying to stop it. If this is true, then the therapist's interpretations, however correct they may be, will not be accepted by the client. This is equivalent to the psychoanalytic concept of *resistance*. It is generally preferable for the therapist to bring the client to the point of realizing what the inner brain is trying to do, rather than press an interpretation on her/him.

Picking up a scent

One of the most important processes in therapy is perceiving and taking note of those issues with which the client's inner brain is preoccupied. The client may repeatedly refer, or come back to, certain incidents or topics. The therapist has to try to discover what these incidents and topics have in common. This is bound up with the idea of concept formation and the inner brain's capacity to think in terms of concepts. In order to comprehend the client's inner brain, the therapist must try to identify its concepts. Take a concept like "nobody likes me". The person may cite a number of examples of her/his not being liked, may make reference to the fact that people can be very cruel, say how unpleasant it can be not to be liked, and yet not be able to pull all these references together into the single phrase, "Nobody likes me". The therapist has to try to discover and to help the client to discover what the uniting concept might be and try it out on the client.

A valuable pointer to what it might be is the show of emotion. If the client begins to show signs of emotion, or to talk excitedly, some underlying concept must be generating the distress or the excitement. If every time s/he refers to a particular person or a particular situation s/he looks or sounds upset, there must be something about that person or situation that is troubling her/him. In tracking down the cause of the client's unrest, it is best to latch on to some show of emotion, however small, and try to follow it to its source.

Anything the client says that carries some hint of emotion is likely to be on the right track and is worth following. It is like picking up a scent. When the client moves in some directions from this point of departure the emotion may start to fade (getting cooler); when s/he moves in others, it may start to intensify (getting warmer). Sometimes the client will just stop being emotional whichever direction s/he moves in. This is a sign that the outer brain, perceiving impending danger, has put a block on the proceedings. The scent is lost, and the therapist can only note the point of departure and try again later.

As words and the emotion linked to them go hand in hand, getting the right words will intensify the emotion. During the exercise of finding the right words to unlock the emotion, client and therapist need to work together. The therapist encourages the client to stay with those words with which s/he is most preoccupied. Slightly rephrasing a sentence can firm up a concept and, at the same time, make the client more emotional. The therapist should cautiously take the client back to what seems to be a useful starting point by saying something like, "You say that people can be very cruel sometimes". The client may respond with, "Yes, they can be very hurtful". On the word "hurtful", there might be a perceptible tremor in the client's voice, which would convey that this particular word carries an emotional charge. The therapist will want to stay with it, by simply repeating the word. Hearing this emotive word spoken out loud may be enough to provoke the client to continue, saying something like, "When people say hurtful things to me it makes me feel they do not like me"; on the phrase "do not like me", the tremor may return. The therapist, confident that s/he is now close to something important, may simply reflect back to the client, "You think that people do not like you". Some part of the client is now aware that the therapist is on the right track. This can free her/him to be more expansive and more openly emotional. In a flood of words and emotion the essential phrase "Nobody likes me" gets said.

This verbalization is like striking oil. Everything becomes clearer. Ideas about not being liked and instances of people not liking the client come tumbling out. The therapist may now allow the client to stop using words and just be emotional. With the emotion comes a whole sequence of related ideas, which will need to be explored and examined further. Which people does s/he believe do not like her/him? Why does s/he believe they do not like her/him? Is it true that they do not like her/him? Are they right not to like her/him? Does it matter that they do not like her/him? Is s/he really a likeable person? Does the therapist like her/him?

How is change effected?

It is a common experience in psychotherapy that the client is aware of what the problem is and can openly talk about it but can see no way of correcting it. Change usually takes place only when emotion starts to be felt. The process of tracking down a scent is a way of picking up an emotional lead and following it to its origin. When the origin is found, work on it can begin. It is like when a miner reaches the coal face. The therapeutic process is a delicate mixture of inner brain feeling and outer brain cognition. The client needs to stay emotional, because that way s/he stays in touch with the problem, but s/he needs, at an outer brain level, to be understanding the problem, seeing what needs to be done to resolve it, and planning strategies for resolving it.

There is no easy, comfortable way to make progress in psychotherapy. Nothing of any value ever happens when therapist and client just sit together and talk about the problem. Sooner or later the going has to get rough; the client has to start to suffer, for only in her/his suffering does s/he come to grips with the problem and start to resolve it. Emotion is frightening. In normal conversation, if a person starts to show emotion, the course of the conversation gets changed in order that the conversation can move away from the emotion. In psychotherapy, it is necessary to do the opposite, to move in on the emotion; but getting emotional or staying emotional is not effective in itself. The client needs to understand what s/he is being emotional about, and it is that that client and therapist have to work on.

Dreams in psychotherapy

The exploration of dreams is a valuable exercise in psychotherapy because dreams provide a freer or more direct access to inner brain activity. Freud (1902) described dreams as "the royal road to the unconscious". In dreams, the inner brain gains fuller expression and the outer brain is forced to take a back seat. In dreams the inner brain comes into its own, and we are privileged to participate in its dramas. If we pay attention to what we do and feel in our dreams, we gain a clearer understanding of what our major preoccupations are, what we really want, what we like, what we are afraid of and so forth. Unfortunately, when we wake, we rapidly lose contact with our dreams, and their content becomes quickly forgotten. When therapy is going well, contact with the inner brain occurs more easily. It is easier to remember dreams during psychotherapy, perhaps because the therapist is able to reassure the client that it is acceptable to do so or because the therapist may provide some protection against the disapprovals and inhibitions of the outer brain. Inner-outer brain conflicts that frequently feature in dreams can be examined and possibly resolved during therapy. Crazy ideas, which often feature in dreams, are better tolerated in therapy, and the meaning that may lie behind such ideas becomes more apparent. They provide important pointers to clients' current preoccupations. Clients often dream about the people they talk about during therapy, which indicates that the interpersonal tensions brought out in therapy continue to preoccupy them between sessions. Therapists not infrequently feature in clients' dreams; in recounting these dreams to their therapists, clients are able, in an indirect way, to reveal their more intimate or less acceptable feelings toward the therapists.

Summary

In evolutionary time, the inner brain was in place before the outer brain. The inner brain is the seat of the relating objectives. It regulates our behavior in ways that enable us to attain them and generates emotions that register success or failure in their attainment. The inner brain operates like a computer, quite automatically and with no self-awareness. The outer brain has self-awareness. It can see what the inner brain is trying to get us to do and can devise new ways of doing things that are more suitable to new situations. It can modify the automatic operations of the inner brain by "writing new programs". The psychotherapist needs to gain access to the client's inner brain and to help the client to be more aware and trusting of it. At the outer brain level, therapist and client need to collaborate in "writing new programs" for the client's inner brain.

Chapter 3

The proximity axis in relating

It could be argued that approach-avoidance conflicts are the most fundamental conflicts of all mobile organisms. Both benefits and dangers are associated with close proximity; consequently, most organisms devote much of their time to moving either toward or away from other organisms. Byrne and colleagues (1963) maintained that people acquire, on the basis of their experiences of life, a generalized expectancy of reward or punishment. If the expectancy of reward is greater than that of punishment, other people will be trusted, valued and sought as companions; if the reverse is true, they will be mistrusted, devalued and avoided. This is perhaps a gross oversimplification, for most people spend part of their time in close proximity to others and part in separation from them. They also trust, value and stay close to some people and mistrust, devalue and stay distant from others. Even within a close relationship, there are times when it is necessary to be close and times when it is necessary to be distant.

It is almost inevitable that when people turn away from others they turn in on themselves. Macdiarmid (1989) drew the useful distinction between what he called *other-cathexis* and *self-cathexis*. This distinction is reflected in the writing of a number of other authors. Freud (1914) and Abraham (1924) distinguished between what they called the *anaclitic object choice*, which takes the form of the infant's libidinal attachment to the mother, and the *narcissistic object choice*, which takes the form of a hypercathexis of the self. Blatt and Shichman (1983) extended this idea to a theory of personality development, which proposed that we have two primary tasks, the one, called *anaclitic*, involving the formation of stable, enduring relationships and the other, called *introjective*, involving the development of a differentiated and consolidated identity. Beck (1983) similarly divided personality types into the *sociotropic*, who are concerned with a positive interchange with others, and the *autonomous*, who are concerned with preserving the integrity and autonomy of the personal domain. Jung's (1921) distinction between the *introvert*, who is more interested in ideas than in people, and the *extravert*, who is sociable and outgoing, must also be related.

Maturation within the proximity axis

Maturation within both axes is characterized by alternate movements from one end of an axis to the other. Although it must be assumed that we are all born with general tendencies toward the four main positions, it is still necessary for us to become acquainted with them and develop competence in them. There is a fuller account of this process in Birtchnell (1993/1996). Ideally, it is during the period of maturation that the child becomes exposed to various states of relatedness, comes to feel comfortable in them, to like them and to acquire a taste for them. In order for this to happen, the parent has to provide these periods of exposure and ensure that they are pleasurable for the child. This the parent can only do if s/he feels comfortable in them her/himself. A parent who is frightened of closeness or distance is going to be reluctant to allow comfortable closeness or distance to happen for the child. S/he will hold back when s/he should be providing and encouraging closeness and hang on when she should be providing and encouraging distance. Largely, therefore, it is the negative relating of the parent that gives rise to negative relating in the child.

On the proximity axis, it could be argued that our first experience of closeness is within the womb; there is accumulating evidence that the infant is affected by intrauterine experiences. The claim, first made by Rank (1923), that expulsion from the warmth and security of the womb constitutes a trauma of some magnitude cannot be substantiated, but birth could be considered our first separation experience.

For the first few months of life, the infant cannot even crawl. In order to survive, it has to attract the mother to it by crying, clinging, gazing, smiling and babbling (Benedek, 1956). MacFarlane (1975) has shown that, after only three days, it can recognize the smell of its mother's milk. Many have considered these first few months to be a period of extreme closeness. Mahler (1961) called it the phase of *symbiosis*. Bowlby (1969) maintained that, from about the age of six months, the infant attains that level of closeness that he called *attachment*. It is through attachment that the infant acquires what Ainsworth (1963) called a *secure base* from which it can explore. Such exploration is positive and pleasurable and represents the infant's first experience of positive distance.

Freud (1914) considered that, in this first period of distancing, the infant withdraws its emotional investment (*libido*) from the mother and directs it into itself. This he called *secondary narcissism*. Mahler (1961, 1963) called this the phase of *separation-individuation*, emphasizing that it is through the process of distancing that the infant starts to become an individual, with a separate identity. This pattern of coming together and separating off is repeated many times throughout infancy, childhood, adolescence and adult life; it is through these alternations that the person acquires the competencies associated with closeness and distance.

The development of a secure sense of self depends upon parents encouraging the child to make decisions about what it likes and what it does not like, what it wants to do and what it does not want to do. Parents need to ask the child questions like, "What do you like? What would you like to do? Where would you like to go?" Parents interfere with the development of a child's sense of self by putting ideas into its head with remarks like, "We like this, don't we? You like that, don't you? You don't want to do that, do you? This would be a better thing to do. Isn't that nice? Let's do this today."

Sullivan (1953) placed great emphasis upon the school as a socializing institution, especially during that period which he called the *juvenile era*. It is there, and at that time, that the child acquires *playmates*, becomes a member of a *peer group* and learns the critical social processes of *cooperation* and *compromise*, During the next epoch of development, which Sullivan called *pre-adolescence*, the playmate is replaced by the *chum*, a close friend of the same sex. It is, Sullivan maintained, in the chum relationship that the child first considers the needs of the other to be as important as its own.

It is an important principle that one cannot become confidently distant without the assurance that there is secure closeness to return to, and one cannot become confidently close without the assurance that there is secure distance to return to. Erikson (1965) maintained that the establishment of a secure identity is both a precursor to and a prerequisite for the development of an intimate relationship; a sentiment echoed by Laing and colleagues (1966) and Raskin (1985). Bowen (1978) wrote of the necessary *differentiation of self* of the young adult from the family of origin before it becomes possible to fall in love and settle into a family of procreation. Many marriages fail because one or both partners have failed to make this disconnection.

Gender differences on the proximity axis

Although there are those within either gender who are close and those who are distant, there does appear to be a tendency for females to be more close and males to be more distant. Even when they are quite small, girls, when left to play together, ask each other personal questions and show more of an interest in dolls and relationships, and boys ask each other fewer questions and show more of an interest in machines and making things. By adulthood, these differences are even more pronounced. There are two kinds of explanation for this difference, the developmental and the evolutionary. The developmentalists (e.g., Greenson, 1968) argue that, during the phase of symbiosis, all infants identify with their mothers, but during the separation-individuation phase, where girls are able to continue identifying with their mothers, boys have to start identifying with their fathers. This, they say, means that boys have to separate more completely and therefore, according to Suttie (1935), more painfully. Hudson and Jacot (1991) referred to this as the *male wound*. The argument goes that, because the break is so much more painful for boys, they remain more afraid of forming close relationships in the future.

The evolutionists (e.g., Buss, 1994) argue that men and women have evolved with different characteristics. It is biologically advantageous for women to be more preoccupied with closeness, for they need to stay close to their children and to hold on to their men, who will protect them and their children and bring them back food from their hunting expeditions. It is, on the other hand, biologically advantageous for men to be distant, for they need to spend long periods away hunting and to have casual sex with as many women as possible in order to spread their genes around. In the course of a year, a woman can bear only one child. In the same period, a man can impregnate a hundred women.

Closeness

In Chapter 1, closeness was offered as an example of a relating objective, and some of the advantages of closeness were described. While some animals are solitary, many are not. There are shoals of fish, swarms of insects, flocks of birds and herds of ungulates; humans, perhaps the most successful of all animal forms, exist mainly in communities of various levels of complexity. Since fish, insects, birds and ungulates have evolved along different lines, they must all separately have acquired the tendency for closeness because of the advantages it provides for them. In its most basic form, it enables animals to group together to retain heat, repel predators and form a more effective attacking force. Animals must have ways of recognizing and being drawn toward members of their own species, which promotes the cohesiveness of the group.

Many gregarious animals have acquired a primitive means of communication, and some show evidence of collaboration. These enable them to work effectively together toward a common goal. By various means, animals are able to put out alarm signals that warn others of imminent danger. Some animals that hunt in packs have evolved hunting strategies whereby they catch their prey by collaborative endeavour. Bees have a means of conveying to others in the hive where a source of nectar may be. Some gregarious insects demonstrate simple forms of division of labor, whereby certain members of the colony are adapted to perform specialist functions.

In humans, forms of communication and collaboration have been carried much further. Through the adoption and evolution of language, humans have become capable of extending their capacity for communication far beyond that of their closest ancestors. Human infants now have what Pinker (1995) has called a language instinct, which enables them, during a relatively short period in their lives, to learn the use and meaning of words at a phenomenal rate. At a less efficient level, humans retain the capacity to add to and improve their linguistic capabilities throughout life. By means of language, people are able to instantly convey to each other what is going on in their heads, what they want and what they feel. They are able to exchange ideas, bargain and discuss ways of sharing responsibilities and working together. With the written language we can assemble vast stores of knowledge that can be spread around the world and passed on from one generation to the next. With telephones, television, communication satellites and email, our capacity to communicate has become even further extended.

Our capacity for collaborative endeavor is far in advance of that of any of our animal ancestors. Even a group of small children, by means of their linguistic and other abilities, are able to organize themselves into a workforce that is more efficient than any group of adult primates. Even the most primitive of human tribes make plans and work together toward common goals, divide themselves up according to specialist abilities and agree about who should do what and who should work with whom. All complex human societies are made up of large numbers of interdependent specialist trade and professional groups, which are meshed together by means of organizing governmental bodies and communication networks. This is not to say, of course, that with complexity there comes harmony. Complexity generates its own problems, many of which will become apparent through the course of this book.

Closeness in relation to reproductive functions

In most animal species, closeness-seeking behavior is a prominent feature of many aspects of sexual reproduction. Even solitary animals need to find a mate. Sexually reproductive animals have evolved particular smells, sounds, forms of appearance and forms of behavior directed toward making their presence known to members of the opposite sex and responding to the mating signals of opposite sex others. In order to ensure that the best possible mates are selected, female animals do not normally accept the first suitor on the scene; this promotes rivalry between competing suitors. There are advantages to mates, once they have been selected, in staying together, at least throughout one period of breeding. Once a pair bond has been established, boundaries to the mating territory are demarcated and subsequent suitors are challenged and expelled. This has the effect of reinforcing the pair bond. In humans, there remain strong drives toward mate selection; often, there is intense rivalry between suitors. Humans establish powerful pair bonds that commonly endure over many years. Though they do not exactly occupy and defend mating territories, they do set up a family home, which powerfully reinforces the bonding process. Human mates are capable of harboring intensely possessive and jealous feelings toward each other and of fighting off and even killing rival suitors. Unlike our animal ancestors, humans of either sex are sometimes driven to killing a mate who has shown an interest in, or has had sexual involvement with, another person.

Whereas the drive toward closeness between mates is specifically directed in animals toward sexual activity, in humans, although there is a powerful propulsion toward sexual activity, there is the additional objective of the promotion of non-sexual, affectional behavior. Falling and staying in love are compounded of these two objectives, though sometimes they remain quite separate. Mainly through the adoption of contraception, human mates may stay together, sometimes for periods of many years, indulging in sex play and having frequent sex but not proceeding to childbearing. In some mates, particularly with increasing age, the sexual component may be minimal or absent, and the relationship may be directed predominantly or entirely toward the maintenance of an affectional companionship. Difficulties sometimes arise when the drive is predominantly toward sex in one partner and predominantly toward affection in the other. Couples may be completely harmonious in one compartment of the relationship and not in the other.

Once the young are hatched or born, equally powerful drives have had to evolve in order to ensure that parents and offspring, and the offspring themselves, remain in close proximity to one another. These drives, which are present in both parents and offspring, involve the accurate recognition and memorizing of smells, sounds and appearances. The young cling, open their mouths to receive food and make plaintive cries, to which parents instinctively respond. The parents nestle up close, proffer items of food and make soothing noises. The young instinctively move and stay close to each other. Human infants cling and gaze into the eyes of their parents. They are programmed to respond to the smiling human face. Parents cuddle and caress, gaze back, coo and make highpitched noises to which infants positively respond. Before learning to speak actual words, infants make babbling noises, which parents try to emulate. In mammals, the bond between parent and offspring is intensified by suckling, during which warm milk passes out of the parent into the infant. In humans, once language is acquired, parent and child talk endlessly together and the process of talking, irrespective of what is actually said, has a powerful bonding effect.

Kinship and altruism

Bailey (1988) made the point that our predecessors in phylogeny that failed to develop effective kinship strategies for distinguishing between *familiars* and *strangers*, and for determining their degree of closeness to familiars, became extinct. It seems likely that some aspects of human closeness have evolved out of such kinship strategies. Animals benefit from treating kin differently from non-kin, for kin are likely to be less harmful. Hamilton (1963) introduced the term *inclusive fitness* to imply that fitness, as considered by evolutionary theorists, might apply to both individuals and their kin. Bailey called the kind of helping that members of the same kinship provide for each other *natural helping* and maintained that, under stress, individuals turn to kin to avail themselves of such natural helping. Much of what parents do to and for their offspring could be considered altruistic; such behavior was called by Hamilton (1964) *kin altruism*. Bailey (1988) observed that self-sacrificial altruism to close kin serves to perpetuate *our* genes in *them* through succeeding generations. It may be that other forms of altruism, called by Trivers (1971) *reciprocal altruism*, may be a derivative of kin altruism. Trivers (1985) argued that helping others may have evolved because the donor would be likely to benefit in terms of subsequent help received from the recipient. Kin selection theory assumes that all behavior is genetically selfish, whether it occurs through reciprocal altruism or inclusive fitness, but reciprocal altruism extends kin selection theory because it includes mutually beneficial relations among non-genetically related individuals (Chagnon & Irons, 1979).

Human closeness

Closeness, the state of being or feeling in the presence or the company of another or others, is a basic human need (Baumeister & Leary, 1995). A person who is starved of closeness may not mind where s/he gets it. The satisfaction of closeness can be derived not just from actual other people. It can be derived from representations of them such as photographs or tape recordings, products of them such as things that they have made or written, gifts received from them, articles that belong or have belonged to them, places where they live or that are associated with them, and so on. It can be also be derived from animals, particularly pets, plants such as a favorite tree, or even inert objects such as treasured possessions or familiar places.

Closeness may not even depend upon the presence of the other person. Feeling close to someone may be due to having a close relationship with that person such that even when that person is somewhere else, the feeling of closeness remains. This is an example of internal relating. It is possible to feel close to someone who is dead. Hearing the voice or seeing a vision of someone who has died is a not-uncommon experience. People sometimes talk to loved ones who have died, especially at their graveside. The need for closeness causes children in particular to create imaginary companions; and certain psychotic individuals, particularly those with erotomania, develop close delusional relationships that have no equivalent in reality. For many, feeling in the presence of God can provide a powerful and reassuring experience of closeness.

Closeness to a group versus closeness to an individual

Closeness from being a member of a group is qualitatively different from closeness from being involved with a single other person. A group provides a sense of belonging and togetherness. More so than in a one-to-one relationship, a person can become immersed within a group and will readily assume the group identity. In a group, individuality is not encouraged because it can be disruptive. The characteristics of a group are solidarity, conformity and uniformity. Human groups have evolved from hunting groups. Group members are rendered confident and strong because they feel and act as one, which makes them less inhibited and more outspoken. When a choir sings, it sings with one voice; and because it is difficult to discern each individual voice, the singers feel able to sing more freely.

A similar distinction may be drawn between sociability and intimacy. Sociability is liking to circulate among people. The most sociable people are vivacious extroverts, who can be the life and soul of the party. They dance with everybody and talk to everybody, but they are careful to keep their contacts at a superficial level and rarely allow themselves to become too serious or too deeply involved with any one person. Their philosophy is enjoy yourself, live for the present; life is too short to take things seriously. Society has a place for people like this; they are excellent organizers and they keep everybody happy, but it is possible that they are this way because they are afraid of being tied down to a single other person.

Closeness to a single other person is a different proposition. With group membership and sociability the closeness is spread around. With closeness to a single other it is much more focused. It is more like putting all your eggs in one basket, though, of course, the degree of closeness in one-to-one relationships is extremely variable, and it is possible to have a number of very close one-to-one relationships. People in very close relationships allow themselves to become needful of and dependent upon each other. This renders them vulnerable, so that if one leaves or dies or the relationship breaks down, it hurts a lot. But although the risks are high the rewards are great. The word *love* is commonly used to describe this kind of relationship. Love does not always have a sexual component, but when it does it is particularly intense and is called *intimacy*. The term *falling in love* applies only to intimate relationships, though something milder applies to all close friendships. It implies that there has to be a definite starting point, when the participants allow it to happen.

Falling in love has evolved from animal mating rituals, many of which include acts of appeasement by the male, which convey the message "I mean you no harm", and acts of submission by the female, which convey the message "I will let you come in". Whereas in animals this means into my body, in humans it can mean into my mind, into my self, or into my trust. In humans, becoming close is a much more psychological process, which has to occur for both the man and the woman. The phrase *opening oneself to love* conveys that there is a letting down of normal defenses to let the other in. The Paul McCartney song *Hey Jude* (addressed to John Lennon's son at the time of his divorce) movingly describes this process with phrases like *let him under your skin* and *let him into your heart*.

At this stage, it need only be mentioned that there are two other important forms of one-to-one closeness: that of the infant to the parent and that of the parent to the infant. They will be dealt with more fully in the next chapter, but it should be said here that, for both of these, there has to be a starting point, which is similar to the act of falling in love.

The physical expression of closeness

Because people do not normally make physical contact with each other, when they do, it has special significance. When friends meet, they commonly embrace. People naturally touch and hold others whom they perceive are hurt or in distress. Being massaged has a soothing effect, though professional masseurs do not need to be close to their clients in order to massage them.

The distinction between sexual and affectional closeness has already been drawn, and the point has been made that these two kinds of closeness may be considered quite separately. Sexual intercourse can occur, and commonly does occur, between total strangers who experience no other kind of close feeling toward each other. In many respects, sexual closeness is a much easier kind of closeness than affectional closeness, and some people can manage sexual closeness when they cannot manage any other kind of closeness.

These considerations apart, it has to be said that physical contact can be a powerful reinforcer of other forms of closeness. The bond between a mother and her infant is enormously strengthened by the physical exchanges that take place between them. Winnicott (1952) emphasized the sense of security gained by the infant from being securely held by its mother. Falling in love is accompanied and reinforced by the acts of holding, touching, stroking, embracing and kissing and ultimately by sexual intercourse. Ideally, there is a constant interplay between the physical and the psychological.

The characteristics of human closeness

Inevitably, closeness involves doing things together, working and playing together, staying together, and moving from place to place together. This accentuates the feeling of togetherness and creates a sense of we-ness, of two (or more) people acting as one. A great deal of closeness is mediated through talking. Even the act of talking, irrespective of what is actually said, has the effect of bringing and holding people together. *Sharing* is an important component of closeness. Close people share living spaces, share experiences and accumulate shared memories. They also share possessions, thoughts and ideas. They are brought together by having common interests and common objectives, but if they stay together, these commonalities become added to and reinforced. This was called by Heard and Lake (1986) *companionable interaction. Exchanging* is another feature of closeness. Close people like to be kind to each other, to give to and to receive. They also like to help and to be helped; this was called by Heard and Lake (1986) *supportive interaction*. A particular form of exchanging is *revealing* and *being revealed to*. Close people not only want to make revelations and disclosures to each other but are also curious about each other. This has the effect psychologically of both getting inside the other person and being got inside. A particularly important feature of this form of closeness is *being understood*. Getting into and being got into facilitate the process of *identification*, and with identification come mutual *concern, sympathy* and *empathy*. Close people, particularly intimates, perform together acts that normally would be performed only in private and say things to each other that people normally would keep to themselves. Close people talk more freely and spontaneously, are more open in their show of emotion, and are more honest and straightforward with each other. Communication therefore is more inner brain to inner brain, with minimal intervention from the outer brain.

Closeness and respectful relating

It may have occurred to the reader that the form of positive relating referred to in Chapter 1 as respectful relating must surely be a form of closeness. Respectful relating is being mindful of, and concerned about, the relating needs of the other and about the effects that one's own relating might be having upon the other. That is part of what closeness amounts to. Since closeness is itself a form of relating, then respectful closeness would surely be what one would have to call close closeness, which does not appear to make much sense. Yet however strange this may seem, it is the case that this particular aspect of closeness is also a way of describing relating in general. This is borne out by the fact, as is clear from the following discussion, that there is such a thing as disrespectful closeness.

Forms of negative closeness

Since closeness was used in Chapter 1 as an example of a form of relating, the main classes of negative closeness were described there. Here these will be developed in a little more detail. A person who lacks competence as a close relater will have difficulty presenting her/himself to others as an interesting and likeable person. Although some close people may "click" from the start, others will have to gradually build up their state of closeness by progressive stages of cautious exploration and testing out trust. Those who do not appreciate the fragility of the early stages of close relationships plunge into them clumsily, unaware of either the encouraging or the repelling signals of the other. An example of such clumsiness were the attempts by Travis, played by Robert DeNiro, to woo the young woman political campaigner in Scorsese's film *Taxi Driver*. Incompetent close relaters experience many rebuffs, which render them anxious and insecure in any relationships they do find themselves in or deter them from trying again. Insecurely close people cling desperately and stiflingly to those they are close to, dreading separation, and in separation, anxiously await the other's return. Afraid that the other may find other people more appealing, they can be jealous and possessive. The extreme of closeness incompetence is *loneliness*. Sullivan (1953) wrote sensitively of what he called the *lonely one*, the child who suffers because s/he cannot find a group to belong to. A particularly destructive defensive response of the lonely one is what Sullivan called *disparagement*, a devaluing of others. In adult life, the lonely one becomes the *avoidant personality*, who desperately wants closeness but is afraid to seek it.

There is no clear-cut distinction between the anxious or incompetently close relater and the close relater who is frankly disrespectful. Essentially, the disrespectfully close relater does not care whether the other wants to be close or not, or how the other might feel about her/his trying to become close. S/he goes ahead anyway and imposes her/his closeness upon the other. It might seen odd that one person can experience closeness when the other clearly does not want it, but this is the case. The person who imposes closeness may deceive her/himself into believing that the other really does want it or will come to like it in time. Extreme forms of disrespectful closeness are imprisoning, forcible stripping, sexual abuse, raping, prying and interrogating.

Another form of negative closeness is abandoning one's own life to becoming excessively bound up with the life of another person. This may be a state either of excessive attachment or of excessive identification. It was called *fusion* or *failure of differentiation* by Bowen (1978) and *engulfment* or *ontological dependence* by Laing (1965). Such a state is normal during the phase of *primary identification* of early infancy (Chapter 5), but not when it occurs in adult life. Some writers (Tabachnick, 1961; Taylor, 1975) have used the word *symbiosis* to refer to a parent who cannot let go of an adult child. Although it is normal for parents or teachers to follow closely the fortunes of those who have been in their charge, it is excessive when they live for and through them. Fans who idolize and emulate public performers are another category of excessive involvement. A psychotic form of the phenomenon is the psychiatric condition of *folie à deux* (Rioux, 1963) in which two individuals become caught up in the same delusional system.

The direction of closeness

As with all states of relatedness, closeness can either be given or received (donative or receptive). Ironically however, the person who gives closeness to someone else cannot avoid also giving some to her/himself. This may be why people who consider themselves to have been deprived of love often have a compulsive need to give love to others, for in the giving of it they are also providing it for themselves. Not only is the giving of love a close experience, but by identifying with the person who is being loved, the giver also feels that s/he is giving love to her/himself. Even though giving closeness does provide closeness to the giver, it is sometimes important to determine who is giving it and who is receiving it, for giving closeness is not the same experience as receiving it. Ideally, people both give and receive closeness, but some people are predominantly donors (they freely offer it but they cannot let it in), and others are predominantly receptors (they suck it up but they cannot give it out). In most close relationships, each partner both gives and receives in equal measure. In some, however, one person predominantly gives and the other predominantly receives.

Distance

Distance is the most primitive of states, for organisms would need to have been solitary before they could become gregarious; yet the advantages of distance are so great that, even today, there are many solitary species. All mobile organisms come together for the purpose of sexual reproduction; but for solitary organisms this is but a brief encounter, and they rapidly separate again. The advantages for solitary animals are that it is hard for predators to find and catch them, they can stalk their prey with less likelihood of being seen and they do not have to share their catch with others, they do not need to compete with other members of the species for food or feeding places, and they are less prone to infestation and infection. Primitive, solitary humans have similar advantages, but even within civilized societies, there are solitary individuals who keep to themselves, limit their objectives, meet their own needs, share nothing, and seek the help of no one.

Distant relating

Much of what has been written about distance could be construed as being about getting away from people or keeping people at bay. In fact, the greater part of relating behavior consists of a mixture of closeness and distance, in which we get neither too close to nor too far away from the people we relate to, and this mixture is called *distant* or *formal relating*. In distant relating we are careful not to reveal too much about ourselves; we withhold personal details, avoid spontaneity, and keep a check on our emotions. We speak more slowly and more carefully than in close relating, sometimes reading from a prepared statement, choosing our words carefully, adopting formal language and observing social conventions. Polite conversation is a form of distant relating. We use distant relating with professional people, tradespeople, people at work, and people we do not know well; but even with people we do know well, we may use it when discussing ordinary, everyday, practical matters. An important feature of some forms of distant relating is its impersonal nature, and much scientific and technical jargon is created in order to eliminate sentimentality from what is being talked about. In its more extreme forms, distant relating requires a certain callousness and disregard for the feelings of others. Murderers, torturers, terrorists, rapists, muggers and members of the armed services have to adopt a distant attitude in order that they can carry out acts of destruction and cruelty.

Distance and exploration

One of the most positive aspects of distancing is the stimulus it provides for the organism to move outwards into the surrounding environment. From an evolutionary point of view, this ensures that the species covers ever larger areas of the earth's surface. For man, it took thousands of years for the species to spread from its supposed origin in central Africa to the remainder of the earth. An advantage of this is that if the species in one area becomes endangered by climatic changes, shortage of food or water or predation, it continues to survive in other areas. All animals naturally explore their surroundings as a means of seeking out less populated and safer areas, new sources of food and unrelated members of the species with which to mate. The last of these reasons is paradoxical, for in moving away from the herd or the family, the individual is moving toward new partners. This paradoxical form of distancing is particularly prominent in humans.

In a species such as ours, in which the young stay close to the parents and the family for long periods of time, it can be disadvantageous for the young to move away too soon; a balance has to be struck between staying and leaving. The first stages of the exploration process begin at an early age; throughout childhood and into the early adult years, there follow successive stages of ever more distant explorations combined with periods of moving back to base. Such explorations are facilitated by the establishment, within the psyche, of internal close objects, which provide an internal source of closeness to sustain the person through periods of separation (see Chapter 5).

Distance and escape

For animals, an essential form of distance is the avoidance of or escape from predators. This they achieve either by taking flight or by remaining still, that, is by freezing, and relying upon their natural camouflage. Many animals can move extremely quickly and many can freeze. Humans have retained the ability to run fast, but they rarely use it for escaping from danger. Humans escape not so much from predators as from situations of intolerable psychological stress. The most extreme form of escape is suicide. Short of this, it is not uncommon for either adults or children to flee the family home to start life anew in a new location, sometimes with an assumed, new identity. A more inner brain-directed form of the same behavior is called the *fugue* (Stengel, 1941, 1943). In this, the person wanders, drives or travels, sometimes for long distances, emerging after a period of time into full consciousness, unaware of where s/he is or how s/he has got there.

It might be said that humans have retained the capacity to freeze, but it no longer serves the purpose for which it was originally intended. Called *stupor*, it is normally viewed as a form of psychopathology. The person, though aware of what is going on, cannot move and often also cannot speak. Fromm-Reichmann (1959) quoted a patient who had recovered from such a state as saying, "Hell is if you are frozen in isolation into a block of ice. That is where I have been" (p. 9).

Humans have evolved many other means of separating themselves off from stress without actually leaving the scene that are many times more subtle and more efficient than the stupor. They can go through the motions of living while not being totally in the situation. They can blot out the whole or part of what is going on by telling themselves that it is not really happening or by not experiencing the appropriate emotion, not feeling the pain, not seeing what is there to be seen or not hearing what is being said. This can apply as much to what they are doing to others as to what others are doing to them. By the process of *dissociation* they can so detach themselves from the action that it is as though they are witnessing it from somewhere outside of their bodies. Laing (1965) described the process of the *self splitting itself off from the body* so that the disembodied self is able to regard the body as though it were just another thing.

Deutsch (1942) wrote of the *as if* personality, who lacks any genuine emotional relationship to the outside world and simply behaves as if s/he had. Winnicott (1956) wrote of the *false self*, which is a kind of pretend self that is pushed out into the action to take all the knocks and rebuffs, while the *real* or *true self* remains safely out of the way. Similarly, Guntrip (1969a) wrote of the *central ego*, which is not capable of being hurt, which is pushed out to take the place of the *withdrawn ego*, which is capable of being hurt.

Distance and defense

Animals do not always flee from their attackers. Sometimes they stand their ground and fight them off. There is probably a great deal of interspecies variation in the extent to which animals take flight or stand their ground and fight. Judging by their propensity for aggression, humans appear more inclined to fight than to take flight, though some clearly are more so inclined than others. There does appear to be a component of the human relating repertoire that has a specific defensive function, and that is *paranoia*. In this, the person is highly aroused, suspicious, vigilant, tense and prepared to strike out. There are circumstances in which it is reasonable and beneficial to adopt this attitude, but some individuals, who have what is called a *paranoid personality*, are paranoid for much of the time or are easily provoked into being so. They may have lived through periods of stress that have primed them to be this way, or they may have inherited a heightened alertness to external threat, which represents an overcharged paranoid defense system. Probably an extreme form of the same defensive process is *paranoid psychosis*, in which the person hears hallucinations of threatening voices and is deluded that others, or gangs of others, are intent on harming or killing her/him.

The establishment of boundaries

A large number of animal species have evolved strategies for establishing and maintaining distance between themselves and other animals. Such distancing occurs both between and within species. Animals mark out their territories by brushing against or urinating upon objects in order that their smell may be left as a marker. They then patrol and defend these territories. Humans too, are preoccupied with defining and maintaining territorial boundaries. Territories are of value for animals largely because they contain sources of food. Territories are of value for humans because they contain sources of food, wood, minerals, energy and other resources. While some animals form colonies and work together for the common good, humans form large and complex conurbations, often with a unifying language and a strong racial and national identity. The members of these conurbations fear and hate the members of neighboring conurbations, and bitter feuds and wars break out between one conurbation and another. These fears and hatreds manifest themselves as *nationalism, racism* and *xenophobia* and give rise to such atrocities as *genocide* and *ethnic cleansing*. The paranoia that develops between nations and groups of nations is acquiring such intensity that the resultant accumulation of weapons of mass destruction is showing signs of seriously endangering the survival of the human species. It should be said that fear and mistrust of others also develops *within* complex conurbations. This has been well documented by Lasch (1984).

Fear of invasion and fear of intrusion

The defending of territory has become for humans much more than simply the preservation and protection of resources. Humans have acquired an intense fear of the invasion and intrusion of others. Properties are surrounded by hedges, fences and walls and have locked gates; people live in secure buildings with locked doors and windows; within these buildings they have their own locked rooms; and within these rooms they have their own locked drawers and cupboards. Besides the function of keeping people warm, clothing also serves the function of keeping other people out and of keeping our bodies out of the sight of others. When we are naked we not only feel cold, we also feel vulnerable. Being stripped, or being forced to strip, is experienced as a shocking invasion of our personal space. Women can find the thought of men *undressing them with their eyes* deeply disturbing.

Even when we are fully clothed, we can experience the gaze of others as penetrating. We sometimes use the expression *x-ray eyes* to describe this experience. The myth of the gorgon Medusa, whose gaze could turn people to stone, may be an expression of the universal fear of the power of the eyes. Laing (1965) used the term *petrification* to describe the state of paralysis that some psychotics experience when they feel they are caught in the gaze of others. He wrote, "In psychotic conditions, the gaze and scrutiny of the other can be experienced as an actual penetration to the core of the 'inner self'" (p. 106). Making *eye contact* is a special experience we reserve for moments of particular significance between ourselves and people we feel close to. Goffman (1963) used the term *civil inattention* to describe the normal practice of respectfully avoiding eye contact between ourselves and most people in most social situations.

Eibl-Eibesfeldt (1989) observed that "Fear of others is one of the universals that decidedly influence our social life" (p. 175). He believed that our personal space is carried about with us like an invisible bubble; most fish, birds and animals can also be seen to maintain a distance between themselves and others. People usually respect the need of others to maintain an area of space around themselves and try to leave a suitable space between themselves and others when sitting on public transport and in other public places (Mazur, 1977). McBride and colleagues (1965) were able to measure the anxiety generated by intrusion upon people's personal space. Altman (1975) observed that the more anxious people are, the less close will they allow others to come to them. Freud (1895) used the term *contact barrier* to refer to the psychological boundary we maintain around ourselves.

The skin is essential for the survival of all animals and serves a number of important functions, including that of protection against attackers. In some animals it is extremely thick or is covered with scales or a hard shell. In humans, it is relatively thin, which renders us vulnerable to the penetration of teeth, spears, swords and bullets. It does, however, provide us with the advantage of being able to preserve heat or lose heat rapidly according to changes in temperature, which enables us to tolerate extreme climatic changes and survive in a range of environments. Anzieu (1989), a French psychoanalyst, wrote of the significance of the skin as both a true and a metaphorical barrier between our inner selves and the outside world. He wrote of the extreme distress we experience when areas of our skin are destroyed, for instance, by burns, but also of the strong emotions we have about the skin. He used the term *Le Moi-Peau*, which translates as *the skin ego*, to describe what he called a psychological envelope that contains, defines and protects the psyche.

There are those who have a heightened sensitivity to invasion or intrusion; possibly because, in earlier years, their personal space was invaded disrespectfully. They may be more than usually fastidious about keeping their bodies covered up, try to maintain a greater than average distance from others, be particularly sensitive to people coming close to them and have a fear of being touched. This might be combined with a fear of dirt and a fear of contamination.

The psychoanalytic concept of the *ego boundary* is more abstract than that of the contact barrier or the skin ego. It is to do with the fact that most individuals experience themselves as being distinct and separate from other individuals. Ego boundaries are spoken of as being strong or weak, and it is as disadvantageous to have an excessively strong one as to have an excessively weak one. A person with an excessively strong ego boundary lives too much inside her/himself and does not easily empathize, sympathize or identify with other people. A person with an excessively weak ego boundary has the chameleon-like characteristic of too readily feeling the emotions, adopting the ideas and assuming the identity of anyone s/he happens to be with. People can remain distant either because they have very strong ego boundaries or because their ego boundaries are so weak that they are afraid of losing themselves within the identity of anyone they allow themselves to get close to.

Interest in the self

At the beginning of this chapter it was explained that when cathexis is withdrawn from others it becomes directed onto the self. Therefore, in the condition of distance, people become interested in and preoccupied with themselves. It seems reasonable and proper that people should pay a great deal of attention to themselves, not just to their own personal survival or to protecting their own self-interest but also to getting to know themselves well and to understanding themselves. Jacobson (1964) maintained that there are not only internal representations of others, but also an internal representation of the self. In this way the self is able to relate to itself, to approve or disapprove of it, to be good to it or hard on it, to console and encourage it or to blame and chastise it. Though people are reluctant to admit that they talk to themselves, it seems likely that everyone does, either quietly, internally, or out loud. It is hardly possible to have a good relationship with oneself if one is not able to have conversations with it. There are those who relate to themselves to the exclusion of relating to others. There are also those who try to avoid themselves and scarcely relate to themselves at all.

To a very large extent, the self and the body are one continuous entity, so that relating to the self also involves relating to the body. Ideally the self is securely wedded to and embedded within the body, but sometimes it is not. Laing (1965) described how, in some schizophrenics, there is a splitting of the self from the body, so that the self feels subjectively outside the body, views it as though it were a thing and is frightened of entering into it. Those who are on good terms with their bodies treat them well and lavish attention upon them. Those who are not neglect and abuse them. Sometimes a person's relationship to her/himself is quite different from that with her/his body: s/he may like her/himself and dislike her/his body, or vice versa. A person may project bad feelings about her/himself on to her/his body, which may result in self-mutilation or seeking to change the body through plastic surgery. People sometimes dislike or dissociate themselves from their bodies because they consider them to be the wrong gender, too old or ugly. It is a principle of Gestalt therapy that people should strive to accept, own and be proud of their bodies whatever their age or whatever their appearance, because their bodies are them and they are their bodies.

Turning in on the self

When people are cut off from external stimuli they are brought more into contact with their psychic interiors. This partly amounts just to the recollection of memories, but it can also involve making contact with internalized others, and such others can be friendly or hostile. Lilly (1956) observed that when normal levels of external stimuli are reduced, the inner life of some people can become vivid and intense. After only a few days, they can experience fantastic dreams or become deluded and hallucinated. The same sometimes happens to people under conditions of solitary confinement (Grassian, 1983).

Being alone with oneself

People are never completely alone, because they are always alone with themselves. Having been with a lot of people for a long time, particularly if the involvement has been fraught and intense, being able to escape to a place where one can be completely alone can, because of the contrast, be a great relief. However, after a fairly short time, most people start wanting to make contact with people again, and the solitude begins to feel unpleasant. Some people, particularly those who have schizoid tendencies, enjoy spending time on their own for quite long periods, and they do so frequently. Others hate the experience, and if they find themselves alone, they try to distract themselves by reading a book or turning on the radio. Whether one likes to spend time with oneself depends to a large degree upon whether one likes oneself.

Identity and the self

In the previous chapter the question arose as to whether the self might be located in the inner or the outer brain. The answer was not straightforward because, although that which we call the sense of self appears to be located in the outer brain, that which we might call the essential self is located in the inner brain. The same applies to identity. Feeling that we are someone distinct and separate from other people is an outer brain experience, but our awareness of all of the ways that we are distinct and separate from other people is an inner brain experience. If we have a secure identity we are able to say with conviction, "I know what I like". We can say this because when we have, or are in the presence of, that which we like, a strong surge of pleasure wells up from the inner brain. We do not need to think to ourselves, "Now, do I or do I not like this?" If we trust our inner brains, the message comes through loud and clear, "Yes, I do", or "No, I don't". What can perhaps be infuriating is that we may not know why we do or do not like it. We may, at an outer brain level, try to work this out, though in the end this can only be a rationalization.

What any one person likes is entirely individual and is not necessarily the same as what any other person likes. This we may find puzzling. "Why", we might ask, "if s/he likes it, do not I like it?" If that other person is important, or knowledgeable or known to have good taste, we may think there is something wrong with us for not liking it. The inner brain has built up its store of things that it does and does not like, and it has perfectly sound reasons, based upon how we have experienced various things, for its judgments. We cannot like what we do not like, and part of having a secure identity is accepting that there are things that we like and things that we do not like. The distinction made in the last chapter between what we like and what we think we ought to like is a crucial one. As far as the identity is concerned, what we think we ought to like is quite irrelevant.

Self-esteem

Having established that each person has something called the self and that that self can become a center of interest for the person, it is sometimes a matter of some importance what s/he may think of her/himself. *Self-esteem* is the extent to which a person like or dislikes, or approves or disapproves, of her/himself. The issue of self-esteem is one of endless interest to psychologists (Baumeister, 1993) and psychiatrists (Robson, 1988) alike. One reason for this interest is the widely held view that low self esteem may predispose people to depression (Beck, 1967). Certainly, depression and low self-esteem commonly coexist, but it has been shown that low self-esteem does not predict subsequent depression (Lewinsohn et al., 1981) and that the self-esteem of recovered depressives is no lower than that of people who did not become depressed (Hamilton & Abramson, 1983). It is believed by writers such as Storr (1983) that people carry around within themselves a kind of generalized self-esteem, which has been carried over from the esteem in which they were held by their parents. Superimposed upon this there must be a kind of moment-to-moment self-esteem, which is a reflection of their assessment of how well they are doing or have done in various situations. Finally, there is the esteem derived from the responses of others to how well they are doing or have done. People very in the extent to which their esteem is self-determined or other-determined. For the ontologically insecure it is entirely other-determined.

Originally and inventiveness

A person who has both a strong sense of identity and well-established sense of autonomy is capable of thinking up new and original ideas and working out new and original ways of doing things. Creativity takes place in that state that Fromm-Reichman (1959) called *constructive aloneness*, but people have to be careful not to carry their originally or inventiveness too far. Artists often use the word *derivative* in a disparaging way, but it is probably safer for creative people to begin by being derivative and then to carry their ideas or creations just a stage or two further. Having made their original contribution in their state of aloneness, they need ultimately to bring it into the real world to test out its feasibility and its acceptability. If it is too original, the world may not be ready for it and it may be rejected. Often it has been said that it is hard to draw the line between genius and insanity; since both are forms of originality, there may be some truth in this. Millon (1981) observed that the more estranged an individual becomes from her/his social environment, the more out of touch s/he becomes with the conventions of reality and with the checks against irrational thought and behavior that are provided by reciprocal relationships.

Ontological security

Laing (1965), who probably understood the state of distance more clearly than most, introduced the term *ontological security*. This term incorporates three distinct though overlapping, ways of being securely separate from others. The first is by having a strong ego boundary. The second is the formation of a *secure identity* and the third is the acquisition of *autonomy*.

Much has been written about the nature of identity (Yardley & Honess, 1987), and here may not be the place to explore the concept in any detail. Whereas character and personality are more to do with other people's views of the person, identity is more to do with the person's subjective experience of her/himself. Many people simply take their identity for granted, and it may be only those who have what might be called *an identity problem* who find themselves asking questions such as, "Who am I?" They may be like this because they have never been encouraged or permitted to make their minds up about such issues as what they like and what they believe in. Instead they have spent their lives following the example of, and conforming to, the opinions of others. A person's identity may be substantial, or insubstantial, which is similar to an ego boundary being weak or strong.

Autonomy is concerned less with preferences, beliefs and opinions and more with a sense of being responsible for oneself and taking the initiative in the making of decisions. It is also concerned with making one's own mind up, with setting personal standards of behavior and with judging oneself against such standards. People develop a sense of autonomy only when they are left to their own devices and when the decision about what to do and what not to do rests entirely with them. Motivation from within moves in to fill the void left from the absence of any direction from without.

Laing explained that a person who is ontologically insecure is torn between two contrasting strategies, either to keep away from others in order to avoid becoming totally overwhelmed by them or to elect to become fused with and parasitic upon an ontologically secure other, living for and through that person, in a state of what Laing called *ontological dependence*.

Causes of negative distance

In psychotherapy, it is important to appreciate that distancing behavior may have a number of different causes, some of which may be more amenable to therapy than others. Some of these (such as paranoia, fear of invasion or intrusion and ontological insecurity) have already been discussed, but one that has not been discussed so far is the limited tolerance of sensory input. It seems that, perhaps even from birth, people may vary in the extent to which they can tolerate involvement with others and that this may be due to as simple a physiological variable as the ability to control the inflow of sensory messages. People with a low tolerance level rapidly attain a condition called *stimulus overload* (Baron & Byrne, 1991), at which further exposure to people becomes intolerable. Eysenck (1947) observed that introverts are less tolerant than extraverts, and Ornitz (1983) observed that *autistic* individuals, that is, individuals who from an early age maintain an extremely limited and tenuous contact with others, have a very low tolerance. Schizophrenics, who probably also have a low tolerance, have a particularly high tolerance of the opposite experience of sensory deprivation and under such conditions may even experience a reduction of hallucinatory experiences (Harris, 1959).

It is important to distinguish between those distant individuals who in the *Diagnostic and Statistical Manual of Mental Disorders* (American Psychiatric Association, 1994) are defined as *avoidant personalities*, and were described by Millon (1981) as being actively avoidant, and those who, in the same *DSM* classification, are defined as *schizoid personalities*, and were described by Millon (1981) as passively avoidant. Those in the first category desire closeness but are frightened of seeking it, mainly out of fear of rejection. Those in the second category, such as those who are being described here, find all but the most limited involvement with others intolerable.

The psychiatric condition of *schizophrenia* is very much a condition of distance (Birtchnell, 1993/1996), and many of the phenomena associated with distance are most clearly observable in this condition. This is not to say, however, that distance and schizophrenia are one and the same thing. Distance is an essential feature of relating. It is simply that in schizophrenia it has come to assume certain extreme and maladaptive forms.

The distinction between the active and the passive avoidant is similar to, though probably not the same as, Bartholomew's (1990) distinction between *fearful avoidant* and *dismissive avoidant* personalities. The first desire intimacy but fear rejection, and the second place value on independence and maintain that relationships are not that important. It is not clear from Bartholomew's description whether the dismissive category has an innate intolerance of closeness or whether, as the name implies, they are an extreme version of the fearful who, out of a once bitten, twice shy or a sour grapes attitude, have decided to steer clear of people because they always let you down.

Lack of trust is a theme that runs through the descriptions of a number of types of distant individuals, though it must be acknowledged that such lack of trust may be as much to do with the untrustworthiness of the other as to the individual's inability to trust. Hayward and Taylor (1956) quoted a patient as saying, "The problem with schizophrenics is that they can't trust anyone. The doctor will have to fight to get in no matter how much the patient objects" (p. 218). Bannister (1987) also maintained that in the psychotherapy of schizophrenia trust continues to be tested time and time again. An inability to trust is certainly not restricted to schizophrenics, and many would consider that schizophrenics belong to that class of individuals who are distant because they have a low tolerance of sensory input, though Millon's (1969) description of what he called the *active* or *avoidant schizophrenic* could be what these writers are referring to.

Much has been written here of the fear of and retreat from others. It needs to be stressed that there is also an active, negative form of distancing that pushes others into distance. This is called *rejection* or, in its extreme form, *ostracization*. The rejector is most usually an upper distant individual, but it may still be that rejection is motivated by a fear of closeness or of the person who is being rejected.

Distant closeness

Distant closeness is a form of distant relating in which people derive closeness from a distance. Its appeal is that it is safer than more direct forms of closeness because it does not carry the same risk of rejection. It can assume many forms, and here it is possible to provide only a few examples. Relating to pets can sometimes be extremely close, but because pets are not human, relating to them cannot be considered to be true closeness. Pets rarely reject their owners. Relating to dolls, imaginary companions, fantasy lovers, photographs, characters in books or films, or on radio or television provides a similar kind of restricted closeness. Relating to God has to be included in this category. Relating that is entirely or almost entirely sexual is limited because it does not extend into other forms of closeness, and many forms of sexual or predominantly sexual behavior such as extramarital affairs, one-night stands and prostitution carry a similar limitation.

Talking to people on telephone help lines provides genuine though transient closeness, but the communication has predominantly to be one-way, and there is little likelihood of the relationship developing into a true and lasting friendship. The limitations of the psychotherapeutic relationship were referred to in the section on closeness; even though patient and therapist can sometimes enter into states of extreme intimacy, psychotherapy itself has to be considered a form of distant closeness because of these limitations.

Summary

It is by way of the proximity axis that we regulate our closeness to and distance from others, but there is more to closeness and distance than mere proximity. It is through closeness that we become caught up in the life of another person; we become part of that person and that person becomes part of us. We feel we understand that person and that we are understood by that person. We feel for that person and are respectful of the needs of that person, and that person feels for us and is respectful of our needs. In negative closeness, we cling desperately and disrespectfully to others. It is through distance that we become caught up in the life of ourselves. We develop a sense of separateness from others and create within ourselves a totally new and original individual. We become aware of, and own, our ideas, opinions and preferences. In negative distance we lack a clearly defined and secure sense of self and fear the encroachment and intrusion of others.

Chapter 4

The proximity axis in psychotherapy

The proximity axis has relevance both within and outside the therapy session. Within the session, both the therapist and the client have relating tendencies that will have a bearing upon what happens between them. Although therapists are likely to be more versatile (as defined in Chapter 1) than clients, they do vary considerably in the extent to which they allow themselves to get close to clients or encourage or allow clients to get close to them. This variation is due to two factors, possibly related. The first is the therapist's personality, the second is the style of therapy the therapist chooses to adopt.

Therapists' personalities and therapists' styles can range from close to distant. Close therapists are more likely to adopt close forms of therapy, and distant therapists are more likely to adopt distant forms of therapy. Clients also range from close to distant. It is possible that close therapists get on better with close clients and distant therapists get on better with distant ones. This is not to say that close therapists are better for close clients and distant therapists are better for distant ones, for close therapists may reinforce the closeness of close clients and distant therapists may reinforce the distance of distant ones. To a large extent, therapists are able to choose the form of therapy they adopt; to a lesser extent, they are able to choose the clients they treat. On the other hand, most clients are probably not aware that there is a range of different forms of therapy; even if they were, they would not normally be offered a range of therapies to choose from. Most clients are not in a position to choose their therapist. It may well be, therefore, that during the early stages of therapy either therapist or client decides that the therapy is not going to work. This decision may well be made on the basis of a (consciously or unconsciously) perceived incompatibility in terms of closeness and distance. There is scope for empirical research that would test some of these possibilities.

The effect of personality on therapists' style

Irrespective of the form of therapy they adopt, close therapists are more inclined to work in restful, informal surroundings, with colorful pictures on the walls, with no desk and with soft, inviting, comfortable furniture. They will be casually dressed and propose from an early stage that they and their clients should be on first-name terms. They are more likely to place themselves in close proximity to their clients, facing them and ensuring that there are no obstacles between themselves and the client. They will adopt a friendly, chatty style and will not concern themselves with elicting symptoms or taking a formal history. Instead, they will invite their clients to tell them their story at their own speed and in their own way. They will not take notes, but will watch and listen intently and respond appropriately, by word or gesture, with amusement, horror or whatever, to the things their clients say to them. They will show emotion themselves and encourage their clients to show emotion. In fact, one of their objectives may be to urge their clients toward a fuller show of emotion, if not a complete emotional catharsis. They will be inclined to touch or hold their clients as a way of offering encouragement, comfort, consolation or support.

Again, irrespective of the form of therapy they adopt, distant therapists are more inclined to work in formal consulting rooms with harder, less comfortable chairs. They will be more formally dressed, expect to be addressed by their surname and by a title if they have one and address their clients by their surname. They may sit behind or beside a desk and ensure that their clients remain some distance from them. They may not look directly at their clients, or they may suggest that their clients lie supine on a couch. They may take notes. They are more likely to elicit symptoms, take a formal history, ask questions and give instructions. They are more likely to call their clients patients. They will try not to respond emotionally to what their clients say to them and to maintain an expressionless attitude toward them. They will try to ignore or avoid any show of emotion and keep the dialogue at a factual level. They will avoid physical contact.

Proximity characteristics of different styles of therapy

There are styles of therapy that correspond to these different ways of relating to clients. The closer styles belong to the humanistic group, the more distant ones belong to the behavioral-cognitive group and an entire range of styles falls between these two extremes. The closer styles are less clearly defined, more accepting of the irrational (i.e., more inner brain orientated), and the therapists are more disposed to allowing the client to lead the way. The more distant styles are more clearly defined and rationally based (i.e., more outer brain orientated), and the therapists are more inclined to direct and instruct the clients. Although it is acknowledged that therapists' personalities vary, it should be emphasized that therapists owe it to their clients to be competent in the entire spectrum of therapeutic approaches, in order that they be capable of applying the most appropriate technique to each client or problem that is encountered. A therapist who proclaims that s/he is a behaviorist, humanist, psychoanalyst or whatever is, in fact, admitting to her/his limitations. Examples of the most close and the most distant forms of therapy will now be given.

The humanistic therapies–the most close

The humanistic group includes person-centered therapy (Rogers, 1961), the body therapies (Liss, 1974), primal therapy (Janov, 1973), and Gestalt therapy (Fagan & Shepard, 1970). The aim of the humanistic therapies is the development of the whole person, sometimes called personal growth or self-actualization (Maslow, 1968). A central assumption is that clients have the capacity to heal themselves provided they are encouraged and supported by the therapist, sometimes called the facilitator. Rogers (1986) wrote, "The more the therapist is himself or herself in the relationship, putting up no professional front or personal facade, the greater is the likelihood that the client will change and grow in a constructive manner" (p. 197). Related to this is the idea that therapist and client should be of equal status. Clients and patients are more likely to address each other by their first names. This enables the therapist to make personal disclosures to the client should they seem appropriate or helpful. Physical contact, particularly hugging, between therapist and client and client and client is common. Nudity features occasionally. A small number of humanistic therapists (Shepard, 1971) have condoned actual sexual involvement between therapists and clients.

In person-centered therapy, the therapist allows the client to lead, and the therapist follows closely behind, for as Rogers (1986) observed, only the client knows where her/his difficulties lie and the therapist requires the client to take her/him there. The section on "picking up a scent" in Chapter 2 is in keeping with the client-centered approach. This form of therapy is in direct contrast to those in which the therapist tells the client what to do. Essential to the person-centered approach is that the therapist trusts the client, which gives the client confidence.

The body therapies rest upon the assumption that the person is the body and the body is the person and that a sense of identity is reinforced by a greater awareness of and acceptance of the body. They aim to enable clients to become more in contact with their bodies. Lowen (1967) wrote, "An ego dissociated from the body is weak and vulnerable, and knowledge divorced from feeling is empty and meaningless" (p. 260). Body therapists stress that emotion gains expression through physical movement and that the muscles are, among other things, organs of emotional expression. When people are anxious or angry their muscles become tense. Therefore, muscles can become the repositories of pent-up feelings. Release of these feelings can be facilitated by breathing deeply, changing posture, unlocking arms and legs and shaking, and by exercises that put the muscles on stretch or by certain kinds of massage that stimulate or relax the muscles.

Expression of emotion is a form of closeness, and it is difficult to release emotion in a state of distance. Therefore, the body therapies require therapists and clients, and sometimes also clients and clients, to work closely together. Physical contact can intensify involvement between people; under the right circumstances, securely holding someone can create a powerful sense of security in that person. It is like the security experienced by the firmly held infant (Winnicott, 1952).

In primal therapy the emphasis once more is upon emotional release, but the approach is different. The therapist aims gradually to break down the client's defenses. The initial phase of therapy takes place daily over a three-week period; during this time, the client is required not to work. For twenty-four hours before the first session, s/he is required to stay alone in a hotel bedroom, preferably without sleeping. The client lies spread-eagled upon a couch and is encouraged to talk freely. S/he is discouraged from intellectualizing (Chapter 2). When moving in an emotional direction, s/he is not allowed to change the subject, and if s/he shows signs of emotion, she is urged to "stay with it". S/he is encouraged to speak to Daddy or Mommy. Janov (1973) wrote "Each day an attempt is made to widen the hole in the defense system until the patient can no longer defend himself" (p. 83). When the emotion comes, it comes in a gush, which is called *the primal scream*. As the days go by, the client becomes "defenseless" and emotions come more easily. Further *primals* follow, and the client goes further back into childhood. Following their three weeks of individual therapy, clients enter a therapy group that meets for three hours, twice weekly, over several months; in this group, members provoke each other into having further primals.

Gestalt therapy incorporates many of the techniques included in the three approaches just described, and in many respects it is the parent therapy from which the others have been derived. It is usually carried out in a group setting, but with the therapist working with one group member at a time. Other group members identify and empathize with the member being worked with, and there is often a two-way emotional interaction between them and that member. This makes it easier for the therapist to move from one group member to another.

A central feature of Gestalt therapy is what is called the *here and now* principle, that emotion belongs to the place and the time at which it is experienced. If clients can be persuaded to re-enact, in the here and now, events that happened in another place and at another time, they will re-experience the emotions generated by that event. There is a world of difference between saying "It was frightening" and saying "I am frightened". Also, if the client can be persuaded to address the person about whom the emotion is or was felt, the emotion can be re-experienced. The remarks can be made to a chair or a cushion used to represent the person or to a drawing of the person.

Saying "I was frightened of him" is much less disturbing than saying "I am frightened of you". The here and now is a more close experience than the there and then.

The behavioral-cognitive therapies—the most distant

The behavioral-cognitive group includes behavior therapy (Liberman, 1972; King, 1986), cognitive therapy (Beck, 1976), and rational-emotive therapy (Ellis and Grieger, 1977). Behavioral cognitive therapists adopt a more formal attitude toward their clients, stay apart from them, do not touch them, and address them by their surnames. Even though the majority of behavioral-cognitive therapists are psychologists, they behave more like doctors. They attach great importance to eliciting symptoms, and much of their treatment involves telling clients what to do. The therapy is appealing to the more distant and also the more passive kind of client. It also induces both distance and passivity in the client. While telling clients what to do is more a power (Chapter 6) than a proximity issue, it is more upper distant than upper close, and it does seem to fit in with a distant posture.

The aim of behavior therapy is the rectification of *current behavioral deficits*. Such deficits must be capable of precise definition and measurement. The practitioners reveal little interest in tracking down the origin of the deficits. They measure them, apply their therapy and measure them again. This leads to what they call *self-correcting feedback loops*, by which they are able repeatedly to modify the therapy and measure again until they find the optimum treatment strategy either for the individual or for the field as a whole. Whereas early treatment strategies were based upon specific theories of behavior (Skinner, 1953), later ones have become empirical.

The so-called deficits appear mostly to be unhelpful and chronic affective states such as anxiety, phobia, panic and depression. To an interpersonal therapist, it would seem odd to separate off an affective state and consider it something to be ameliorated. Doing so might itself be considered a form of distancing. It needs to be said, however, that fears of particular states of relating commonly exist, and such fears represent one form of negative relating (Chapter 1). Therefore, there is no reason why behavioral techniques should not be effective in enabling clients to overcome such fears. Evans (1996) observed that "Sullivan's ideas about learning and psychotherapeutic change bear a conspicuous similarity to behaviorism" (p. 172). Although there may well be certain similarities between, say, a fear of heights and a fear of upperness, it could be argued that the fear of a state of relatedness (such as upperness) is a more complex and far-reaching phenomenon than the fear of a specific experience (such as heights) and may require more extensive exploration and understanding.

Many behavioral-cognitive therapists, perhaps as another form of distancing, maintain that the therapy is not dependent upon the quality of the therapist/client relationship. Therapists do, however, work collaboratively with their clients and do praise and encourage them when they do well. They perform the important function of directing clients toward specific tasks and holding them to them. Phobias, for example, can be eliminated by the forced exposure of the individual to the feared object or situation without avoidance or escape taking place. When this is carried out in the presence of a competent therapist, 70 percent of subjects show full remission after a single session (Ost, 1989). When the same procedure is adopted by the client, in the absence of a therapist, using a self-help manual, the therapy is far less effective. Therefore, despite their distant posture, behavior therapists have a beneficial effect upon their clients by their very presence. In fact, Bandura (1986) stressed the importance of the behavioral-cognitive therapist as a model for the client to observe, imitate and learn from.

The assumption behind most of the behavioral-cognitive therapies is that certain unhelpful attitudes are the result of faulty learning. Therefore therapists' interventions are designed to be instructive or educational, and therapy is called a *corrective therapeutic learning experience*. In the longer-term forms of therapy, progress is made not so much within the treatment session as during the period between sessions, when clients complete specific homework assignments. Clients are often required to keep diaries, to provide a daily record of the frequency and severity of their symptoms. The therapy is not always carried out on a client who has come to a therapist for help. Sometimes a behavioral regime is carried out on the patients in a hospital. In this instance, the treatment goals are set by the hospital staff, who carry out observations upon the patients and record data.

When the behavioral-cognitive therapies were first introduced, because results were achieved by such simple methods in so short a time, the more psychodynamic therapists felt threatened by them. They claimed that because no attention had been paid to resolving the conflicts that underlie the symptoms, either the effects would be short lived or symptom substitution would occur. In fact, studies have now shown that the effects are not short lived and symptom substitution does not occur. Therefore, instead of turning a blind eye to the behavioral-cognitive therapists, it is useful to examine with some care what they do and why their methods work. At the simplest level, what they do is relax the client and move progressively toward the elimination of the symptom by introducing the client, in simple and manageable stages, to increasing doses of a feared stimulus. This is no more than the good parent might do with a frightened child.

However, the cognitive therapists have carried the process a lot further. In some instances, the therapy would appear to be a way of using the outer brain to reprogram the inner brain. Carrying on from the theorizing of Beck (1976), Salkovskis (1995) explained that it is not the situation itself that produces an undesired emotion, it is what the person thinks and believes about the situation. As everyone becomes emotional under certain circumstances, becoming emotional is not the problem. The problem is that the person erroneously sees the situation as one in which s/he should feel emotional. S/he feels anxious, phobic, panicky or depressed when realistically s/he has no need to. The belief has been established some time earlier in life and has been passed down to the inner brain. Once there it has become automatic. The therapy involves revealing to the person the irrationality of her/his belief and using the outer brain to interrupt the inner brain's automatic thought processes. For example, a person may be shown that s/he experiences panic when s/he misinterprets a normal bodily sensation as a sign of a serious condition.

Rational-emotive therapy is a further extension of this way of thinking. It aims not so much to alter behavior as to alter attitudes. Ellis (1986) maintained that people disturb themselves by thinking, feeling and acting in ways that defeat their own best interests. They *awfulize* both the conditions of their lives and themselves. He wrote of the *irrational beliefs* that clients hold about themselves that lead to self-defeating and self-sabotaging consequences. The therapy involves revealing the irrationality of their beliefs by way of a *disputational dialogue*. Some forms of rational-emotive therapy come close to interpersonal therapy. For example, a client may harbor the belief that nobody enjoys her/his company because s/he is so boring. S/he therefore avoids talking to people or makes excuses to terminate the conversation if someone starts talking to her/him. The therapist may challenge the client to justify this belief and to offer evidence of people who did not enjoy her/his company. The therapist may try to de-awfulize the situation by asking "Who said you always have to be interesting? Is it so terrible if sometimes you bore people? Don't people sometimes bore you?" The therapist may ask the client to imagine the worst possible scenario of someone being utterly bored by her/him and ask if s/he could survive this. S/he may set her/him the task of talking to at least three people a week for ten minutes at a time. The therapy appears to be a mixture of friendly reassurance and firm pressure. By this stage it is no longer a distant form of relating.

Closeness in psychotherapy

Orlinsky and Howard (1986), concluded from a review of over a thousand outcome studies that the crucial factor in all cases of effective psychotherapy is the bond that therapists form with their clients. Rogers (1957) placed the therapist/client relationship above all else as the factor responsible for the efficacy of psychotherapy. He believed that, in comparison, the various theories of psychopathology were of minor importance. He considered the three most important therapist characteristics to be genuineness, unconditional positive regard, and empathy, all of which are facets of closeness. Similarly, Ferreira (1964) believed that the therapeutic value of what is talked about is secondary to the experience of the fulfillment of the client's intimacy needs. Lambert and colleagues (1986) concluded that certain *common factors*, such as attention, warmth and understanding, are central to all forms of psycho-therapy; Mitchell and colleagues (1977) found, from a research review, a significant link between genuineness, warmth and empathy in the therapist and positive therapeutic outcome. Luborsky and colleagues (1988) showed the therapist's quality of closeness to the client to be the best predictor of a favorable outcome; and Strupp and colleagues (1969) observed that what clients valued most in psychotherapy were the warmth, friendliness, respect and interest of the therapist. Bailey (1988) maintained that what clients seek most from their therapists is kinship, namely, the warmth and friendliness of being with their own kind (see Chapter 3). This he called *familiness*. He considered that most psychotherapists withhold such kinship, which creates what he called *kinship asymmetry*. In fact, therapists vary greatly in the extent to which they allow themselves to become naturally warm and friendly toward their clients. Some of the most kin-like therapists belong to the humanistic category.

Sullivan (1954) introduced the term *interpersonal security* to describe the setting, created by the therapist, within which it becomes safe for clients to be openly themselves and to examine and modify the assumptions they hold about themselves and others. It is a term he also applied to the mother-infant relationship, suggesting that the mother's secure presence reduces anxiety and enables the infant to apply itself to the task of learning new inter-personal competencies, which is similar to Bowlby's (1969) concept of secure attachment. Sullivan believed that the therapist should be engaged, respect-ful, interpersonal and empathic. Evans (1996) likened this to Fairbairn's (1952) *genuine emotional contact*. All interpretations made either by client or therapist should be subjected to systematic enquiry and consensual validation.

In a lecture, Smail (1995) maintained that "One of the principal things, and sometimes the only thing, psychotherapy, and even good psychotherapy, offers its clients is a commodity which is not widely or plentifully available elsewhere: that is love". It was Ferenczi who most openly and unashamedly acknowledged that what clients both expected and needed from their analysts was love. He used terms such as *maternal friendliness*; real, sincere sympathy; *transference love* and *active tenderness*. When he considered it necessary, he was prepared to touch and caress his clients and to permit them to express physical affection toward him (though never to the extent of sexual inter-course). For this he was sternly admonished by both Freud and Ernest Jones. He believed that those who have been brutally, sexually abused as children need to be held tenderly when regressed to this stage (Stanton, 1990). Dublin (1985) described a similar approach to the treatment of terrorized or brutali-zed clients. Of one client he wrote, "When she kissed me on the cheek and I could feel her slight trembling, I held her as tenderly as I ever have my own daughter" (p. 79). Considering how closely the psychotherapeutic relation-ship approximates to amorous love, it is not entirely surprising that actual sexual intercourse between therapist and client sometimes does occur (Pope and Bouhoutsos, 1986; Jehu, 1994).

Transference and countertransference

In psychoanalytic psychotherapy in particular, much has been written of the nature of the client's feelings toward the therapist, commonly referred to as the *transference*, and of the therapist's feelings toward the client, commonly referred to as the *countertransference*. Freud (1895) first used the word transference to refer to the sometimes intensely loving feelings that his female clients developed toward him. He explained these as feelings that the client more correctly felt toward an important other person in her life, such as a parent, but which, in the course of therapy, had become displaced onto him. Some (e.g., Shlien, 1984) have argued that the nature of the psychoanalytic encounter, involving as it frequently does the revelation of highly personal and erotic material, is sufficient to promote such feelings in the client and that Freud resorted to the concept of the transference as a means of dissociating himself from the true nature of the developing relationship between himself and his clients. When Freud later experienced the expression by his clients of intensely negative feelings toward him, he found it necessary to adopt the adjectives *positive* and *negative* to describe the transference. In place of transference, Sullivan (1954) used the term *parataxic distortion*. He considered that such distortion was not restricted to the client's relationship to the therapist. It was observable in the client's reporting of her/his relating to others. It was a form of relating that had become established in early interactions with important others and had become generalizable to later, similar, interpersonal situations.

The countertransference was first conceived of as the therapist's response to the transference, but was later extended to include the therapist's sometimes irrational feelings toward the client. These too could be either positive or negative and might also represent the displacement of feelings held toward some important other person. Unlike Freud, who believed that countertransference reactions should be eliminated through personal analysis, Sullivan saw the strong feelings of therapist toward the client as inevitable and part of the human dimension of treatment (Evans, 1996).

For many, the continued examination of transference and countertransference are the most important component of the psychoanalytic procedure (Smith, 1991). Milton (1997), attempting to contrast the behavioral-cognitive approach with her own psychoanalytic one, considered that the cognitive therapist was inclined to try to reason the client out of her/his unreasonable stance. She wrote,

> When I as an analyst ... find myself trying to be reasonable with a patient, who is disagreeing with me, or hating or despising me, and trying

to justify myself by explaining something, alarm bells ring (or should ring) in my mind. . . . If I do manage to do this and we are a cosy duo again, I will become nice but weak for the patient, and he will be left with his unmodified bad internal figure, ready to arise again in his life. . . . I want to stress that being the recipient of hatred, contempt, and so on is really awful. There is nothing as if about it, and if there is, there is something wrong, somehow the therapy has gone too intellectual too quickly.

(pp. 33–34)

Her contention is that unless the hate, contempt or whatever is actually expressed in all its true intensity to the therapist during the session, no effective linking with the original figure of hate or contempt is possible.

It may be easier for the psychoanalyst to allow her/himself to be the recipient of real hate than to be the recipient of real love or of real sexual desire. At least with hate, it is possible for the analyst to reassure her/himself that the hatred belongs elsewhere. With love, or sexual desire, it may be more tempting to believe that s/he is the true and deserving recipient of these feelings and to want to reciprocate.

Analysts and other therapists must also accept that the countertransference feelings that they experience in the session toward their clients, whether they be hateful or loving and desirous, are also real feelings and that their clients may all too easily become aware that these feelings are being directed toward them. Does the therapist acknowledge them to the client and accept their possible origins, or does s/he try to conceal or deny them?

The direction of closeness

In psychotherapy, the direction of closeness is predominantly one way, from therapist to client (Waldroop & Hurst, 1982). Psychotherapy is the process of *being there for the client* but not the other way round. It is possible that some people become psychotherapists because they have a need to be givers of closeness but cannot tolerate being receivers of it. Those therapists who rely heavily upon transference and transference interpretation make a point of not revealing aspects of themselves to their clients. This way they present themselves as a *blank screen* upon which their clients may project their ways of relating to significant others (Freud, 1912), but the idea of the therapist being impenetrable and serving as a mirror to the client ran counter to Sullivan's (1954) idea of the psychotherapeutic relationship. Feifell and Eells (1963) observed that what clients find most helpful in psychotherapy is simply the opportunity to talk. They like to be allowed to make self-revelations to the therapists but they do not like it when therapists make self-revelations to them. They wish to be understood, to be *got right*. They resent it when therapists make interventions that take them off their own track or when therapists say things that do not feel right (McLeod, 1990).

While there are good reasons why, generally speaking, therapists should not make disclosures to clients, there are arguments against therapists being totally un-self-disclosing. Just as some therapists enter therapy out of a need to give rather than to receive closeness, some therapists find the self-disclosures of clients gratifying but find it difficult, even in non-therapy situations, to make disclosures about themselves. Laing (1965) has argued that, in some cases at least, it is therapeutically counter-productive to avoid self-disclosure. When clients ask me personal questions, more often than not I answer them, because I feel it is unreasonable to expect clients to do what I am not prepared to do myself. If they do this to excess, I question their motives and suspect this might be a way of deflecting my attention away from them. Once a young male client, who turned out to be homosexual, said that he could not work with me unless he knew something about me. He considered that therapists hide from their clients behind a professional facade. He had already shed one therapist because he thought she did this to him. He said he wanted to experience me as a real person. I told him a limited amount about myself, which had the effect of strengthening the bond between us. He did not persist in asking me about myself, and for the remainder of the therapy the focus of attention was upon him.

Spinelli (1994) adopted what he called an *existential-phenomenological* approach to therapy. In this he emphasized the distinction between *doing* and *being* and between the doing and the being qualities of both clients and therapists. He considered that humans were overly preoccupied with doing and insufficiently concerned with being. He asked how it could be that clients can claim substantial benefit from therapy when the therapist has done absolutely nothing. He concluded that the being qualities of therapists must be more important than their doing qualities. He considered that the being therapist should both *be with* and *be for* the client. In being with the client the therapist is staying with the experienced truths of the client as they are being related and is accepting the client's reality as it is described. In being for the client the therapist agrees, for the duration of the session, to seek to inhabit the client's experiential world. He described the sometimes unpleasant, disturbing or even frightening experience of being temporarily lost or swallowed up in the client's world.

Another feature of the one-way nature of the psychotherapeutic alliance is that clients become much more attached to their therapists than therapists do to their clients. Clients incorporate therapists into their dreams much more frequently than therapists incorporate clients into theirs. Clients remember much more of what is said during sessions, are much more affected by what is said, spend much more time between sessions thinking about what was said, are much more affected by discontinuities in therapy and experience much greater difficulty terminating therapy. This has led to the suggestion that the closeness that therapists show to their clients is a sham. How much, it could be asked, are therapist prepared to put themselves out on behalf of their clients? Though it must be acknowledged that a degree of professionalism is required in psychotherapy that makes it difficult for therapists to extend their help beyond the confines of the session, many therapists do feel strongly about their clients and show great concern for them. One explanation for the difference is that being the recipient of closeness is a much more addictive experience than being the giver of it.

Kohut (1984) emphasized the powerful therapeutic effect of the therapist conveying to the client that s/he has been correctly understood. Rowe and MacIsaac (1989) introduced the term *empathic attunement* to describe the process by which Kohut considered that such understanding takes place. Kohut defined empathy as the capacity to think and feel oneself into the inner life of another person. He stressed the difference between the interrogative approach of, say, the conventional psychiatrist, who takes a psychiatric history and carries out a mental state examination to obtain the information necessary to reach a diagnosis, and that of the empathic therapist, who gives the client the time and space to be her/himself and to develop her/his story, which enables her/him to convey to the therapist what it feels like to be her/himself. He called the first approach *experience-distant* and the second approach *experience-near*.

There is one system of therapy, developed by the humanistic therapists, which is truly bi-directional. It is called *cocounselling*. In this, two people elect to work together and take turns to be the client. For this to be possible, each person must have an understanding of the general principles of psychotherapy.

The form of psychotherapy called interpersonal is more likely to result in a two-way interaction between therapist and client than most other forms. Sullivan, in a reaction to the formality of Freudian psychoanalysis, tried to dispense with jargon in psychotherapy, to use simple words and to conduct the therapeutic session in a way that more closely resembles a normal conversation (Evans, 1996). Throughout this book, but particularly in Chapter 10, a form of psychotherapy is described that is called *relating therapy*. It is an extension of interpersonal psychotherapy and uses the relationship that develops between therapist and client as the framework within which the therapy takes place. The therapist observes a certain relating deficiency in the client and encourages the client to try out a new way of relating within the interactions that take place in the session. The therapist might try out a way of relating to the client that might entice the client into relating back in a particular way to the therapist. In this respect, the interrelating that takes place between therapist and client *is* the therapy.

The integration of therapist and client

Certain therapists, most commonly humanistic therapists, propose a form of closeness by which, it is claimed, they are able to experience clients' feelings.

It is also claimed that clients are able to experience therapists' feelings. Mackie (1969) wrote, "These empathic, or telepathic, phenomena have been, usually somewhat warily, reported by other workers; so far as I am concerned their existence is a fact of life, which while not being able to explain, I have to take account of in my clinical work" (p. 375). Mahrer (1983) described what he called *altered states*, "wherein the therapist and patient can integrate with one another. The personhood and identity of one can assimilate or fuse with that of the other" (p. 138). Rogers (1986) also wrote of altered states, in which "my inner spirit has reached out and touched the inner spirit of the other" (p. 199). Van Deurzen-Smith (1988) wrote of the *I-Me relationship* in which there can be a perfect merging of therapist and client who totally identify with each other. Rogers (1986) observed that, in these altered states, he sometimes behaved in strange and impulsive ways that he could not justify rationally and that had nothing to do with his thought processes, but which in some odd way turned out to be *right*. This suggests that what these writers are referring to is a direct communication between the inner brains of the therapist and the client. There is no reason to implicate anything so supernatural as telepathy.

Sexual closeness in therapy

In Chapter 3 it is explained that although affectional closeness and sexual closeness overlap, they are in many respects quite separate. There is general agreement that while non-sexual closeness between therapists and clients is highly desirable, sexual closeness is unacceptable. All professional organizations prohibit sexual closeness. Nevertheless, around 5 percent of therapists both in Britain (Borys and Pope, 1989) and in North America (Pope, Tabachnik and Keith-Spiegel, 1987) do not consider it unethical. Over half of male therapists admit to being sexually attracted toward or having sexual fantasies about clients (Pope, Tabachnik and Kieth-Spiegel, 1987). It seems likely that a substantial proportion of clients are sexually attracted toward or have sexual fantasies about their therapists. Eight percent of male therapists and 1 percent of female therapists admit to having had sex with a client, the majority of these to having had sex with more than one (Holroyd and Brodsky, 1977). Clients who enter therapy having had sex with a previous therapist are more likely to have sex with their new one (Folman, 1991).

Humans are programmed to have sex, and sex frequently happens when men and women work closely together. The circumstances of the psychotherapeutic session are particularly conducive to sex happening. Therapist and client meet regularly over long periods. They are always alone together. The client may be lying on a couch, or there may be a couch in the room. The client makes highly personal revelations to the therapist. It is perhaps the essentially one-way nature of the transaction that prevents sex happening more often. Another limiting feature is the sense of responsibility that the therapist feels toward the client. This is similar to the inhibition of the father's sexual feelings toward his daughter that result from his sense of responsibility. The similarity of the therapist/client relationship to the father/daughter one perhaps leads to an overlapping and reinforcing of the two senses of responsibility.

In a survey by Garrett (1994), all therapists who admitted to having sex with clients maintained that it had been by mutual consent and that, in a third of cases, it had been initiated by the client. Clearly, both therapists and clients are capable of acting seductively toward the other, and very rarely do therapists actually rape their clients. However, the capacity of therapists to influence their clients is infinitely greater that the capacity of clients to influence therapists. It is difficult to know how much harm results from therapist-client sex, since only those clients who have experienced it as harmful seek further treatment. That clients do seek treatment for it indicates that it can cause harm, and Pope and Bouhoutsos (1986) have described a *therapist-patient sex syndrome*, which includes ambivalence and guilt, inability to trust, suppressed rage and increased risk of suicide. This issue is discussed further in Chapter 6.

Clients should be able to talk about sexual feelings, even toward the therapist, and sometimes they do. The therapist should be able to tolerate being told about these feelings without experiencing it as an invitation to participate in sex. In one session I asked a young woman what she was feeling toward me. She replied that she was trying to think of how she could seduce me. I said "You mean here, in this room?" It was a clinic room, and there actually was a bed in it. She said "Yes". In the next session she told me that she had had a dream in which she had had sex with me, and that she had written in her diary that she could not continue to see me because it was not right. She did continue, and later she admitted that she was relieved that she had failed in her attempt to seduce me.

The difference between non-sexual and sexual closeness

It is common in therapy for clients to differentiate between people they love and people they are turned on by. It is usual for people to both love and be turned on by the same person, but this is not invariably the case. It seems as though affectional closeness and sexual closeness run in parallel and that progress in one does not necessarily mirror progress in the other; sometimes one begins to fail while the other remains unaffected. Clients are sometimes tormented by the fact that those whom they love they cannot be turned on by and those whom they are turned on by they cannot love. Love is a more integrated form of closeness than being turned on, and while it is possible to be turned on by a complete stranger, it is not possible to love a complete stranger.

A man who admitted to being a distant individual had difficulty having sex with his wife but could, and did, freely have sex with prostitutes. He experienced his wife as being possessive, which drove him away from her. Because the prostitutes made no demands upon him, it was easier and pleasanter to have sex with them. He chose to stay with his wife and go with the prostitutes.

A woman had two man friends. One was tall, smartly dressed, confident but bossy. He took life as it came. He did not talk very much, and what he did say was superficial. The other was small, shabbily dressed, lacking confidence and obedient, but he thought a lot and she could talk to him for hours. She even talked to him about the other man. The tall one she found exciting, and she had regular sex with him, but he enjoyed being single. The small one did not excite her at all, though she did have sex with him once, when they were out walking. He would do anything for her and wanted to marry her, but she chose to pursue the tall one.

Another woman had left her husband because she felt stifled in the relationship. She met up with a man whom she described as going nowhere. On the other hand, the very thought of him made her go weak at the knees, and whenever they met they had sex. They never went places or did things together and never had a serious conversation. After a time he began to be more attentive toward her and to talk of the possibility of marriage. She went into a claustrophobic panic, and shortly afterward she left him. She met another man who was kind and sympathetic. She could talk to him for hours, but she could not even let him kiss her. She spent a very uncomfortable evening lying beside him in bed. The next day she had the compulsion to contact another man, specifically for the purpose of having sex with him. This she did, and gained much relief from it. She was determined to overcome her fear of intimacy and to allow herself to be sexual with the kind and sympathetic man. She did have sex with him soon after, but she found it distasteful. She realized that the only man she could really get anywhere with was the man who was going nowhere. She re-established contact with him. In fact, he was not really going nowhere; he had a reasonably promising job. She explained her fear to him, and he seemed to understand. This time they proceeded more cautiously and started to live a more normal existence. At this point I terminated the therapy. A year later she contacted me again and said that she had finally given up this man and was living with a man she could both love and have sex with.

Enabling close clients to become capable of distance

In Chapter 1, it was stated that, from an evolutionary point of view, no position within the octagon should be considered more or less important than any other. Distance therefore is as important as closeness. It was stated further that psychotherapy should be directed toward helping clients become more competent in those areas of relating in which they are demonstrably incompetent. The most striking form of incompetence is the fear and avoidance of a particular state of relatedness. Clients may cling excessively to their therapists and to certain others in their lives because they are afraid of distance. An objective in therapy then is to enable them to understand that distance is something they fear and to support them in their attempts to overcome that fear.

The fear of distance

Distance may be feared for a variety of reasons. A person may fear being alone in public places because once, when s/he was alone, s/he was attacked, or because s/he knows of a friend or more than one friend who were. If, in the location in which s/he lives, attacks on people are common, her/his fear may be reasonable; but if they are not, s/he may need to be helped to regain her confidence in walking alone in public places.

Another person may have a fear of travelling far from home because s/he had a parent who was always afraid of being separated from her/him. S/he was never allowed or encouraged to explore her/his surroundings or to spend time away from her/his parent. Here, the therapist will have to enable her/him to make the connection between her/his fear of travelling and her/his parent's behavior toward her/him and to make it possible for her/him to give expression to the feelings of restriction, and even imprisonment, that her parent's enforced closeness has given rise to in her/him. At this stage, s/he may also need to experience some sympathy for her parent's position and to express some guilt at wanting to break away from her/his parent. If s/he is able to pass beyond this, s/he may accept from the therapist the encouragement and reassurance that her/his mother was never able to give her/him, to try to go places on her/his own and to make progressively longer excursions to distant places.

The inability to become distant may be secondary to the absence of what Ainsworth (1963) first described as a *secure base*. The psychotherapist may be able to provide that secure base from which the client can risk making excursions into distance. Developmentally, the infant masters closeness before it ventures into distance. It is able to tolerate periods of distance only if it is sure that it can return to the security of a relationship with its parent, a condition referred to by Erikson (1965) as *basic trust*. From this point on, throughout childhood, and even into adult life, the individual alternates between periods of closeness and periods of distance. It is as though, during the periods of distance, the individual is able to draw upon internal reserves of closeness that were "taken on board" during these periods of closeness.

The adult is able to tolerate periods of distance only if s/he is sure that s/he can return to the security of a relationship with a close other person. A possible strategy, therefore, is for the therapist to help to strengthen the client's closeness either to her/him or to a key other person, who can then become the client's secure base. A man came to therapy because his wife was threatening to leave him. The relationship had reached this point because he persistently objected to her going out without him. Despite his objections, she did, from time to time, spend evenings out with her friends, but she paid dearly for this. As the moment of her going out approached, he became increasingly unpleasant to her, and on her return, his unpleasantness was even worse. He would shout at her and sometimes hit her. The therapy was able to progress after he had acknowledged that he was frightened of losing her. The emotion he experienced as the moment of her going out approached was fear, and this fear persisted all the time she was away. Understandably, she was angry and bitter about the way that he had treated her, but when she was able to reassure him that it was he whom she loved and that she would never leave him, he felt able to tolerate her going out without him.

Distance in psychotherapy

With such an accumulation of evidence that the therapist's warmth and intimacy contribute significantly to a successful outcome in psychotherapy, how can it be argued that establishing and maintaining distance from the client can also contribute to a successful outcome? Admittedly, there is not the same weight of evidence to be offered in support of this point of view; nevertheless, there are sound reasons for believing it to be the case. Although what is offered in psychotherapy is closeness, it is a highly controlled, if not contrived, form of closeness and occurs predominantly in one direction. While the client is free, and even encouraged, to make personal revelations to the therapist, s/he does not expect the therapist to make personal revelations back to her/him. While the client is permitted to become dependent upon and needful of the therapist, the therapist rarely allows her/himself to become dependent upon or needful of the client. This is not to say that the therapist does not enjoy spending time with the client or look forward to their meetings. It is entirely because the therapist is able to maintain an outer brain dominated, objective detachment from the proceedings, observing what is happening in the client's life and between client and therapist and planning what should or should not happen next, that psychotherapy is possible at all. This is why the therapist's distance is such a key factor in the psychotherapeutic process.

Just as some clients in psychotherapy need to be given (exposed to) satisfactory closeness, others need to be given (exposed to) satisfactory distance. They may have been clung to or intruded upon by parents and never known what it is like to be given distance or to have their distance accepted and respected, to be allowed to have a private place that is their own, to have secrets, to have an inner world that others do not wish or try to enter.

Insecure distance

It is important to recognize that the process of venturing into distance from a position of secure closeness (Ainsworth's secure base) is reflected exactly in the process of venturing into closeness from a position of secure distance. That secure distance (which is the distant equivalent of Ainsworth's secure base) is Laing's (1965) ontological security. "When two people have secure identities they are able to *lose themselves in each other*, creating a state of total we-ness, but being confident that should they need to, they can extricate themselves from this and regain their autonomous separateness" (Birtchnell, 1993/1996, p. 92). Raskin (1985) wrote of such people, "Secure in their knowledge of themselves and their values, with firm boundaries that make merger unlikely and therefore nonthreatening, these individuals are capable of mutuality, empathy, and interdependence without threat to autonomy" (p. 205).

The psychotherapy for insecure distance involves turning insecure distance into secure distance. It is primarily concerned with building up and reinforcing the three components of ontological security, namely, a strong sense of identity, autonomy and firm boundaries. A person may be deficient in any one or any combination of these three components.

Someone who has a poor sense of identity is frustrating to work with because where a real and solid person should be, there is just a nobody. Such a person may be what Laing (1965) called *ontologically dependent*. S/he compensates for having no ideas of her/his own by borrowing ideas from other people and presenting them as though they were her/his own. The therapist finds her/his own ideas being borrowed in this way. The frustration is compounded by the fact that outside of therapy the borrowing habit continues unabated. A client who never has had a secure sense of identity is confused by the very concept and does not know what having an identity feels like. The therapy involves seeking out such fragments of identity as there are and encouraging the client to recognize and add to them. The therapist needs repeatedly to ask questions like "Yes, but what do *you* believe/like/want?" Progress will not be made until the client begins to feel that s/he has the beginnings of an identity, likes the feeling and wants to feel it more strongly.

A person who lacks autonomy is not self-motivating and behaves like a becalmed boat, waiting for a wind. S/he is like this because s/he has no sense of what s/he wants or where s/he wants to go. S/he is unable to take responsibility for herself. Like the person with a poor sense of identity, s/he looks to others to tell her/him what to do and happily goes along with whatever they suggest. S/he is gullible and easily influenced. The therapist needs to take a hold of any kind of wish or intention, however small, and encourage her/him to see it through. The therapist needs to make remarks like "No, *you* decide". Because of her/his lost and helpless expression, outside of therapy there are others, particularly parents, who are all too willing to assume responsibility for her/him and point her/him in a particular direction.

Insecure boundaries can be the result of intrusions of many kinds. Such intrusions include parents who do not respect the right of their children to have a secret inner world, to cover themselves in clothes when they want to or to have private rooms and private possessions or who pry into their children's personal affairs, read their diaries and ask penetrating questions. People who have had such experiences do not easily make personal revelations in therapy and are resistant to the therapist's wishes to know more about them. The therapist will need to provide the opportunity for them to express the distress that such intrusions have caused them and to reaffirm their right to secrecy and privacy. The therapist must make clear to them that privacy is important and show respect for their privacy.

People who have been the victims of sexual abuse or rape are concerned more with the invasion of their personal space than of their psychic interior. A client who had had such an experience worked as a school teacher. She told me that she drew a chalk circle on the floor around her desk and forbade her pupils to cross it. She found it frightening to be in the same room as me, expressly requested that I should never touch her and was upset if I stretched my legs out in front of me in her direction. A feature of the therapy was the respect I had to show for the space around her.

Distance and self-centeredness

The issue of ontological security does not focus sufficiently upon the idea of the person being the focal point of her/his existence. People whose parents have not focused sufficiently upon them and have not emphasized enough their individuality do not experience themselves as being the center of their universe. They are perhaps ashamed of paying themselves too much attention. One of the more positive features of psychotherapy is the way that clients, perhaps for the first time in their lives, become the center of attention. Some clients will resist this because they feel they do not deserve it, and the therapist can help them by assuring them that everyone, sometime, needs to be the center of attention. An important feature of self-centeredness is *self-ishness*, the willingness to put oneself first, to pay attention to one's own needs, to indulge oneself. People reveal their need to be selfish by remarks such as "What about me?" and "When is it going to be my turn?" but though they make such protests, they do not act upon them, because they do not have a sufficiently strong sense of entitlement.

People are able to reinforce their self-centeredness by accumulating things around them and asserting, "All these things are *mine*". The feeling of never having had things of one's own can be particularly acute for people who have always had to share things with their siblings. One of the strongest reinforcers of self-centeredness is having *a place of one's own*. A couple came into therapy because the wife had lost all feeling for her husband and had become besotted by another man. The situation became complicated when the man moved to a new place of work two hundred miles away. The wife admitted that his appeal had been that he had lavished attention upon her. Although, at an outer brain level, she accepted his need to go to the new job, at an inner brain level she protested against the loss of attention. She did not follow him to his new place of work because she did not want to uproot her two young children or separate them from their father. She said that what she wanted more than either of the men was time to be by herself and the opportunity to *find herself*. She moved into a house on her own, from which she was able to share the care of her children. She later divorced her husband and lost interest in the other man.

The existential therapies

The existential therapies are concerned with establishing a sense of self and setting the self securely within the environment. There are a number of existential therapies, including existential psychoanalysis (Holt, 1986), existential humanistic psychotherapy (Bugental, 1978) and existential phenomenology (Spinelli, 1994). Existential psychoanalysis distinguishes among three stages of being-in-the-world (Binswanger, 1968): the inner world of thoughts and fantasies, the world in relation to other people and the experience of the surrounding environment. These are said, by Holt (1986), to correspond to MacLean's (1973) three brains, but this is not in accord with the distinctions drawn in Chapter 2 or with the distinction drawn there between the inner and the outer brain. One object of therapy is to enable the client to move freely between these stages. The humanistic psychotherapist's aim is quite different. It is to assist the client to become more alive, more spirited and more vital. Bugental (1978) used the term *presence* to mean the state of being as aware and participative as possible. Spinelli's existential phenomenology is introduced in the earlier part of this chapter that was concerned with closeness, and although the therapist's technique is one of attentive closeness, the objective is to enable the client to assert and identify her/himself as a separate and unique being. The therapist aims to enter the client's meaning-world in order to interpret it in such a way that the interpretations approximate the client's experience rather than something imposed by the therapist.

Enabling distant clients to become capable of closeness

People remain distant for a number of reasons. They may find human contact overwhelming; they may feel that they are a malevolent or harmful presence; they may fear that if they get close to someone they will get lost in the identity of the other; they may feel that others intend to harm them; they may be untrusting; they may feel they are not likable; they may feel they have nothing worth saying; they may fear that if they let themselves get close, they will get hurt if the relationship breaks down. Any one or any combination of these is possible. It may take weeks or months of therapy before the reasons become apparent. Only when they do is it possible to trace their origins and seek forms of reassurance.

Essentially, people are distant because they have had either no adequately satisfying closeness experiences to enable them to feel comfortable and secure in closeness, or they have had disturbing closeness experiences that make them wary of further closeness. They have come to assume that there is no such thing as pleasurable closeness or that the unsatisfactory closeness experiences they have had are typical. Over time, they may come to experience their closeness to the therapist as different from and better than what they have experienced before, which may encourage them to let themselves get closer to others.

Treating the schizoid client

People who have a limited tolerance of sensory input (e.g., those who may be called schizoid) are extremely sensitive to the encroachment of others. They withdraw into themselves and watch others cautiously from behind their barricades. It may be necessary to spend long periods of time with them, saying little to them and respecting their own need to remain still and silent. While they may not speak, they remain acutely aware of what the therapist is doing and saying. The therapist needs to remain constantly aware that behind the expressionless facade there sits a frightened person. Moving too close too quickly may arouse alarm and drive the person further into her/himself. When the person does not speak, there is no way of knowing what is going on inside her/him, and there may be little or no sign that alarm is being aroused. There is also little to indicate whether the therapist's actions or words are having any beneficial effect.

Schizoid people may both want and appreciate closeness even though they may have no way of asking for it or registering that they are receiving it. I was invited to work with a young man in an art therapy department. Once a week, he and I sat together while he drew pictures. Little was said by either of us, and I was unable to perceive any sign of improvement in him. When I moved to work in another center, the art therapist wrote to tell me that he had been noticeably upset.

Perhaps the only indication that a schizoid person wants help is that s/he turns up regularly for therapy. When the person does not speak, what do you do—sit in silence, or speak unilaterally? Sitting in silence for long periods may not be a problem for a schizoid person. The presence of the therapist alone may provide an acceptable degree of closeness. When one does speak, asking questions is a pointless exercise, because the person is not going to answer them. Furthermore, s/he may experience being asked questions as a form of intrusion, like someone knocking on a door, trying to get in. It is better to make statements, but even some statements can be experienced as intrusive, particularly when they convey the message, "I know what you are thinking". The kinds of statements that are helpful are friendly, accepting and non-demanding, like "If it helps, I am happy to stay here with you". Hopefully, as the person begins to feel safer, words can be exchanged, but it is better that the initiatives come from the client.

Treating the avoidant client

The major difference between the schizoid and the avoidant client is that the schizoid client is easily overwhelmed by closeness and can tolerate only a limited amount of it, but the avoidant client likes closeness but is afraid of seeking it, for fear of being denied it or of having it and then losing it again. What the avoidant client dreads is the pain of rejection or separation. It has to be assumed that at some time in her/his life, the avoidant client has known the pleasure of closeness but has suffered the painful experience of having it taken away.

Avoidant people vary in the extent to which they are prepared to give humanity another chance. Some have given up entirely and have decided to be self-sufficient. They live alone, keep to themselves and do not socialize. They indulge in vicarious forms of closeness like reading novels and watching plays, films, sitcoms and soaps in which others enjoy close involvements, or they keep pets that are always loyal and affectionate. Others continue to make cautious approaches to others, but in these approaches, as Kantor (1993) pointed out, they orchestrate their own rejections. They are excessively choosy of the people they deign to be associated with; they present themselves as unattractive; they make only half-hearted approaches to people; or they get their own rejection in first.

In therapy, avoidant clients adopt various positions within this range of posibilities. The therapist must assume that, however much the client may try to conceal it, s/he really does want closeness and also, ultimately, to be able to get close to other people. The client is aware that an enormous advantage of therapy is that s/he does not have to win the therapist's favor in order to get taken on for treatment and that the therapist will not reject her/him. Within the therapy, the client is able to indulge in the closeness that s/he is afraid of seeking from other people, though s/he is aware that eventually the therapy will come to an end. The termination of therapy must be carefully planned, and the client may need to be given the option of making further contact if s/he needs it.

More often than not, when seeking the origin of the avoidant attitude, the therapist unearths a whole series of occasions when the client experienced painful rejections or separations. The avoidance is a defensive reaction to the cumulative effect of these. The rejections and abandonments have left the client with the conviction that there is something defective or unappealing about her/him. The therapist needs to suggest to her/him that the rejections and abandonments could be as much to do with defects in those who rejected and abandoned her/him as with any defects in her/himself. It sometimes helps to enable her/him to re-live some of the experiences to feel the pain again, but within the closeness of the session. This brings her/him closer to the reality of what actually happened and provides her/him with the opportunity to re-evaluate the circumstances.

This humanistic approach may be combined with a more behavioral-cognitive approach in which some of the client's negative views of her/himself are challenged. S/he should be helped to accept that rejections and abandonments sometimes do happen, but that they do not always happen, and s/he should be encouraged to try starting conversations with people in order to discover that people are likely to respond positively when they are spoken to in a friendly manner.

Summary

Therapists and therapies vary in the extent to which closeness or distance is established and maintained between therapist and client. Therapy can be conducted either by close or by distant strategies, the humanistic approach representing the closer ones and the behavioral approach representing the more distant ones. The good therapist should be capable of adopting all approaches. In therapy, the close client can be helped to overcome the fear of distance, and the distant client can be helped to overcome the fear of close-ness; the insecurely close client is enabled to become securely close, and the insecurely distant client is enabled to become securely distant. The importance of closeness in therapy is that the therapist can be there for the client, can be accepting, perceptive, responsive and understanding. The importance of distance is that the therapist can maintain an objective and respectful detachment and can encourage the client to become a separated and autonomous being, with clearly defined boundaries and a consolidated, personal identity.

Chapter 5

The power axis in relating

Although the terms "upper" and "lower" are used to refer to the extremes of the vertical axis of the interpersonal octagon, and although these are spatial terms, more often than not these terms do not define the organism's position in space. One organism is not literally higher up or lower down than another. Upperness and lowerness refer to the degree of advantage or disadvantage that one organism has in relation to another. Even the most primitive animals seem to be capable of recognizing this. When two reptiles confront each other, one backs off. However many times the same two reptiles confront each other, it is always the same one that backs off. The reptile that backs off must have concluded, according to some criterion, that if there were a fight between the two reptiles, the other would win. Obviously, reptiles do not actually conclude, and what they do must be more automatic than that. The judgment of the reptile that backed off may not have been correct, but a judgment was made. This simple piece of decision making has been carried right through the evolutionary chain to humans. Animals, including humans, are constantly making judgments about their position in relation to each other. The criteria by which humans make these judgments are much more complex than those of the reptiles, but the process is the same.

The upperness/lowerness judgments of humans are based upon a broad range of criteria. A person may consider her/himself upper to another in respect of, say, height, strength and fitness but lower in respect of, say, intelligence, academic attainment and social position. Although humans may sometimes make judgments about upperness and lowerness in order to determine who might win if there were a fight or some other form of competition, they are much more likely to make them for other reasons.

Far more frequently than animals, humans use their upperness in a helping, rather than a conflictual way. For this reason, being lower in humans is frequently not a disadvantage. Much more than animals, humans are interdependent. As they exchange one form of upperness for another, within a short space of time two people can be both upper and lower in relation to each other. Humans are also collaborative. They enter into complex enterprises, in which people with different forms of upperness (strengths and capabilities) work toward a common goal.

From an early stage in human history, money became a substitute for upperness. In fact, money stores upperness, as a battery stores electricity, but just as electricity is soon divorced from the sun, wind and water power from which it was generated, so money is soon divorced from the possessions, skills and abilities for which it was first donated. The acquistion of upperness in the form of money has become an end in itself; by complex financial manipulations, people use money to generate more money.

Money frequently plays a part in the transactions that take place between psychotherapists and clients. Private psychotherapists rely upon payments from clients for their income. To this extent they are dependent on their clients, which gives clients power over them. Either consciously or unconsciously, therapists can be motivated to keep clients needful of them in order that the clients will continue to attend and pay them. They may persuade them to attend more frequently, to extract more money. Therapists sometimes maintain that, because therapy costs money, clients who pay place greater value upon therapy and are motivated to work harder at therapy. It is not always the client who pays for the therapy. Sometimes it is a parent or marital partner, and the client may perceive this as a way of extracting something from or even punishing the parent or partner. Alternatively, or at the same time, it may make the client feel indebted to them.

Maturation within the power axis

It is observed in Chapter 3 that parents need to provide the child with adequate and satisfactory exposure to the main positions and that they cannot do so unless they are themselves comfortable with and competent in these positions. A parent who is not comfortable or competent in the position of upperness cannot provide the child with an adequate exposure to lowerness. S/he may try to reverse the process and persuade the child to be upper to her/him. A parent who is insecurely upper may feel threatened by the child moving into upperness and may try to push the child back down. A fuller account of the maturation process appears in Birtchnell (1993/1996).

It was also observed in Chapter 3 that maturation within both axes is characterized by alternate movements from one end of the axis to another. The child begins its life in a position of lowerness. In certain respects, it may remain lower in relation to its parents for the rest of its life, though in others it may rise above them. The lowerness of childhood extends from lower closeness to lower distance. In the state of lower closeness, if it has fond and adoring parents, it feels loved, cherished and protected. All its need are met, and it feels safely and securely lower. It knows that its parents will never knowingly let it down and that it can always turn to them to be comforted, consoled, encouraged and praised. In the state of lower distance, if it has responsible parents, it acquires a clear understanding of what is and is not permissible. Coopersmith (1967) observed that children with high self-esteem have parents who set clearly defined and enforced limits. The close and distant forms of lowerness reinforce each other. If the child feels loved by its parents, it will be accepting of the limits imposed by them, understand that they are for its own good and not defy or challenge them.

Just as when, if the child feels securely close, it will feel confident to make excursions into distance, when it feels securely lower, it will feel confident to make excursions into upperness. It will begin to be loving and protective toward dolls, pets and younger children and to impose rules and restrictions upon them. Just as the securely close parent will not hold the child back but will encourage it to explore its surroundings and move into distance, so the securely upper parent will not hold the child down but will encourage it to try out new skills and move upward toward accepting responsibilities. Just as the securely close child will know it can always return to the parental base and feel welcome and wanted, so the securely lower child will know that if it runs into difficulties in its upward endeavors, it can always return to the parental base to be consoled and indulged to regain the confidence to try again. In late adolescence and early adult life, just as the parents will be happy to say goodbye to their child and let it go off and make its way in the world, so they will praise and congratulate the child for all its upper successes and be happy for it to draw level with them and even overtake them. As the result of these experiences, the mature adult will be as capable of leading and nurturing as s/he is of accepting the leadership and nurturance of others.

Gender differences on the power axis

While there are those within either gender who are predominantly upper and those who are predominantly lower, there does appear to be a tendency for males to be more inclined to upperness, particularly toward females, and females to be more inclined to lowerness, particularly toward males. This is apparent in mate selection. Buss (1994) has shown that, in the wide range of cultures he studied, women express a preference for taller, older, stronger and more powerful partners, and men show a preference for shorter, younger, weaker and less powerful partners. Even women who have attained high professional status prefer their partners to be of higher status than they are or of higher status in some other domain. During courtship, women may pretend to be younger, weaker, less capable and less intelligent, and men may pretend to be older, stronger, more capable and more intelligent. Partly because male attractiveness is linked with being older and more powerful, men retain their sexual attractiveness to a later age than women. In most societies, more men occupy positions of authority and high status, and women are accorded lower status than men.

The influence of the horizontal axis

A distinction should be drawn between distant upper-to-lower relating and close upper-to-lower relating. It will be remembered that distant relating is more self-directed and close relating is more other-directed. In animals, most upper-to-lower relating is distant, the major exception being that which takes place between parents and their young. In distant upper-to-lower relating, the upper animal is a threat to the lower one; in close upper-to-lower relating, the upper animal is more of a help to the lower one. It must have been an evolutionary breakthrough when parents began to protect and feed their young, for this would have been the first time in biological history that upperness was used for the advantage of others. Because close relating is so much more advanced in humans, close upper-to-lower relating is as well. In animals it has remained restricted almost entirely to the parenting of the young, which, both for the parents and for the young, occupies a relatively brief period in the animal's lifetime. In humans, it has become vastly extended to cover broad areas of human interaction and is not restricted to one particular part of the life cycle. In fact, in humans, close upper-to-lower relating is at least as common as distant upper-to-lower relating.

A feature of parenting is raising the status of the young from lower to upper. As young animals are fed, they become bigger and stronger. The same applies to humans, and a stage is usually reached when the young draw level with, and even overtake, the parents. Well-adjusted (securely upper) parents find this an exciting experience. They welcome the young into their adult world and treat them as equals. When the young pull ahead of them, they feel proud of them. Teachers commonly have a similar experience. In contrast to animals, for adult humans, many forms of upper-close-to-lower-close relating share this important characteristic, by which the upper person helps to raise the lower person from a lower toward a relatively more upper position.

Upperness

Three points need to be stressed about upperness: (1) it is a relative condition, (2) the respect in which one person is upper in relation to another has to be specified, and (3) upperness must be viewed in terms of how a particular characteristic can be seen as carrying advantages for the individual in any particular environment. The gap between the upper and the lower person can be small or large, and the ratings by which each is defined can be high or low. The best can feel upper to the second best, but the worst but one can feel upper to the very worst. There need only be one other who has less of a particular characteristic for a person to feel upper in respect of that characteristic. A person who feels lower at the bottom of one league can drop into a lower league where s/he can feel upper at the top. As long as s/he does not look beyond or outside that league, s/he will be a big fish in a small pond and experience the pleasure of being so. Adults can feel upper in relation to children, but older children can feel upper in relation to younger children, and younger children can feel upper in relation to their dolls or their pets.

Because one person can feel upper in relation to another in so many ways, everyone has the opportunity of sometimes feeling upper. The way to feel good about oneself is to find an area in which one is upper. When size is important, an elephant is upper to a flea, but when jumping power is important, a flea is upper to an elephant. Furthermore, people need to find the physical or social environment in which their particular capabilities can be applied to the greatest effect. In a desert, the cactus is the upper species, because it can survive when other plants cannot. In a polar region, the penguin is the upper species, because it can survive when other birds cannot.

Objective and subjective upperness

In this section, upperness is being considered quite separately from lowerness. In reality, there is a constant interplay between the upperness of some people and the lowerness of others. Upperness involves feeling better than or superior to someone else, or to others in general. It carries the subjective experience of being above others, of being in a position to look down upon them. Being up, on top, like being on top of a mountain, can be an exhilarating experience. A person with her own internal standards can be her/his own judge of her/his upperness; but more often than not, upperness is generated or reinforced by the reaction of others.

There can be a discrepancy between the upperness of people as determined by certain objective criteria (their true worth) and the upperness that people believe themselves to possess. Some people feel more upper than they really are and some feel less upper than they really are. Some people have been made to feel more upper by unwarranted praise or flattery from others. Others have been made to feel less upper by unwarranted derision and putting down by others. Some people have acquired an exaggerated sense of upperness by having lived among lower people, and some have acquired an exaggerated sense of lowerness by having lived among upper people.

Some characteristics of upper people

Upperness is the assumption of high status, and people who believe themselves to be of high status (like upper animals) often adopt postures such as holding the head high, pulling the shoulders back and thrusting the chest out that create the impression of having greater height, breadth and power. They strut and swagger and take big strides. They use their arms and hands in a gesture of putting or keeping people down. (Hitler had two forms of salute: one with the arm stretched out and the palm turned down, in a manner that suggested that people should stay in their place beneath him, and one with the arm bent back in a manner that suggested he might be going to hit someone). They talk loudly, with a particular tone of voice, and in an accent which, in their particular culture, would be regarded as upper. They use particular expressions like "My dear fellow".

In many cultures, upper behavior has come to be more and more associated with wealth. Upper people do things that require a lot of money, like live in big houses, drive expensive automobiles, go to expensive holiday resorts, stay in expensive hotels, eat in expensive restaurants, become fat, wear jewelry and expensive clothes.

Like upper animals, upper people expect to be treated with respect, listened to when they speak and obeyed when they give instructions. They speak with authority and believe themselves to be right, leaving no room for doubt. They adopt an attitude of entitlement, expecting certain privileges, like people stepping aside to let them pass and opening doors for them. They are intolerant and inclined to lose their temper easily. They become annoyed, if not affronted, when people do not defer to them. All of these characteristics are exaggerated in people who are insecurely upper, but the fact that upper people behave like upper animals suggests that the upper attitude has passed through evolution relatively unchanged.

Upperness and personal attributes

When we compare ourselves with others, we become aware, or are made aware by the responses of others, of those attributes that we have that may be or become for us potential sources of the subjective experience of upperness. Certain attributes, like parental cultural group, social status, wealth, area of residence and size of house, we derive from the family we are born into. Certain others, like height, physical appearance, strength, speed of running, skill at games, learning ability and mental aptitude, are part of our genetic makeup. These bestow upperness upon us, even though we have done nothing to acquire them.

Upperness and achievement

We acquire new attributes through our own endeavors, which become sources of upperness for us. We develop our physical and mental potentialities, accumulate skills, abilities, knowledge, experience, qualifications, wealth and possessions; we get promoted and gain the recognition, approval and admiration of others. Some who do not progress through conventional channels gain upperness through the alternative route of criminality. While many criminals do have skills, knowledge, experience and abilities, they also take the short cuts of deception, intimidation, stealing and murder.

It is possible to attain states of upperness without reference to other people at all. An autonomous individual may set her/himself targets and achieve certain targets such as climbing a mountain, running a particular distance, or attaining a particular level of technical or aesthetic performance that gives her/him personal satisfaction. Such satisfaction may or may not be further enhanced by the praise and acclaim of others. A person who lacks autonomy may depend entirely upon the judgments of others, whether they may be correct or not, for confirmation of whether any particular achievement is worthy of praise.

Upperness and self-esteem

Self-esteem was described in Chapter 3 in the section on distance. Undoubtedly, when people develop a separate self, they also acquire a degree of self-approval, self-worth or self-esteem. It is hard not to apply such judgments also to various attributes and achievements that contribute to upperness. Therefore, there must be both a distant and an upper component to self-esteem. Harter (1996) observed that "perceived physical appearance consistently heads the list as the number one predictor of self-esteem" (p. 13); next comes social acceptance; and beyond this are academic and athletic competence. The association with physical appearance may be a spurious finding. Since Lasky (1979) observed no relationship between observed physical attractiveness and self-esteem, it is more likely that people with high self-esteem consider themselves to be physically attractive, whether they are or not. Academic and athletic competence are more likely to be genuine predictors of self-esteem, though even here high self-esteem, in terms of believing in oneself, may improve performance.

Being one-up

Stephen Potter, the English author of a number of popular books on what he called *one-upmanship* maintained that if you are not one up you must be one down. Potter, writing very much in the tradition of Adler (1931) and Berne (1975), considered that the predominant strategy in life is to do one better than, or get one up on, other people. Adler (1931) believed that the feeling of being weak, impotent and inferior stimulates in the child an intense desire to seek power. Berne (1975) was concerned with winners, who accomplish what they set out to do, and losers, who fail to accomplish what they set out to do. It cannot be denied that such competitive attitudes exist and that in some situations they are useful and relevant, but they are not sufficiently removed from the behavioral systems of animals and belong only to the distant side of the interpersonal octagon (Chapter 1).

Forms of positive upperness

Upperness is a natural consequence of utilizing personal attributes, acquiring knowledge and experience and developing skills. People gain in confidence from their achievements and successes. They take a pride in the things they do well and respond with pleasure to the acknowledgment by others of their abilities and accomplishments. From an early age they discover that they can be of use and assistance to others who respond appreciatively to what they are able to do for them.

An important form of upperness in humans is that which is called *benevolence*, that is, when someone uses her/his upperness for the benefit of others. At the more distant end of the horizontal axis, this includes leading, managing and assuming responsibility. Beyond showing the way, the good leader inspires confidence and brings out the best in those s/he leads. The good manager seeks out the opinions of those s/he organizes, ensuring that everyone moves together toward agreed objectives. By assuming responsibility, leaders and managers free workers to concentrate upon their allotted tasks. Sometimes, particularly in a war situation, the good leader is required to be harsh and ruthless. Around the midpoint of the horizontal axis, upperness includes teaching and training. This involves increasing the upperness of others. The good teacher or trainer is not afraid to bring others up to her/his level and even encourage them to overtake her/him. At the more close end of the horizontal axis, upperness includes being protective, caring, nurturant and restorative.

Concern, compassion and care

The positively upper close person feels concern for and compassion toward a needful and weaker other. Her/his motives are initially to console and comfort, but subsequently to build up and strengthen, to restore to health, and eventually to encourage the other to take off and fend for her/himself. These are the qualities of the good psychotherapist. Sometimes a person can behave in a truly selfless way: seeing another in difficulties, s/he goes out of her/his way to help, even to the extent of disadvantaging her/himself or risking her/his life. This happens with greater compulsion when the other is a child, which suggests that such behavior originated in the relating of parents to their offspring. Many voluntary helping agencies aim to help others in need. This extends to helping other species, like protecting birds and preventing cruelty to animals. Thus humans, unlike any other animal, have an innate tendency to help the needy, even of a different species. Compassion is the motivation to help needful others. It has powerful rewards. Witnessing the gratitude of someone who has been helped is deeply moving. It is because compassion is so powerful that pleading and begging (forms of lower closeness) are so effective. Cynically put, the gratitude of others generates in the helper the satisfying experiences of closeness and upperness.

Forms of negative upperness

Negatively upper people are not sufficiently confident of their ability to acquire and hold on to upperness through the normal channels and are afraid of losing such upperness as they have. They may have been exposed to negative upperness themselves, not being praised for the good things they did and being ridiculed for their deficiencies or for being clumsy and incompetent.

One form of negative upperness is an *unwillingness to be lower*. Some people set up their own businesses because they cannot tolerate working for someone who tells them what to do. People with an *antisocial personality* need to defy authority, cannot accept instruction from anyone, and willfully break the law. A story is told by Webster (1996) of the young Theodore Roosevelt, who was in a Washington hotel when the fire alarm went. Hotel staff instructed residents to evacuate the hotel. As he was walking up the stairs, he was challenged by a member of the hotel staff, and he shouted, "I'm the Vice President and I'm going to my room". The staircase is an interesting metaphor for the vertical axis.

The negatively upper distant person behaves in an egocentric and unscrupulous manner to gain, or grab, whatever upperness s/he can. S/he may derive the satisfaction of upperness from cruelly and remorselessly torturing, tyrannizing, intimidating, taunting, insulting, exploiting or manipulating others. This is called *malevolent upperness*. The recipient other can try either to retaliate or escape, but sometimes s/he can do neither and simply has to take it. Her/his response will be either one of hatred and a determination to gain revenge or of defeat, despair and despondency.

Insecurely upper people have to keep stressing their upperness to others by being conceited, pompous and boastful. They try to push others down to increase the gap between their relative upperness and other's relative lowerness. They ridicule, humiliate and insult others, overlooking their strengths and exaggerating their weaknesses. They threaten, taunt and intimidate them, destroy their possessions, torture and injure them and even ultimately kill them.

Negatively upper leaders are tyrannical and use their position of power to impose their will upon and intimidate others. They may have what is called a *narcissistic personality disorder* (Birtchnell, 1997). They reveal a callous disregard for the rights and feelings of others and view those who fail to respect them with contempt. They are not prepared to accept that they are wrong and try to place blame on others. They remove from office those who criticize or threaten them and accumulate around themselves sycophantic and solicitous subordinates. They employ spies and bodyguards. Negatively upper managers dictate how things should be done and manipulate and exploit those under their control. Negatively upper teachers mystify rather than clarify, by holding back vital information. They become anxious if those in their charge become as knowledgeable as they are.

Negatively upper carers thrive upon the weakness and helplessness of those who depend upon them and prefer to keep them in their state of dependence, rather than encourage them to become stronger and more capable. Some psychotherapists, either consciously or unconsciously, frequently draw attention to their clients' inadequacies in order to maintain them in a regressed and dependent state. There have been examples of negatively upper nurses who murder their patients. Feldman (1976) described what is probably a largely unconscious strategy, adopted by some marital partners, of making apparently innocent remarks that happen to touch upon particularly sensitive spots in the other, which undermines the other's confidence and precipitates her/him into a depressed state. They then indulge in rescuing and nurturing behavior toward the other that brings her/him back to normal.

A parent who derives gratification from fussing over her/his child will continue to do things for the child long after the child could have been capable of doing such things for itself. One marital partner may behave in a similar way toward the other, in order to prevent the other becoming too capable. S/he may say such things as, "Why don't you let me do it. You know I'm better at these things than you are". S/he would never say, "Why don't you have a try?" or "Let me show you how to do it".

One form of negative upper closeness is unscrupulously using upperness to enforce closeness, with no concern for the effects of such behavior upon the other. The rapist, child abductor or child abuser acts in this way. In the novel *The Collector*, by John Fowles, a man captured a woman, just as he might have caught a butterfly, and kept her in a specially constructed house from which she could not escape, in the hope that one day she would come to love him. A parent can keep a child close by warning the child of the dangers of becoming distant. A mother who was inside a shop looking at some clothes told her daughter that if she stood too near the shop door a stranger could come along and snatch her away. A parent can also enforce closeness by denying the child privacy and by being intrusive. A client said proudly that her children never kept secrets from her.

Gaining upperness at the expense of others' lowerness

Reacting to the setbacks and misfortunes of others is gaining upperness as a consequence of others losing it. When someone drops in position, another's position in relation to her/him rises. Potentially this is a source of pleasure, but the pleasure can be diminished, or denied altogether, out of concern for the plight of the other person. Distant people are more able than close people to permit themselves such pleasure. Tantam (1988) observed that those with a schizotypal personality disorder, which is an extreme form of distance

(Birtchnell, 1996), can allow themselves to respond with pleasure to the suffering of others; probably many of those with an antisocial personality disorder, another form of distance (Birtchnell, 1996), are able to do so as well.

Feeling sorry for another who is in difficulties is not normally considered pleasurable, yet insofar as it is a form of upperness, it could be. Pitying someone is getting closer to a pleasurable experience, particularly when it assumes a smug or gloating quality; in fact, others often do not like to be pitied because of the possible implication of smugness. When we are close to someone who is in difficulties we cannot easily allow ourselves to experience pleasure because we feel for them, sympathize with them, even empathize with them. This conflict between wanting to experience pleasure yet feeling concerned sometimes generates laughter, and laughter frequently arises out of a conflict of emotions. Clowns place themselves in positions of mild misfortune in order to make us laugh. In fact, we might allow ourselves to laugh at a friend who has had a mild mishap, such as tripping over the edge of a carpet. Such laughter is a celebration of our upperness. If the misfortune or mishap gets worse and, say, the clown or the friend breaks a leg, the laughing stops. It is no longer a laughing matter, because the clown's or the friend's misfortune is too serious and our concern takes over. Comedians need to steer a delicate path between not being cruel enough and being too cruel.

Methods of persuasion

Persuasion is influencing the behavior and thinking of another by means that do not involve compulsion. Although it is possible for a lower individual to persuade an upper one, more commonly it happens the other way round; and although persuasion may be achieved by logical argument, usually less scrupulous means are adopted. The British psychiatrist Sargant (1957) wrote "Intellectual indoctrination without emotional excitement is remarkably ineffective" (p. 100). He linked together in one book a series of settings in which powerful (upper) individuals resorted to a variety of unscrupulous approaches. His starting point was the Pavlovian conditioning of dogs. Dogs, he wrote, are rendered more conditionable by being subjected to repeated stress. In this state, they can be conditioned to hate what they previously loved and to love what they previously hated. Sargant showed how this principle was applied in religious and political conversion.

He observed that rhythmic drumming is found in the ceremonies of many primitive religions of the world. The excitement and dancing are maintained until a point of physical and emotional collapse is reached. Belief in divine possession is very common at such times, and there is a feeling of being freed from sin and of starting life anew. Sargant compared this with the methods adopted by John Wesley, the eighteenth-century British preacher and the nineteenth-century evangelists of the southern states of America. The basic principle underlying these methods is to generate in the congregation a state of excitement that leads to fatigue and collapse. The upper person (preacher) then draws attention to the person's sinful life and, at the same time, offers redemption from sin by belief in a Savior, another upper person who, in a sense, is an extension of the preacher. Wesley warned that failure to achieve salvation would condemn the sinner to hellfire forever. The American evangelists relied upon prolonged singing, hand-clapping and dancing to loud, rhythmic music to produce states of high excitement and physical exhaustion. The tension was intensified by thrusting live, poisonous snakes into people's hands. It was not unknown for people to be killed by them.

Sargant drew parallels between these rituals and the elaborately orchestrated political rallies of Nazi Germany in which states of high excitement were generated by large crowds, flags, marching military bands and repetitive chanting. In his dramatic speeches, Hitler offered himself as a savior, who would deliver the people of 1930s Germany out of their economic misery to a land of plenty, where there would be only healthy and beautiful people. With their emphasis on guilt, the methods of the Chinese Communist revolutionaries of the 1950s came closer to those of the religious revivalists. Mass trials were carried out in public places, in an atmosphere of high emotional tension. In these, victims were publicly denigrated and then publicly shot. The Communists also perfected *brainwashing* techniques in what were euphemistically referred to as training groups. Young people were separated from their families and subjected to taxing work schedules, which reduced them to a state of physical and mental exhaustion. Then they were required repeatedly to make detailed confessions of past mistakes. Every endeavor was made to arouse intense guilt and anxiety. For many, a moment of breakdown was reached when suddenly they found a surprising illumination in Communist party slogans.

Sargant (1957) maintained that the same principles could be applied to certain forms of psychotherapy, particularly psychoanalysis. He believed that by repeatedly reliving past traumas and experiencing strong emotions, clients are rendered fatigued and debilitated. This weakens their resistance to the analyst's interpretations. They cease to fight and at last are "granted a novel and fascinating insight" into their condition (p. 151). Sargant was not a psychotherapist; he was a tall, charismatic figure who had many disciples. However, it is hard to discount entirely his explanation of the power of certain psychotherapeutic processes.

Lowerness

An important characteristic of humans is that they help one another. It is out of the satisfactions of being helped that the state of lowerness in humans has expanded and developed. But lowerness involves more than simply receiving help. It is immensely reassuring to know that certain things are being taken care of. In a complex society people need to know that they are in good hands, that those who are running the country know what they are doing, that the economy is being managed responsibly, that the armed forces are strong, that the legal system is fair, that the news is being truthfully reported, that there is an effective health service and that adequate supplies of food, water, gas and electricity are coming through. In North America and in most European countries, it is possible to be reasonably reassured on most of these points, which creates a sense of collective lowerness. However, there remain many other countries in which this is not the case.

Some characteristics of lower people

It is a common misunderstanding of relating theory that lowerness is the loss or absence of upperness. It might be thought that if upperness involves feeling better than or superior to other people, lowerness should involve feeling worse than or inferior to other people. It is undeniable that lower people commonly, though not always, experience a form of emotion that renders them at least subdued, and even cautious or respectful. This arises out of their awareness of the power that upper people have over them and the knowledge that such power can be used either for their good or for their ill. Because lower people can benefit in so many ways from the benevolent acts of upper others, they are capable of feeling wonderfully safe and secure. The elation of many religious beliefs and the bliss experienced by happy children are of this nature. In an earlier version of the theory (Birtchnell, 1987), the lower position was called the *receptive* position. This term was abandoned because not all aspects of lowerness are receptive. Receptiveness can be a good and positive experience, which is in keeping with the important principle of the theory that no position within the interpersonal octagon is either better or worse than any other position. It can also be a bad and negative one.

Adler (1931) considered inferiority to be something to rise above or escape from. Lowerness and inferiority are far from being the same thing, and lowerness is not necessarily something one might wish to rise above or escape from. In fact, dissatisfaction with one's present position, the wish to better oneself and ambition are more characteristics of the drive to upperness, rather than components of lowerness. Lower people need not necessarily have these characteristics, and the more positive features of lowerness are humility, satisfaction and contentment.

So how do lower people feel and behave? They are quieter and less conspicuous than upper people. Their gestures are more restrained and they speak more quietly. They tend to tilt the head forward and downward rather than backward and upward. Because they are conscious of the power of upper people, they treat them with caution, perhaps suspicion, but sometimes with respect, even deference, and they are careful not to provoke or annoy them. They may bow, kneel or curtsey. They are more inclined to apologize if they cause offense. They say "please" and excuse me" when they approach upper people, and they express gratitude to them for what they have done.

Pride can be a characteristic of lower people. Though their attributes and achievements may be modest they are proud of them. People can be poor yet proud. Pride carries with it the expectation of being treated respectfully and decently by upper people. Many lower people are aware that they have rights to be properly governed, led, helped, advised, protected and cared for; they can feel angered, though not indignant, if their rights are not respected.

Lowerness and vulnerability

The lower person frequently needs to rely upon someone who is able to offer her/him help. If s/he does not know the way, s/he has to find someone who does. S/he cannot be sure that the other person really does know the way but s/he has to trust this person. The other person may intentionally or unintentionally mislead her/him. Being led astray may or may not be serious. Being told the wrong way to the docking berth of a ship could cause a person to miss her/his departure. Agreeing to board an airplane is an act of lowerness. Is the airplane safe? Does the pilot know how to fly it? What's that smoke coming out of the ventilator? The air stewardess says it's all right. Is she telling the truth? Does she know what she is talking about? Being admitted to a hospital is one of the most critical forms of lowerness. The patient has to agree to being rendered unconscious by the anesthetist and cut open by the surgeon. S/he has to assume that the surgeon is competent and will not unnecessarily remove a vital organ. Lowerness works in societies only because various safeguards have been built into the system. Airplanes have to be frequently tested. Pilots need to qualify. Air stewardesses have to be trained. Doctors do not get to be anesthetists and surgeons without satisfying their examining authorities. Even so, pilots and doctors can be tired, drunk or overworked, and accidents can happen.

Lowerness and trust

Because, in so many situations, lower people are reliant upon others and have to place themselves in the care of others, trust is an important component of many forms of lowerness. As it is not possible to trust someone who is untrustworthy, it is sensible, before entering into a lower-to-upper relationship, to try to determine the trustworthiness of the upper other. Beyond this, people can have a general level of trust toward others. Some people are too trusting and overinclined to trust people who are obviously untrustworthy. As a consequence they are frequently let down. Others are excessively untrusting and cannot place themselves in a position in which they need to trust someone else. As a result they limit their needs and do without rather than invite someone to help, guide, teach or care for them.

Pleading and begging

Pleading and begging are lower close activities. They are not necessarily forms of negative relating, though when feigned or exaggerated they can be. If a lower close person desperately needs help, it is reasonable to plead and beg for it. Saying "please" increases the lower person's chances of getting help; so do pouting and sobbing. Pleading and begging work because upper close people are moved by it (see the section on compassion). Being needed is a gratifying experience, and the closeness element of upper closeness generates sympathy, putting oneself in the place of another. The upper close person *feels for* the lower close person and is moved to help.

Admiration and adoration

One form of lowerness is looking up to another in an admiring way. In this form of relating, nothing is actively done by the upper person to or for the lower person, yet the lower person takes something from the upper person. The lower person acknowledges the superiority of the upper person but does not feel daunted or discouraged by this. S/he feels that what the upper person has achieved poses no threat to her/him, though it is not necessarily advantageous to her/him either. There is a lot of closeness in admiration. The lower person identifies with the admired person, though not necessarily wishing to emulate her/him. In this identification the lower person gains some of the status of the upper person, as in reflected glory. There is also an alignment with the upper person; it is as though the lower person is saying, "I am with you. I am on your side. I am behind you".

The lower person may adopt the upper person as her/his idol, rather like adopting someone as a parent. This proceeds to a condition of we-ness, to the idea that we are somehow united. The lower person may or may not communicate her/his admiration to the upper person. If s/he does, it becomes a two-way relatiionship, in which the upper person's experience of upperness is enhanced or reinforced by what Price (1988) has called "up-hierarchy anathetic communications". Certain upper people, particularly those with a narcissistic personality disorder, thrive upon such communication and depend upon the admiration of lower people.

Loyal servants are happy to work for their masters in exchange for their keep and a small income. Their relationship to their masters is similar to that of the admirer. They are proud to be associated with them and share in their success and status.

One kind of admirer is called a fan. Public performers inevitably attract fans, and fans sometimes unite to form fan-clubs. The lower person may follow the upper person about, as when sports fans follow their teams to away matches. Fans are sometimes called supporters, which implies that they actually benefit the upper person or the sports team. Public performers perform better when praised and encouraged by their supporters. This is an example of how lower people can be to the advantage of upper people.

Adoration is a stage beyond admiration. It is accompanied by a powerful and positive affect. In adoration the upper person is idealized and her/his upperness is exaggerated. The adorer feels somehow that s/he shares the upperness of the other while remaining in her/his position of lowerness. In fact, in the act of worship, the worshipper stresses how small and insignificant s/he is compared with the adored other. Adoration is sometimes a feature of romantic love. It has been directed toward kings and other charismatic figures. The adorer lives by and through the adored other, demonstrating absolute loyalty and obedience. The ultimate in adoration is the deification of the adored person and the imparting to her/him of supernatural powers.

Lowerness and religion

In religion, adoration and worship are directed toward a fantasized other, and once the other becomes fantasized the ascribed upperness can be boundless. The Christian God created the universe, knows everything, is everywhere and is accessible to everyone. Freud (1927) described religion as a regression to infantile dependence and the projection of the parental image onto the universe. This was discounted by Guntrip (1969b), who believed it referred only to what he called neurotic religion, but he did not explain what he considered non-neurotic religion to be. He preferred religion to be mysterious and incomprehensible. For some, certain nuns and monks for example, God is the equivalent of Millon's (1981) magical helper, and they devote their lives to worshipping Him.

One of the features of religion is the contrast that is stressed between the greatness of the deity and the smallness of the worshipper; to this end, places of worship are built to be large and magnificent. Another feature of religion is that the deity is able to convey to followers, via intermediaries (holy men, church leaders, priests and ministers of religion, who are substitute upper figures) rules that must be obeyed. Such rules are of a restrictive nature. The lowerness, certainly of the Christian religion, is concerned with an awareness that there are deeds (sins) that must not be committed and with the sense of wickedness that is experienced by people who commit them. A tension is created in religion by people having the free will to commit these sins, but by their experiencing badness, wickedness or evil if they should.

Most religious attitudes (humility, respectfulness, admiration) are those of lowerness, and lower attitudes are fostered and encouraged, particularly in the Christian religion. The phrase "Blessed are the meek, for they shall enter the Kingdom of Heaven", conveys that through lowerness, upperness is attained. This is akin to the feeling of oneness of the adorer with the one who is adored.

Lowerness and the law

In all societies, legal systems exist that closely resemble religion, and in some societies, the legal and religious systems are closely interconnected. Conformity to the law and being punished for breaking it are forms of lowerness that everyone experiences. Laws are laid down by parliament and the judiciary and enforced by the police. A legal system is a more distant form of control than religion, and confession and forgiveness are not normally an option within it. People do not normally worship and adore those who lay down and enforce the law. However, judges often describe criminals as evil, and religion features prominently in prisons. Prisoners who have committed serious crimes frequently feel wicked, turn to religion and seek their salvation through a renewed belief in God.

Being lower to an internalized upper other

Most people have the experience, at least some of the time, of being in relation to an *internalized upper other*. Their relation to it is undoubtedly lower. It ranges in character from severe, persecutory, disapproving, directive, inhibiting and punitive (upper distant) to benign, caring, approving, encouraging, comforting and tolerant (upper close). It is likely to be an amalgam of the various upper figures, particularly parents and teachers, we have encountered over the course of a lifetime. We do not have an equivalent, internalized lower other, although a narcissist might have a generalized view of "my admirers" as a king might have of "my subjects" or a teacher might have of "my pupils". For some, the internalized upper other may assume the form of an actual person, who talks to them and to whom they are able to talk. For some this is God; for others it is the conscience, which makes them aware of what they should and should not do. It causes them to feel guilty, or even sinful, if they have done what they know they should not have done. For Freud (1923), it was the *superego* and definitely parental, which was assumed to have grown out of a conflict between greedy or incestuous feeling and the fear of parental disapproval and retaliation (see also Chapter 2). This is similar, and obviously related, to the conflict presented by religion.

Being judged

Being judged is a lower experience. A person can be judged externally by a religious or legal representative, some authority figure such as a parent or teacher or simply someone who chooses to do so, like a passing stranger. The person may ignore or accept the judgment, depending upon how much respect s/he has for the person making the judgment, how justified it seems to be and how susceptible s/he is to the judgment of others. A person can also be judged internally, either by some version of an interalized upper other or by her/his own considered view about whether an action is fair or unfair, reasonable or unreasonable. There are times when the external and internal judgments differ, but the impact will be greater when they correspond.

Blame, guilt and shame

The distinction between guilt and shame is not clear. Lewis (1986) argued that guilt is generated from within and shame from without, but since we speak of the pointing finger of guilt and of being ashamed of ourselves, this is not the whole story. Guilt is more linked with a legal judgment and shame with a moral one. Being blamed or made to feel guilty is a painful experience, largely because of the implied disapproval and rejection of others. The emotion is the same whether the blame or guilt are from an external or an internal judgment. While colored by the experience of feeling bad, evil or wicked, it is essentially a depressed state, resulting from loss of positive closeness and positive lowerness. Commonly the blamed or guilty person is disowned, cast out, shut away, punished or executed. When the judgment is made internally, the person may distance her/himself from others, hide her/himself away, punish her/himself or "execute" her/himself by committing suicide.

The self-deprecating personality

People with an overly harsh internalized upper other have marked feelings of personal inadequacy and are inclined to downgrade themselves. Blatt and Shichman man (1983) used the term *introjective personality* to describe people who subject themselves to self-scrutiny, expect to be criticized and disapproved of, have a sense of morality and are disposed toward feelings of guilt and shame. Murray (1938) used the term *abasement* to describe an excessive tendency to feel inferior to others, a need to confess errors and be punished for wrongdoing. Simons (1987) wrote of people with a masochistic personality, who find ways to spoil and take no satisfaction in any good that comes to them. In psychotherapy such people induce their therapists to abuse them. People of this kind are prone to episodes of severe depression in which they believe that they have sinned or brought ruin to their families or to the whole world, that they should be punished or killed. They are capable of serious and brutal acts of self-punishment and suicide.

Being forgiven

As with judgment, forgiveness may be granted from without or from within. A person may, in all humility, approach the person s/he has offended, admit her/his guilt, apologize and seek forgiveness. The offended other may or may not grant it. In the Roman Catholic faith, a person may confess what s/he has done to a priest, who, in his capacity as an agent of God, will forgive her/him.

It is possible to be forgiven by an external source while not forgiving oneself. Even after absolution, a person may continue to blame her/himself, for the only true forgiver is the internalized upper other.

Imposed lowerness: downness

For a number of writers, particularly those who call themselves ranking theorists (e.g., Gilbert, 1992; Price & Sloman, 1987; Price et al., 1994), the vertical axis is concerned predominantly with rising up and dropping down hierarchies. They view lowerness as that place where the victims of domination, suppression, humiliation and defeat end up. This view is a variant of the Stephen Potter concept, if you are not up you must be down. What the ranking theorists are describing here is only one restricted way of viewing lowerness. A possible term for it is *imposed lowerness*. An important feature is that the person is being put or pushed down and held down and has no option but to stay down. In this condition of what might be called *downness*, the person may continue to be abused, ridiculed, insulted and tortured and remains a victim of all that is included under the heading of malevolent upperness. Gardner (1982) introduced the term *omega humans* to describe the most downtrodden members of social groups or societies. He clearly saw a connection between these and animals who come at the end of the pecking order (see Schjelderup-Ebbe, 1935).

Victims of certain forms of degradation, particularly rape and sexual abuse by an adult or older child, can feel so soiled, defiled or branded that they continue to experience shame and depression for many years afterward, even though they had no part in what was done to them. Sometimes this is because they believe, or they think that others believe, that they may have offered some encouragement or experienced some pleasure from it.

Lowerness as a fear of upperness

Just as people who fear closeness stay distant, and people who fear distance stay close, some people who fear upperness stay lower. Since upperness bestows power, why should people fear it? They fear it for a number of reasons: because they fear what they might do with the power, that they may be too destructive or too ruthless; because they cannot handle the responsibility or bear the thought that they hold the fate of others in their hands, that one wrong judgement could cause distress or hardship for those for whom they are responsible; because by gaining uppernes they are overtaking someone whose authority they fear. A client used to swing from times when he thought that he was the greatest, when he was boastful and reckless, to times when he thought he was a failure and had no confidence in himself. He was troubled by the fact that his father got only a third-class degree and became a headmaster, but he got a first-class degree and became a university lecturer. He felt guilty that he had done so much better than his father. Why, he asked, could he not have settled for a second-class degree? Psyhoanalysts would say that his fear of challenging, and even overtaking, his father was manifestation of his oedipal guilt, resulting from his unconsicious wish to compete with his father for his mother's affection and his fear of his father's retaliation. He sometimes thought that life would be easier for him if he were in a junior rank in the armed services, where he simply had to do what he was told.

People who fear upperness will avoid seeking promotion or, if promoted, will perform badly out of an unconscious wish to be demoted again. Schafer (1984) gave examples of people who pursue failure and avoid success, and Gilbert (1992) described the condition of success depression.

Insecure lowerness

Insecure lowerness is a consequence of the vulnerability of the lower position. Insecurely lower people are afraid that either the upper person will abandon them, so that they will no longer be led, guided, advised, protected or cared for, or that the upper person will abuse her/his position of power and do them harm. People who are insecurely lower close have what is called a *dependent personality*. Part of this is similar to what Rochlin (1961) called the *dread of abandonment* and Bowlby (1973) called *anxious attachment*. Dependent people form close ties with others, but they are constantly afraid that something will go wrong. Consequently, they keep checking that the other still approves of them and wants to be with them. They try to ingratiate themselves to people and are extremely careful not to cause offense. They may be willing to demean and humiliate themselves in order to retain their dependent position. Not infrequently, those upon whom they depend become fatigued by their repeated requests for reassurance and are overcome by the urge to shed them. At this stage their anxiety level rises and their demands become intensified. They may even threaten or attempt suicide. By their actions, they may bring upon themselves the rejection they have always dreaded.

People who are insecurely lower distant do not make such demands; instead, they withdraw into themselves trying to be inconspicuous and unappealing to others. They maintain their position of lowerness by being respectful, deferential, obsessional, dutiful, obedient, conformist and laborious, hoping that others will find no fault in them.

Dependence and passivity

The term *dependence* is open to many interpretations (Birtchnell, 1988a, 1991a, 1991b). Its various definitions have largely been absorbed within the descriptions of lowerness. It is always necessary to distinguish between what might be called normal dependence, which is, in effect, positive lowerness, and pathological dependence, which is largely covered by the term *insecure lowerness*. A form of dependence that does not strictly come within the category of insecure lowerness is that which might be called *extreme passivity*. Millon (1981) described how certain dependent people try to find for themselves a single, all-powerful, *magical helper* who will take care of them and allow them to remain in a state of secure lowerness. As such people are not confident in their ability to function as responsible adults, they try to replicate with the magical helper the blissful relationship of the young child to its parent. They adopt a posture of pathetic helplessness, which certain upper others can find seductive. In psychotherapy, such people may try to turn the therapist into such a person. To this end they may praise, flatter, and even adore her/him. Initially at least, the therapists may find this appealing and play along with it.

Another component of extreme passivity is *suggestibility*. The suggestible person accepts as true what another person tells her/him, particularly if this other person is someone s/he has adopted as her/his magical helper. A related condition is that which Laing (1965) called *ontological dependence* (Chapter 3). In this, a person who has a poorly developed sense of self and personal identity attaches her/himself in a clam-like way to another who has a better-established identity and becomes an extension of that other person. People who become members of cults also demonstrate extreme passivity. They give themselves up to the cult leader, adopt his attitudes and beliefs, adore him and blindly obey him. I know of no female cult leaders.

Some lower distant people are passive individuals who find it easiest to tag on to another in a loyal and obedient manner, doing whatever is expected of them, accepting whatever abuses and insults may come their way, in order to remain in some kind of a relationship. They may do all this because they feels they deserve no better. Sometimes a sadomasochistic and mutually gratifying alliance will develop between a negatively upper distant and a negatively lower distant person, as was depicted between Pozzo and Lucky in Samuel Becket's play *Waiting for Godot*.

Another form of lower-distant passivity is called *institutionalization* (Barton, 1959). People who spend long periods in prisons or other institutions, which run strict regimes and where personal initiative is restricted and blind obedience is demanded, lose their ability to function as autonomous individuals and are helpless and become depressed when they are discharged.

Illness behavior

Being ill, either physically or mentally, is one of the most reliable ways of evoking sympathy from others. Szasz (1972) observed that, "Like the infant's cry, the message 'I am sick' is exceedingly effective in mobilising others to some kind of helpful action" (p. 172). What Pilowsky (1969) called *abnormal illness behavior* is used by lower individuals in a variety of ways. In what

Barker (1962) called *hospital addiction*, the person may intentionally injure her/himself, swallow dangerous objects or poisonous substances or break open wounds to endanger her/his health and keep her/himself in need of medical attention. S/he may put blood in urine specimens or claim to have the symptoms of a condition that requires surgical attention.

In the condition called *hysteria*, the individual would like to feign illness or disability in order to avoid an unwished-for experience, but is too afraid of public disapproval to do so. The inner brain resolves the conflict by putting a particular bodily part out of action while denying awareness of this to the outer brain. The outer brain perceives the resulting disability but does not appreciate how it has come about. It therefore concludes that it is a genuine physical disorder. The objective is achieved without the individual being aware that s/he has caused it to happen.

Generating and maintaining concern

The lower person may behave in ways that keep the upper person concerned. Such behavior may occur simply because being looked after is such a gratifying experience or because the lower person is frightened of fending for her/himself. The most blatant form of this kind of behavior is when a person threatens to do or actually does physical harm to her/himself (like self-mutilation or taking tablets) in the presence of another, in order to frighten the other into some form of protective action. The message conveyed by such action is complex, but it is something like, "Look what you are making me do to myself". Threatening suicide or making suicide attempts is a similar and effective means of maintaining the attention of a caregiver. In a hospital setting, Schwartz and colleagues (1974) observed, "The more suicidally the patient behaves, the more parental will the hospital staff become". The self-harmer or suicide attempter is encouraged by witnessing the shock or distress of the other. Acts that may have begun as genuine expressions of desperation become taken up by the lower individual as a means of regenerating such shock and distress. This often sets up a vicious circle, such that whenever the upper other appears to be losing interest the lower person intensifies the self-harming behavior.

Summary

In humans, much more so than in other animal species, those with certain advantages or capabilities (i.e., who are upper) can be of benefit to those who lack such advantages and capabilities (i.e., who are lower). Positive upperness often helps lower others to become more upper. Because there are so many ways in which people can be upper, upper to lower relating is happening between people all of the time. Often, a person who is lower to another in one respect can be upper to that other in another respect, so exchanges between people are common. At the distant end of the proximity spectrum, upperness involves assuming responsibility for, judging, managing and taking charge of; in the middle part, it involves leading, guiding, teaching and helping; and at the close end, it involves protecting, supporting encouraging and caring for. Negatively upper people are dominating, suppressive and possessive. They fear assuming a lower position. Negatively lower people are meek, helpless, passive and dependent. They fear assuming an upper position.

Chapter 6

The power axis in psychotherapy

The power axis differs from the proximity axis. On the proximity axis, the therapist's being close imparts closeness to the client, and the therapist's being distant imparts distance to the client. On the power axis, the therapist's being upper imparts lowerness to the client, and the therapist's being lower imparts upperness to the client. Therefore, when writing about the power axis, it is important to be clear whether the concern is with what the therapist does or gives to the client or what the client does to or receives from the therapist.

In considering psychotherapy on the vertical axis, it is important to bear in mind the general principle that no one position should be considered preferable to any other position. Thus, being upper and being lower are of equal importance. A person who is being rigidly upper might be helped, therefore, not necessarily to be less upper and more lower, but to be capable of being lower as well as upper. A person who is being rigidly lower might be helped, therefore, not necessarily to be less lower and more upper, but to be capable of being upper as well as lower. Therapy should aim at versatility rather than rigidity. The cause of rigidity in one direction is largely a lack of competence in the opposite direction. When there is lack of competence in one direction, there is invariably negative relating in the opposite direction. Thus the improvement of relating in the opposite direction should also reduce the negative relating in the direction in which rigidity is being manifest.

In general terms, people remain fixed at one pole of the vertical axis out of fear of, or lack of competence in, the opposite pole. The therapy involves attempting to understand the nature of the fear or lack of competence and allaying the fear and increasing the competence. It has always to be borne in mind that the client may be forced into or maintained in a particular pole of the axis by someone outside of therapy who is adopting the opposite pole in relation to the client. The therapy may as much involve helping and supporting the client in her/his efforts to persuade this other person, at least sometimes, to change positions.

It must always be remembered that occupying one pole is neither better nor worse than occupying the opposite pole. Sometimes a client may swing from being stuck in one pole to being stuck in the opposite pole, which is no improvement. The object of therapy is to enable the client to move freely between the poles.

It may be not so much that the client is stuck in a particular pole as that s/he is adopting a particularly negative form of relating within that pole. In that case the therapy should be directed toward enabling the client to adopt more positive ways of relating within that pole.

Power characteristics of different styles of therapy

Psychotherapy would normally be considered a form of upper-to-lower activity, but it need not be, and sometimes it is not. Insofar as the psychotherapist is an expert to whom the client, who is not an expert, comes for help and advice, it has to be, for helping and advising is an upper activity and being helped and advised is a lower activity. Whatever takes place during the course of psychotherapy, the client places her/himself in the hands of the therapist and assumes that the therapist knows what s/he is doing. Most psychotherapists, by their actions, gestures, remarks and tone of voice, convey to the client that they are in charge, and most clients are willing to have it this way. However, there is a difference between being in charge and knowing what one is doing and adopting upper attitudes and behaving in upper ways toward clients. Although therapists sometimes do give advice, they generally hold the view that therapy does not work that way, though when pressed, they often find it difficult to explain to clients exactly how it does work, and clients often find that bewildering.

In Chapter 4, evidence was provided, from a number of sources, that closeness plays an important part in psychotherapy. It seems likely that upperness also plays a part, though there is less evidence available to support this view, and it is more difficult to define the part that upperness might play. Lerner (1972) provided suggestive research evidence that there is a positive correlation between therapists' democratic and non-authoritarian attitudes and beneficial therapeutic outcome, but this cannot be the whole story. Leaving aside the argument that the psychotherapist is the expert and that the client has come to her/him for help, does the therapist during the course of her/his work need to adopt a position of upperness? As with closeness, therapists vary considerably in the extent to which they elect to be openly upper in relation to their clients. Some consider it important to present themselves as upper; some try to maintain an egalitarian posture; and some, for short periods at least, try to adopt a lower posture.

In considering the posture of the therapist, one cannot ignore the position adopted by the client. Spinelli (1994) wrote, "The abdication of a position of authority or superior knowledge is no simple task at the best of times; it becomes even more problematic when, not unusually, one's clients seem to demand such of the therapist" (p. 231). Some clients like the therapist to be in charge; some believe that the relationship should be an equal one; and some try to stay in charge of the therapist. Sometimes the position adopted by the client is part or all of the client's problem, but sometimes the position adopted by the therapist can be a manifestation of a personal problem for the therapist.

Psychoanalysis

Psychoanalysts would argue that the predominant behavior of therapists during therapy is neutral. They sit in silence, listening attentively. They would say that clients come to therapy to talk, not to listen. Some analysts believe that, in the course of their talking, clients work things out for themselves, in the way that some art therapists believe that, in art therapy, clients paint themselves through and out of their problems. The therapist remains a reassuring presence. Stone (1984) observed that responses should be restricted to clarification, interpretation and other "neutral" maneuvers. He maintained that it is not even appropriate for the therapist to register an emotional response to what the client says or does. How then can the therapist be upper? Psychoanalysts would argue that, by not speaking, they do not influence the direction in which the clients choose to move, maintaining that only the clients know where their difficulties lie and, when given their head, sooner or later find their way to them. Freud (1912) observed that therapists should be opaque to their clients and, like a mirror, should show them nothing but what is shown to them. Psychoanalysts believe that, by remaining silent, they present to clients a *blank screen*, onto which clients are able to project attitudes they feel toward other people. It is because of the blank screen that clients come to relate to therapists in ways that replicate the way they relate to significant others, that is, they develop transferences (Chapter 3). If these transferences are of upper others, then it is the clients who are placing the therapists in a position of upperness, and not the other way around.

Ironically, although psychoanalysts go to such lengths to present themselves as neutral toward their clients, their clients still experience them as upper. They are popularly conceived of as powerful and frightening beings who have the capacity to see into and read other people's minds. Clients go to them with this understanding and expectation. Requiring clients to lie on a couch carries an implication of upperness, as does encouraging them to regress. Laying down rigid rules of conduct is another act of upperness. By withholding so much of themselves and by speaking so little, psychoanalysts are creating a mysterious and enigmatic image that causes clients to feel lower to them. On those occasions when they do speak they make authoritative pronouncements, sometimes couched in a vocabulary of jargon. Parker, Georgaca, Harper and associates (1995) maintained that the danger of psychoanalysis is that it binds the person into a relationship that requires absolute subordination. They wrote, "The analyst is put into a position of power in which meanings can be imposed instead of being cooperatively reached" (p. 22).

By interpreting what the clients say and do they are conveying the impression that they understand the clients better than the clients know themselves. Strupp (1989) concluded that there is little room for the large array of interpretations used by psychoanalysts. He considered that, when such interpretations are used with resistant clients, they often have a blaming or pejorative quality and are experienced as such by the client. Wile (1984) expressed a similar opinion and considered that interpretations may result in negative therapeutic reactions. Lomas (1987) concluded that interpretation is rarely helpful and favored abandoning it altogether.

The behavioral-cognitive therapies

It is perhaps in the behavioral-cognitive therapies that the therapist is most openly and unapologetically upper, though even here, the behavior of some behavior therapists has a strikingly egalitarian appearance. For example, when a client is afraid of travelling on public transport, the therapist may be willing to abandon the security of the consulting room and accompany the client on her/his travels. This is something a psychoanalyst would never do; but even though therapist and client may be sitting side by side on the train or the bus, the therapist is still able to remain an upper figure, and the situation is remarkably similar to a parent accompanying a frightened child; it is this which makes the therapy effective. It is when the behavior therapist is adopting more of a schoolteacher role, telling the client exactly what to do, giving the client homework assignments and checking that they have been carried out, that s/he is being quite unambiguously upper, and the client is being quite unambiguously lower.

As was mentioned in Chapter 4, although most behavioral-cognitive therapists are psychologists, their posture is sometimes strikingly medical. Clients come to them with specific symptoms, and they prescribe specific therapies for the removal of these symptoms, which often are remarkably effective. That the origin or the significance of these symptoms is frequently ignored is an indication of an even more authoritarian position than that adopted by most medical men, who would consider it dangerously irresponsible to concern themselves simply with the removal of symptoms. In relaxation therapy, the client who is tense and anxious is required to lie receptively on a couch, while the therapist makes soothing and calming suggestions to her/him. The client feels better for this but never gets to understand what the tension and the anxiety were all about.

Hypnotherapy

Hypnotherapy is the most obviously upper form of therapy. Not only is it appealing to those therapists who have upper personalities, it also brings out upper tendencies that may be latent in some therapists. Wolberg (1986) observed that the seeming helplessness of clients and their apparent susceptibility to suggestions may liberate omnipotent, sadistic and sexual feelings in therapists that normally they are able to hold in check. If they find they cannot, they may need to consider refraining from this form of therapy. The danger is that they may find this new-found power so exciting that they have little motivation to give it up. Hypnotherapy is appealing to those (lower, passive) clients who prefer to offer themselves up to the therapist to work on them, rather as a surgeon would operate upon an unconscious patient. Thus, the therapy they seek might not be the best therapy for them. On the other hand, hypnosis can induce the most perfect state of lower closeness, and clients who have never had such an experience may find this immensely comforting.

Particularly during the induction phase, but also during the trance itself, the therapist needs to speak with authority and certainty, that is, to present him/herself as a securely upper person. A persuasive attitude (upper close) rather than a dictatorial one (upper distant) is most effective since some clients are likely to defy orders or commands. There are certain similarities between hypnotherapy and behavioral-cognitive therapy, and there are reports of suggestions given under hypnosis reinforcing those made during behavioral-cognitive therapy (Lazarus, 1973). Hypnotherapy can also be used as an adjunct to psychoanalysis. As in normal sleep, hypnosis has the effect of diminishing the influence of the outer brain. Therefore, the hypnotherapist has a more direct access to the inner brain. Free association, the recall of past traumatic incidents and emotional catharsis can sometimes be facilitated, and hypnosis often puts the client into closer contact with her/his more repressed thoughts, emotions and impulses. Following a hypnotic session, a client may be able to dream more freely and to recall the content of the dream in a subsequent session (Wolberg, 1964).

Interpersonal therapy

Sullivan, the father of interpersonal therapy, was a humble man who tried to relate on equal terms to his clients. On the other hand, he did acknowledge that the psychotherapist is an expert to whom the client comes for help. One way of keeping upper to the client is to speak in professional jargon and to use obscure and mysterious concepts. Evans (1996) wrote, "Sullivan believed that there was more than enough to learn from the patient's description of his or her own experience and perception of the world without resorting to speculation about unconscious fantasy" (p. 57). He was highly critical of psychoanalytic jargon, which he thought only confused the client, and he tried to use simple terms that the client could understand. He shunned the neutral, blank screen approach of the psychoanalysts and adopted a normal, conversational style of psychotherapy.

Because most interpersonal therapists are not concerned with the removal of symptoms (the school of Klerman et al., 1984, referred to in Chapter 1, being a notable exception), they have no investment in relating from a position of upperness. In fact they try to avoid relating in any particular way toward their clients, because they wish to remain *neutral* observers and to make assessments by way of how the clients behave in the session, what they say about how they relate to others and how others relate to them. They are, however, not blank screens. Unlike psychoanalysts, they certainly do make appropriate emotional responses to what their clients say and do, because they want to appear *normal*. They try to enter into relationships with their clients by interacting with them and having normal conversations with them. They observe, in the natural setting of normal discourse, the way their clients relate to them (active relating) and the way their clients respond to what they say and do to them (reactive relating).

An important feature of interpersonal therapy, as Kiesler (1986) pointed out, is that the therapist is bound to enter into a relationship with the client because the client comes to the session with particular relating tendencies and is bound to apply these tendencies to her/his relating to the therapist. The client is used to others responding to her/him in a complimentary manner and can only relate to those who do respond in this way. Kiesler proposes that, initially at least, the therapist should elect to respond to the client in this way, in order, as he puts it, to get the client *hooked*. Interpersonal therapists may differ in their view as to what should happen next. Some (e.g., Kiesler, 1986) would then elect intentionally to modify the way they relate to their clients as a way of easing them out of what they see as a fixed style of relating. If, for example, a client is being excessively distant, the therapist would intentionally try to relate more closely to her/him as a way of drawing the client into a closer form of relating. A less confrontational interpersonal psychotherapist would try to understand why the client has difficulty relating in a particular way and help her/him overcome this difficulty. As part of this helping, the therapist may try to expose the clients to a particular form of relating, such as being close, in order to increase the client's confidence and competence in this form of relating.

The humanistic therapies

As was explained in Chapter 4, the humanistic therapists try, more than most other forms of therapist, to maintain an egalitarian relationship with their clients. This they do largely out of a wish to remain close to them. However, many of the things that humanistic therapists persuade their clients to do (rebirthing, for example), require the therapist to remain well and truly in the driving seat. Spinelli (1994) graphically described his disenchantment with the humanistic therapists when he wrote, "However, not long after I had begun to immerse myself in such approaches, I was perplexed to discover that they seemed to engender the most prominent abuses of therapeutic power I had yet encountered" (p. 276). It may be because the humanistic therapies were forced into the private sector that many of the abuses of therapeutic power arose. Therapists began to realize that they could command high fees for workshops that were offered to the general public. In these, they had free rein to manipulate workshop attenders as and how they pleased, which sometimes went to their heads. The most aberrant and destructive of such workshops were those that were founded by Erhard and carried the name *est*. In these, the leader would openly insult and humiliate attenders, with the objective of breaking them down.

The fact that the humanistic approach has been misused by certain power-crazy practitioners should not detract from the value of much of the work that is carried out by humanistic therapists. Principles of the humanistic approach, such as encouraging clients to accept, own and celebrate themselves, do not instil upper attitudes in therapists; it is probably true that humanistic psychotherapists are some of the most egalitarian. The Gestalt therapist is described as a *coexplorer* who encourages the client to fully experience who s/he is at any one time, never leading or pushing and never asking or encouraging the client to be different (Simkin, 1982). Gestalt therapy differs from most other forms of therapy in that the therapist does not side with the client's wish to change and does not encourage change. In fact, the therapeutic breakthrough sometimes comes when the client realizes that s/he does not have to change.

Existential therapy

Existential therapy has much in common with Sullivan's form of interpersonal therapy and certain forms of humanistic therapy. Laing (1965), who drew heavily upon the existential philosophy of Sartre (1969), insisted on viewing the patient as a person with her/his own unique experience. He considered the task of the therapist as articulating what the other's world is and ways of being in it. In this sense, the client leads and the therapist follows. We experience reality not as it is but as it appears to be to us. Sartre argued that it is never possible fully to comprehend what it is like to be the other person. One person's experience of the world can never be fully shared by another. The experiential therapist attempts to explore the client's experience of being-in-the-world by seeking to enter into her/his world view (Spinelli, 1994). From this point of view experiential therapy is the most respectful and least imposing form of therapy. It emphasizes the *being* quality rather than the *doing* quality not only of the client but also of the therapist. A number of therapists (e.g., Nacht, 1969) have argued that it is not so much what the therapist does as what s/he is that determines the effectiveness of therapy.

When the therapist is upper

Much psychotherapeutic activity comes under the heading of benevolent upperness. The therapist uses her/his upperness for the benefit of the client. This, strangely enough, applies whether the client has a problem of upperness or of lowerness. Even when the client has a problem of upperness, and, in at least some sense or for some of the time, is behaving in an upper way toward the therapist, the therapist is maintaining a position of upperness in a quite different sense (for, from one moment to another or even at any particular moment, upperness may assume a number of different forms). S/he is using her/his knowledge, training and experience to understand the client's upperness and think of ways of helping the client to modify certain unhelpful upper attitudes.

Upper close aspects of therapy

Whether they mean to or not, psychotherapists do many of the things that loving parents do. They listen attentively to what their clients say to them, console them, encourage and praise them, reassure them, and forgive them. That process, which is called *regression*, is defined as reversion to an earlier state or mode of functioning. It occupies a central position in psychoanalytic psychotherapy. In fact, Giovaccini (1990) considered it to be an essential component of the treatment. One of the justifications that analysts provide for requiring clients to attend for five days per week is that it helps them to remain in a prolonged state of regression. It is argued that regression enables the analyst to gain access to early phases and levels of development in order to facilitate the reorganization of personality into a new pattern.

Sometimes, a period of extreme regression, in which an adult client is totally indulged by the therapist and allowed to behave as though s/he were a helpless infant, can have a beneficial effect. Such indulgence normally requires hospitalization. An example of it is provided in Barnes and Berke (1971). Mary Barnes, the patient, was supported through a protracted period of regression (over a number of months) by Joseph Berke, the therapist, in the extraordinary therapeutic center called Kingsley Hall, located in the east end of London. In any therapy that involves regression, particularly when it is as extreme as this, it is essential that eventually the therapist takes time to return the client, through gradual stages, back to her/his true age.

Some analysts (e.g., Anna Freud, 1937) regard regression as one of the ego's mechanisms of defense. When used in this way, regression is usually considered in terms of Freud's (1905) theory of psychosexual development. The understanding is that, in order to avoid the anxieties of the more recent phallic or oedipal stage of development, the individual regresses to the anal or oral stage. Rycroft (1995) observed that this rarely succeeds, since at the earlier stage, new anxieties are encountered. In simpler terms, people may remain regressed because they are afraid of assuming the responsibilities of adult life. Anorexia nervosa, particularly when it occurs in young women, is sometimes considered to be a condition of regression, for by staying thin the young woman is avoiding adopting the curvaceous appearance of the sexually mature adult.

The benefits of lower closeness

There is something soothing about being in the safe hands of another, and although psychotherapists do not normally give advice, they do maintain, either consciously or unconsciously, an upper position in relation to their clients, which clients find pleasurable. It will be remembered from Chapter 4 that Smail (1995) observed that the love (closeness) that clients obtain from their therapists is not widely or plentifully available elsewhere. The same can be said of the more tender kinds of lowerness. The quality of this lowerness is enshrined in the title of the Gershwin song, "Someone to Watch over Me".

Much of what clients derive from psychotherapy is similar to that which people derive from a belief in a Christian god. God watches over us in a protective and concerned way, ensuring that no harm will come to us. It seems likely that much of the appeal of both the Christian religion and psychotherapy is that it replicates the protecting and caring attitude of the loving parent. People may seek psychotherapy either to re-experience or to experience for the first time the bliss of being a lovingly protected infant. As a corollary to this, people may seek to be psychotherapists because it provides for them the opportunity to behave in a lovingly protective way toward others, which is one of the satisfactions of upperness.

In Mary Chase's (1952) play *Harvey*, the main character, Elwood P. Dowd, was admitted to a mental hospital because he had as a companion a giant white rabbit that only he could see. He told the psychiatrist that the rabbit could stop the clock and transport you wherever you wanted to go, for as long as you wanted, with whomever you wanted, and when you came back, not one minute would have passed. The psychiatrist said that he would want to go to a grove of maple trees, with a beautiful, young, quiet woman, and he would tell her things he had never told anyone, and she would stroke his head and say "Oh, you poor, poor thing!" He would want this to last for three weeks. Dowd asked if this would not be monotonous. He said it would not. It would be wonderful. This is as good a description as any, albeit a fictional one, of the soothing nature of lower closeness. While prolonged exposure to this kind of lowerness is undoubtedly pleasurable, if not reparative, it cannot be all there is to psychotherapy. It seems likely that, within the security of protective lowerness, clients are more easily able to explore the disturbing experiences of their past and present lives, express hurts and grievances and consider possible ways forward.

Upper distant aspects of therapy

Just as in good parenting, so also in psychotherapy it is sometimes necessary for the upper person to impose limits on the lower person. Coopersmith (1967) observed that one of the characteristics of children with high self-esteem is that their parents, in the most reasonable way possible, imposed clear and firm limits on their behavior. This created for them a sense of security, in that they knew where they stood. They felt that their parents cared enough about them to impose rules that they understood to be for their own good. Such rules were not only imposed, they were also consistently enforced. When limits are not imposed, children feel confused. Adults who have had this experience say, "We were just left. We ran wild". A woman wept as she described an occasion in her childhood when her mother failed to turn up for her birthday party. They party broke down into chaos, and the children threw the food at each other. Clients who as children did not have such limits imposed upon them are inclined to take liberties with their therapists by failing to keep appointments, arriving late, trying to extend sessions beyond their termination time, phoning between sessions, trying to negotiate additional sessions and so forth. An integral part of therapy for such clients is setting and consistently keeping rules, irrespective of clients' attempts to break them.

Therapists, especially behavior therapists, sometimes give instructions to their clients or prescribe specific exercises for them to do. A therapist might say to a client with snake phobia, "Touch the snake". The definiteness of the instruction makes it easier for the client to respond. In hypnotherapy, therapists speak in an authoritative way to their clients, commanding them to do certain things, either while they are in the hypnotic state or later, in response to a specified cue. In may particular version of Gestalt art therapy (Birtchnell, 1998), I sometimes tell a client to draw what s/he is talking about. If s/he protests that s/he cannot draw, I repeat the instruction in as friendly a way as possible. Usually, then s/he does the drawing with surprising clarity. When a client has drawn a picture of an important person in her/his life, I sometimes tell her/him to talk to the drawing. This is a strange instruction, but, quite often, s/he will do what I say, with considerable benefit. In a couples therapy session, an obsessional man related how he could not propose to his partner. I said, "Do it now". He said, "Will you marry me?" She said, "Yes". It is not normally therapeutically effective to give instructions to clients, because it take away from them any responsibility for their actions. In these rare instances in which it works, it gives the client the confidence to do what s/he might have doubted that s/he could do. It is the suddenness and the definiteness that makes it work. If the behavior therapist had said, "Do you think you might now try to touch the snake?" the client would have said, "Certainly not".

The harm done by the therapist's negative upperness

Masson (1989) took the extreme view that since the therapist inevitably assumes a position of power in relation to the client, all therapy must be abusive, because where there is an imbalance of power rarely can there be compassion. Therefore, no good can come from psychotherapy. This view denies the existence of positive upperness, that form of relating upon which all civilized societies depend. In Chapter 5, under the heading of upper closeness, the tendency of humans to respond to the misfortune of others, even of total strangers, was described. This leaves no doubt that the necessary motivation for psychotherapy exists in most people. It does not however deny that some people are capable of deriving satisfaction from the abuse of their power by showing off to others, intimidating them, bullying them, making fun of them, putting them down, pointing to their deficiencies, causing them embarrassment or distress, gloating over their misfortune, or witnessing their distress or desperation; and psychotherapists are not immune from any of these forms of behavior, which lie at the very heart of sadism.

One important view that Masson (1989) did express is that therapy attempts to impose structures upon clients and, by so doing, disregards client's own views of the world. Parker, Georgaca, Harper and associates (1995) argued that, in psychoanalysis, clients are required not only to say what the analyst wants to hear but also to believe it. They must realize the falsity of what they had told the analysts just before. Winter (1997) expressed the view that much of the harm done in therapy is the result of therapists' endeavors to combat what they consider to be the resistance of their clients. He proposed that when therapists meet with resistance they should modify their approach in order that it will be less invalidating to the client. If instead they persevere with their original approach, but with renewed vigor, they are likely to precipitate reactions that are more detrimental than is the resistance. He quoted Grieger (1989), a rational emotive therapist, as saying the therapist should try to do violence to the client's resistant thoughts and search out and destroy their phony ideas. He also referred to a client in an encounter group reported on by Yalom and Lieberman (1971), whose negative experiences were considered to be "a function of aggressive, intrusive leadership style which attempted to change her according to the leader's own values by battering down her characterologic defences" (p. 23).

The Sadomasochistic relationship

The situation is complicated by the fact that some people derive satisfaction from being harmed or humiliated by others or from having their distress or desperation being witnessed by others. This lies at the very heart of masochism. Just as some therapists are sadists, some clients are masochists; and when sadistic therapists and masochistic clients match up with each other there is little prospect of change occurring in either party. Sometimes sadistic therapists match up with clients who are not masochistic, and their clients resists the therapist's attempts to humiliate them; and sometimes masochistic clients match up with therapists who are not sadistic, and their therapists decline their invitations to humiliate them.

There are many opportunities for experiencing the distress or desperation of others in therapy. If these are uncovered simply for the gratification of the therapist, they will contribute little to the therapeutic process. If, on the other hand, they are uncovered in order to reveal the nature of the problem, they will contribute much to the therapeutic process. The therapist who simply finds the revelations of the client gratifying will have little incentive to improve matters for the client. S/he will simply want to hear about them over and over, perhaps under the pretext that it will be good for the client to become more familiar with them.

Sadistic therapists will not want their clients to improve or to stop attending. They are able to prolong the client's attendance simply by maintaining, possibly quite correctly, that the therapy takes time; they can also contrive, though not necessarily at a conscious level, to provoke setbacks in their clients by touching upon or returning to sensitive spots, such as refering to past disturbing experiences or to client's weakness or deficiencies, that cause them to become less confident, more disturbed and more needful of them. The therapists are then able, quite legitimately, to institute reparative measures that restore the clients to a more stable state. This cycle of pushing clients down and helping them up again can go on indefinitely.

The narcissistic therapist

Narcissistic therapists find their client's adoration and even idolization of them gratifying, and they may reinforce such behavior in their client by their own narcissistic posturing. Narcissists love and reward people who love them, and their clients provide a mirror that reflects their grandeur and splendor back at them. Their clients become their disciples, and they reward their clients by complimenting them on being so perceptive of their worth. Their adoring clients find such rewards gratifying, and a vicious circle is set up that has the effect of pushing the therapist further into the adored position and the client further into the adoring position. The client will now be open to, and accept, whatever interpretation the therapist may choose to make about her/him. Beyond this, and even more damaging, the client will accept what-ever identity the therapist may choose to impose upon her/him. In effect, the client will abandon her/his own identity and any sense of autonomy and will become a creation of the therapist, an extension of the therapist's inner world. This is a version of *ontological dependence*. It has been called *trans-forming directiveness* (Birtchnell, 1987) and *constructing upperness* (Birtch-nell, 1993/1996). The tragedy of this development is that the therapist is so in love with her/himself that s/he has no concern or respect for the client's own needs or the client's fragile, emerging identity. The client's needs are ignored, and the client simply becomes a fulfillment of the therapist's dreams.

The abuse of the lower client

One of the characteristics of dependent clients is that they are so desperate for closeness that they will pay whatever price they have to in order to get it and keep it. Sadistic therapists find such clients seductive because they become aware that the clients will take whatever they throw at them, which they find gratifying. They realize that they can say or do whatever they want to the client and the client will take it. They may find it amusing to see how far they are able to go in this direction. The dependent client will never argue or disagree with or contradict the therapist, because this may turn the thera-pist against her/him and s/he will lose her/his closeness. If the therapist chal-lenges what s/he says, s/he will back down. If s/he appears to have annoyed or offended the therapist, s/he will apologize. When the therapist mocks or laughs at the client, the client pathetically mocks her/himself and laughs with the therapist at her/himself (Kubie, 1994). The client will perform whatever demeaning act the therapist may ask of her/him. It is in a setting such as this that a therapist may touch, kiss or even have full sex with the client. While this may not be what the client wishes to do, s/he may do it on the presumption that the therapist knows best, so as not to offend the therapist or in the belief that this confirms that the therapist really loves her/him. The therapist may interpret such non-resistance as consent. Such abuse of clients is similar to the abuse of dependent adults in general or to the abuse of children by adults. At some level, the client may know that it is wrong and be tormented with guilt about it, but be unable to acknowledge, or give expression to, such guilt for fear of getting the therapist in trouble.

Upper aspects of clients in therapy

Since therapy is primarily an upper activity, the therapist's lowerness does not feature as prominently in the therapy as her/his upperness does. Insofar as the therapist is always the one who is planning and controlling the course of the therapy, there is always a sense in which the therapist never totally gives up her/his upper position. Even when s/he is deciding to allow the client to behave in an upper way toward her/him, s/he is usually in a position to determine for how long or by how much this should continue. One of the principles of therapy based upon relating theory is that positive forms of relating should be accentuated and negative forms should be eliminated.

Letting the client lead the way, be in control

In a very real sense, the therapist always has to be lower to the client, because only the client has the facts. The therapist is helpless unless the client reveals the facts to the therapist. The client has to *lead* and the therapist has to *follow*. Only the client has been where s/he is taking the therapist. Only the client has had the experiences that s/he is describing. Only the client knows what it felt like or is feeling like. It is perhaps true that the client would be afraid to venture into the places s/he is taking the therapist unless the therapist were going there with her/him, but even so, the client is leading the way.

In many respects, it is the client who *sets the agenda*, for it is the client's own personal problems, not the therapist's, that have to be put right. Therapy often breaks down because the therapist tries to set the agenda. Extreme examples of this are when the therapist abuses her/his power and uses the client for her/his own personal gratification. Both throughout the course of therapy and within the setting of every session, it is dangerous for the therapist to have carefully thought-out plans about where the therapy should be going. Alarm bells should start to sound when the therapist finds her/himself thinking that s/he knows the client better than the client knows her/himself.

Taking a personal history, making a diagnosis and prescribing a course of treatment are forms of behavior that have served the physician well. The physician has a specific agenda that needs to be followed, which requires her/him to be in control of the proceedings. Medical psychotherapists and also behavior therapists, particularly when they are concerned with identifying and treating specific diagnostic categories or symptoms such as depression and anxiety, sometimes fashion themselves upon the physician. Even for the physician, there are dangers to keeping too precisely to a predetermined script, and the good physician may well give the patient her/his head.

Taking a history can amount to a form of interrogation, which is negative upper distant behavior. By asking questions, the interrogator controls the areas covered, but also remains detached from the person being interrogated. When being interrogated about highly personal matters, a client will not feel comfortable about revealing the truth and may resort to lying, simply because it is less embarrassing. I recall a young woman on the ward of a mental hospital where I was working. She had been subjected, by a colleague, to a full personal history, including a sexual history, but during the course of this, she had not been able to reveal that she was pregnant.

It is an important principle of therapy that the client has the right (power) to reveal or not to reveal certain information about her/himself. The physician, or even the therapist, does not have the right (power) to ask for it. If the client has chosen not to reveal certain information, I believe I have no right to know about it. Until it is brought up by the client, it is none of my business. I try not to ask a client personal questions, however relevant or important I think these questions might be.

Generally in therapy, but particularly during the early stages, I invite the client to just start talking. I am confident that whatever is on the client's mind inevitably will come to be talked about. The young girl would certainly have told me that she was pregnant. It sometimes surprises me that, even after several years of therapy, there are sometimes quite major items of information, for instance, that the client has a brother, that I do not know because they have not been brought up. This does not trouble me, because I know that there is a lot of other information that I would never have known had I not adopted this nondirective approach.

One of the strongest arguments against asking clients questions is that it is not the information that is important, but the context in which the information is imparted and the way it is imparted. During the course of a conventional personal history, a question that is often asked is "How old were you when you started having periods?" This is a fact I do not normally know, nor do I want to know. However, if a client should tell me of the day she came home from school bleeding and worrying that there was something wrong with her, and of her mother giving her a pack of sanitary towels and saying to her, "You will have to start using these", this is a revelation of some importance.

Treatment of the negatively lower client

The majority of people who seek therapy have lower characteristics. Seeking help is an act of lowerness. The lower client takes easily to therapy and feels comfortable in it, because that is the position s/he most commonly adopts in relation to others. S/he is also more appealing to the therapist. Whereas it is difficult to persuade upper clients to accept therapy, it is often difficult to persuade lower clients to give up therapy. Whereas therapists find working with upper clients hard work, they find working with lower clients easy and are often sorry to let them go. The object of therapy is not to turn negatively lower clients into negatively upper clients, for being negatively upper will cause them as much difficulty as being negatively lower. Lower clients need to be encouraged to hold on to the positive aspects of their lowerness. At the same time, they need to be helped to acquire the competence to adopt the more positive forms of upperness.

Bringing out and reinforcing the client's upperness

In the management of the lower client, it is important for the therapist to try to find ways of being lower to the client, for if the client is going to be exposed to the experience of positive upperness s/he is going to have to do it in relation to the therapist. The therapist needs to seek out upper aspects of the client in order to feel genuinely lower, for it is never acceptable for the therapist to pretend to be lower. If the client should realize that the therapist is pretending s/he will conclude that the therapist could find no genuine upperness in her/him, which will be demoralizing for her/him.

In Ken Loach's film *Kes*, a schoolteacher, played by Colin Welland, befriended a pupil who felt downtrodden and helpless. The teacher went home with the boy who showed him his pet kestrel. The teacher watched in admiration as the boy stood in the middle of a field encouraging the kestrel to swoop down to feed from the dead mice that he held in his hand. At this moment, the teacher, normally upper to the boy, was adopting a genuinely lower attitude toward him, which made the boy feel important. The teacher was also able to appreciate the upper close relationship that the boy had developed toward his kestrel. It would be helpful if the therapist could find opportunities to adopt such an attitude toward a lower client.

Fear of doing better than a parent

It is a characteristic of the (benevolent upper) good parent or good teacher that s/he teaches the child all s/he knows, in order to bring the child up to her/his level. S/he then encourages the child to do even better, and even to overtake her/him. The insecurely upper parent or teacher sometimes conveys, though not necessarily by any direct communication, that the child/client could never, or even should never, aspire to be as good as s/he is. In the area of social class, there used to be an understanding that one should not try to *rise above one's station*. This implied that it was improper to aspire to rise into a class higher than that which one was born into. The child/client may sometimes feel something pulling her/him back (or down) when s/he tries to better him/herself, which may become apparent during therapy. Remember the client who expressed to me how guilty he felt because he got a first-class degree when his father got only a third-class degree. Giving expression to these feelings is therapeutic in itself, but exploring their origins and encouraging the client to question and defy them is also necessary. By adopting a more encouraging attitude toward the client the therapist may be able to neutralize them.

Feeling unworthy

Another, similar, understanding was that of *knowing one's place*, that is, one experiences oneself as a lesser being in relation to certain others. This carries the assumption that one should behave with due deference and respect toward those certain others. In present-day Western society, it is not always easy to determine what one's place is, or whether one should behave with deference toward certain others. The concept of worthiness implies that one has to earn one's place, that one needs to have certain qualities, talents or capabilities in order to be worthy of being looked up to or admired. Feeling worthy or unworthy is not always linked to having qualities, talents and cap-abilities. If influential others treat one as being worthy or unworthy one tends to accept that judgment and behave accordingly. Certain lower people (that is people who experience themselves as lower) have an unjustified feeling of unworthiness (just as certain upper people have an unjustified feeling of worthiness). The origin of this feeling needs to be sought and its justifiability questioned. The therapist may enable the client to reach a more appropriate assessment of her/his worthiness.

The behavioral cognitive therapists adopt a procedure called *assertiveness training*, by which clients are encouraged to practice standing up for them-selves, within a group setting. Undoubtedly this will help the unworthy client, though it would not enable her/him to explore the origin of her/his experience or permit a re-evaluation of her/his judgments.

Incompetence

Realistically, people vary in how competent they are in various skills and abilities. Negatively lower individuals have a pervasive attitude of incompe-tence that they apply in a variety of situations. Such apparent incompetence contributes to their dependent behavior, for if they believe themselves to lack the competence to do certain things, they will ask others to do them for them, which only reinforces their belief that they are incompetent. It is extremely difficult to persuade such people to try to do these things or to try to learn to do them. In fact, they are inclined to interpret such persuasion as rejection, as though the therapist is saying to them, "No, I will not help you". They are afraid that if they try and fail this will only confirm that they cannot. In fact, they are afraid of the depression that they experience when they do fail. The therapist needs to be caring and concerned and to explain to them that nobody gets things right the first time and that failures are only to be expected at the beginning. It is important to set them simple tasks and to praise and encourage them when they succeed. They may well be amazed at themselves for being able to do even these, which may give them the confidence to try something a little more difficult.

Behavior therapists tend to focus only upon this practice and encouragement approach, but more psychodynamic therapists will wish to explore the origin of clients' conviction of their incompetence. Invariably they will tell stories of occasions when others, particularly parents or school teachers, made them feel useless for having failed at various tasks, particularly in front of others. They may have actually failed in certain examinations or competitive events, and they will offer these as evidence of their incompetence. The therapist should not be deterred by these stories, but instead should point to evidence of their successes in other directions. They might be persuaded to re-enact these humiliating experiences with some release of emotion and perhaps to speak out against their humiliators.

Passivity

Many clients, initially at least, assume that the function of the therapist is either to tell them what to do in order to get better or to do something to them that will make them feel better. Thus, they adopt the passive (lower) attitude of offering themselves up to the therapist in order to be cured. Most clients soon learn that this is not the way that therapy works, but some continue to adopt a position of extreme passivity, which can pose considerable problems for the therapist. They do and believe whatever their therapist tells them. They are putty in the therapist's hands. They adopt whatever postures or attitudes are suggested to them, and by so doing, they create the impression that they are responding to treatment. They invite the therapist to tell them what to do, and they try to do things that they believe will please the therapist. It is extremely difficult to resist responding to these invitations or appearing pleased when clients do things that look as though they are making progress. They are always asking the therapist, "Is this right or is that right?" The therapist needs to keep throwing them back upon themselves, saying, "You decide", or, "What do you think?"

Passivity can be a problem in the lives of clients. A man who, from an early age, had a poor opinion of himself, grew up just letting things happen to him. He seemed incapable of influencing the direction his life should take. He felt that his opinion counted for nothing. He drifted into relationships with girls he did not like and did not respect. He felt trapped in these relationships, without the power to end them. With little enthusiasm, he drifted into a marriage in which he also felt trapped. His wife experienced him as weak. She told him to leave, and he obediently did so. His passivity was linked to the overpossessiveness and overcontrollingness of his parents. His main preoccupation in therapy was carving out a true identity for himself and learning to like and respect the emerging real person.

Fear of disapproval

Almost as infuriating as the blind obedience of negatively lower individuals is their fear of causing offense. They are careful always to agree with, and never to contradict, the therapist. They apologize for any slight mistake or misconduct. When they behave in this way, it is necessary to invite them to make whatever association may come to them about this. They are likely to describe a family situation in which they were expected to be obedient and conforming and where any disrespectful behavior was severely dealt with. They should be encouraged to recognize that this is not the normal expectation of other people. It comes as some relief to the therapist when they begin to show signs of disrespect or disagreement.

Combatting the internalized upper other

While people have internalizations of all kinds of other people who have, at different times, significantly interacted with them, the internalized upper other seems to play a particularly important part in shaping people's relating behavior. This presumably occurs because, in both childhood and adult years, upper others dominate and control people in a variety of ways. The internalized upper other is an amalgam of the various upper others who have influenced a person. Negatively lower people are often profoundly influenced by their internalized upper other, which causes them to be subdued, timid, deferential, obedient, self-criticizing, self-blaming and self-punishing. Because the upper other is located within the inner brain, clients are not aware of its existence, and perhaps it does not help to tell them that it exists. However, it is important for the therapist to be aware of its existence, for a major component of the therapy of the negatively lower person is correcting the effect that this upper other is having upon her/his attitudes and behavior. Because the therapist is an upper person, over time, s/he will become internalized and will have the effect of modifying the impact that the internalized upper other has.

The affects of the negatively lower client

Lower clients experience mainly two kinds of affect: anxiety and depression. They experience anxiety because they feel they are at the mercy of upper others, who may abuse, reject, exploit or humiliate them. They experience depression in response to such malevolent behavior of upper others. They also experience depression if they feel they have caused offense to their internalized upper other. As was discussed in Chapter 5, ranking theorists (e.g., Price and Gardner, 1995) view depression as almost synonymous with adopting a lower rank, a view that has been challenged (Birtchnell, 1995).

Whereas certain behavioral cognitive therapists might choose to treat anxiety and depression without reference to their origins, interpersonal therapists would wish to examine those interpersonal circumstances, either past or present, that have given rise to them or are maintaining them.

There appear to be some lower individuals who are stuck in their affective state, particularly if it is one of depression. Others accuse them of *wallowing in self-pity* and respond to them with irritation. Their state appears to be one of defeat, of having given up, and they see no way out of it. Encouraging them to take control of their situation and to find ways out of their entrapped state will dislodge them from their inertia. They may derive such gratification from the consolation they receive from others that they have no motivation to change. Their protest that they want to get better may simply be a camouflage for this gratification. If this is the case, therapy must involve revealing to them the greater gratifications of a more varied lifestyle. It may also involve disconnecting them from the consoling upper others who enjoy maintaining them in their miserable state.

The disposition to guilt and shame

Throughout our lives we are assaulted by accusations by others that various mishaps are our fault, that we are to blame. Upper people are reluctant to accept blame and are all too ready to impose or displace blame on to others. The Christian concept of sin is an extension of this blaming process. Lower people become the ready recipients of blame, and through their internalized upper others they are excessively inclined to load blame on to themselves.

Kaufman (1996) called shame the affect of inferiority. He believed that shame is instilled into the individual by shaming experiences in early life. In these experiences, powerful (upper) others mock, ridicule, humiliate and accuse the individual. These shaming attitudes become attached to the internalized upper figure, which continues to work on the individual throughout life. Kaufman offered as an extreme example a man who, as a boy, had been beaten every day and who, on one occasion, had been forced to kneel before his father and tell him that he was God. Kaufman maintained that shame can only be expunged by reliving these experiences in the presence of the therapist, who can help the client to defy and fight off the shamer and re-evaluate and reassess her/himself.

Resisting the behavior of external upper others

It is possible that some clients have come to acquire lower forms of behavior because they have never been encouraged to become upper, particularly by their parents. Parents who have succeeded in keeping their children lower often continue to maintain them in this condition long into adult life. A man who had a rich father was indulged to the extent that he did not have to work. Whatever he wanted, his father bought. His father paid for his therapy, but ironically, it was in therapy that it became clear to him that his father was simply buying his submission. He refused to receive any more money from his father and by this means he was able to escape from his father's hold on him. Parents often have subtle ways of putting or keeping their adult children down. Often, when their adult children return from a visit to such a parent they feel weak, helpless or worthless and are angry that their parent has done it to them again. Confronting their parent simply evokes the response of bewilderment. Such parents do not want to acknowledge what they are doing because, if they do, they will have to release the child from their (upper close) grip. More often than not, the child, with the support and encouragement of the therapist, has to make a unilateral break from the parent.

Treatment of the negatively upper client

For one reason or another, negatively upper people sometimes do find their way into therapy; when they do, they present a challenge to the therapist. Much that is relevant on the topic of such clients is contained in Travers (1991). Upper distant clients easily take offense and demand apologies from the therapist, and therapists may have to offer their apologies. They will not tolerate criticism, or even anything that might be construed as criticism. They will try to dictate how the therapy should be conducted, telling the therapist what s/he should and should not do and what they are and are not prepared to talk about. They will not be told what to do. They dislike people in authority and try to intimidate them, humiliate them or put them down, which includes the therapist. They will search for ways of presenting themselves as superior to the therapist or of getting one up on the therapist. If there is a difference of opinion they must always be seen to be right. If there is an argument they always have to win.

Problems of engaging upper clients in therapy

Because psychotherapy is primarily an upper-to-lower activity, people who manifest negatively upper ways of relating rarely present themselves for therapy. As they tend to cause others to suffer rather than to suffer themselves, they do not feel the need for help. Many forms of negative upperness, such as vandalism, arson, assault, blackmail, murder (upper distant), abduction, pedophilia, sexual abuse and rape (upper close), are regarded as crimes, for which punishment rather than therapy is the appropriate response. People who behave in these ways may or may not wish they did not do so, but even if they do, they may not feel able to ask to be helped to stop. They may believe that no one would want to help them, or they may be too proud to ask for help. *Pride* is a particular problem for upper people.

Upper people find it difficult to allow themselves to enter into therapy because they perceive therapy as a form of lowerness, and they are often frightened of assuming the lower position in relation to someone else. They see accepting the position of a client as an acknowledgment that there must be something wrong with them, which they may interpret as a kind of insult. They may say, "Do you think I'm mad or something?"

Upper close clients deny any weakness or failing in themselves and try to concern themselves with the welfare of others, including the therapist. They are used to others coming to *them* for help. They cannot tolerate any show of care toward them, for this would place them in the lower close position, a position that they find intolerable.

It sometimes happens that a person who enjoys a position of high status within society will seek therapy for a specific difficulty, one that may not be a manifestation of her/his upperness. Such a person may find it difficult to adopt the lower position of client, though s/he may find this easier if s/he is paying a substantial fee for the therapy, for this places her/him in the position of the therapist's employer. From her/his position of upperness, s/he may watch the therapist at work on her/himself, which prevents her/him from being an active participant in the therapy. Strangely, s/he may also adopt a kind of passive attitude, saying, "I'm paying you to get me better, so go on then, get me better".

Upper clients are much more common in marital therapy, in cases where the marital relationship has broken down because one partner has tried to behave in an excessively controlling or possessive way toward the other. In many respects, upperness is easier to cope with in marital therapy because the upperness is directed more toward the marital partner than toward the therapist. This issue will be addressed further in Chapter 8.

When the client imposes lowerness on the therapist

When the client is functioning excessively at an outer brain level, s/he may choose to direct operations in ways that s/he may think should be productive, but which turn out not to be productive. The client's policy does not work because her/his outer brain can only make guesses about where the trouble is. My response to this behavior is to encourage the client to relax and just talk freely. This way we are able to get in touch with the inner brain, which does know where the trouble is.

There are times when the client assumes the upper position, either calmly or in a state of high emotion, and takes over the session, refuses to do what the therapist suggests, starts to interrogate the therapist, criticizes the therapist, tells the therapist what s/he may or may not do, gives the therapist instructions, rants and shouts at the therapist and even intimidates, threatens or attacks the therapist.

There are also times when the client assumes an upper close attitude toward the therapist, wants to know what is troubling the therapist, asks if the therapist is all right and wants to calm, console or comfort the therapist.

There are no hard and fast rules about how the therapist should respond to such reversals of position. Most probably, the client has moved into the upper position because s/he has felt threatened by (or in the case of the move to upper closeness, concerned about) the therapist, and it has seemed safer for her/him to move into the more powerful position. Although the therapist is in the lower position, s/he is still the therapist and still has a degree of control over how things should proceed. The client remains aware that the therapist is still the therapist and, to some extent, is looking to the therapist for some kind of resolution to the situation.

The insecure therapist may interpret such an event as a power struggle and may feel compelled to regain the position of power as soon as possible. Such action may be effective, but it carries the risk that the client will feel suppressed. Alternatively, it may lead to an escalation. In general, such an approach is not to be recommended. It seems more sensible, initially at least, that the therapist should accept the lower position that the client has imposed upon her/him. The therapist should obey the client's instructions, answer the client's questions, accept the client's criticisms, even apologize if that is appropriate, respond honestly to the client's concerns and even accept the client's consolation and comfort. Suspecting that the client has been frightened or threatened by her/him, the therapist should try to understand the nature of the fear or the threat and to say something that will reduce it. If there has been a misunderstanding, s/he should clarify it.

More often than not, the client's shift into upperness is only temporary. Sometimes it is appropriate for the therapist not even to comment upon it, but at other times it will be necessary to go back over the experience and try to understand what it was all about.

As Kiesler (1986) correctly pointed out, if in the early stages of therapy the therapist attempts to challenge or confront the upper client, or stop the client behaving in an upper way, the client will either intensify her/his efforts to become upper or simply stop attending, for her/his upperness is most usually an expression of a fear of being lower. Therefore, initially, the therapist has no option but to allow the upper client to assume the upper position.

It helps to discover the origin of the excessive tendency to upperness. Most usually it appears to have developed out of a response to the attempts of others to force the client into a position of downness (Chapter 5). This could have been a tyrannical parent, who demanded that the client submit to her/his authority, or a sibling who was determined to come out on top in order to win the favor of the parents or who excluded her/him from games with other children. Alternatively s/he might have had some conspicous disadvantage such as small stature or disability that other children could poke fun at. Any of these circumstances could have led to the client turning into a lower individual, but something must have given her/him the strength to resist and to fight back. That something could have been the discovery of some compensating attribute such as physical strength or high intelligence. The physical strength could have enabled her/him to bully and intimidate others. The intelligence could have enabled her/him to outwit or outsmart others. The client needs to be given the opportunity to relive some of these earlier humiliations and to give expression to the lingering pain and resentment that s/he continues to harbor toward those who tormented and persecuted her/him. Unfortunately, negatively upper people tend to be very unforgiving and to hold on to grudges. It is unlikely therefore that the client can be persuaded to give up her/his resentments, but they may lose some of their intensity.

The therapy should have two primary objectives: first, to reduce the client's negatively upper tendencies, such as being boastful and contemptuous toward others, and to reinforce her/his positively upper tendencies, such as being able to accept responsibility for others and to lead and teach them; and second, to give the client the confidence to be lower in relation to others, by being prepared to seek their help and advice. To a large extent, the therapist has to offer her/himself as an alternative other who has no interest in putting the client down and who can appreciate her/his upper qualities and encourage her/him to put them to constructive use, and who can tentatively offer her/him help and advice and encourage her/him to seek the help and advice of others.

Reinforcing and enhancing the client's positive upperness

In many respects, the client is often superior, or upper, to the therapist. The therapist may be more knowledgeable, experienced and skilled as a therapist, but the client may have knowledge, skills, experience and talents in other areas that are far greater than those of the therapist. It is not unusual for the client to describe feats and achievements that would be beyond the capabilities of the therapist. Even within the interpersonal domain, a client may reveal insights, capabilities, social skills and courage that are greater than those of the therapist. The secure therapist will acknowledge all of this and adopt an appropriately humble attitude toward the client.

There really are times when the client knows or understands a person or a situation better than the therapist does, and it helps both the client and the therapist if the therapist can make clear her/his lack of understanding by asking such a question as "What did she mean by that?" (Not "What do you think she meant by that?" because that implies that the therapist knows the answer and is just testing the client.) It enhances the client's confidence and sense of effectiveness when s/he is made aware that the therapist is treating her/him as an expert and is seeking and respecting her/his opinion and that the therapist cannot function without her/his help.

In any therapeutic endeavor, it is the client who struggles, who finds the solutions, who does the suffering. In terms of relating, the therapist's functions are to appear interested, be concerned, reveal a willingness to help, make suggestions, encourage, support, share the client's sadnesses when things go badly and delights when things go well and watch with approval and admiration as the client finds her/his own way through and out of her/his difficulties. It sometimes seems that the most satisfactory outcome is when the client tells the therapist that s/he was useless and that, in the end, s/he had to do it all her/himself.

The affects of the upper client

Whereas shame and unworthiness are the emotions of lowerness, anger and entitlement are the emotions of upperness. Whereas shame is turned in on the individual, anger is turned outward at others. This leads to complications. Others get shouted at, hit and injured, and sometimes even get killed. Objects get thrown, and property and possessions get smashed and destroyed. Such behavior is both offensive and frightening to others, and upper people frequently are deserted by friends and relatives. It is such experiences that sometimes prompt upper people to seek therapy.

Upper behavior can also assume various forms of criminal activity, and upper people are frequently charged and punished for their behavior. Whereas society feels sorry for the lower individual, it is intolerant of and angry toward the upper one. When property gets damaged and others get hurt or killed by upper people, society demands revenge and retribution. It is only under exceptional circumstances that upper people are recommended for treatment rather than punishment; even when they are, such treatment has to be carried out in places of high security. Upper people are not likely to cooperate when treatment is imposed upon them by a court of law; but sometimes, under conditions of high security, they may think about their lives and wonder whether there might be ways of behaving differently.

Within the criminal world, and certainly within penal institutions, certain upper attitudes serve a protective function. The upper person is sensitive to any sign of insult or abuse and maintains an attitude of constant vigilance. S/he is tense and alert and ready to strike out at anyone who appears likely to insult or harm her/him. In fact, s/he may make a preemptive strike in order to put another person out of action before the other is able to do her/him any damage. Such behavior may be directed toward a therapist. It may not be easy to persuade an insecurely upper person that it is safe to let down this protective vigilance.

It is likely that, during the course of therapy, the client will take offense at remarks made by the therapist and demand that the therapist retract them. In the early stages of therapy it would be as well for the therapist to do as the client demands, but as the therapy progresses, the client may be persuaded to examine objectively the nature of the remarks that were made and view them as less offensive. It is also likely that the client will describe occasions and events outside of therapy when the client considers that others have behaved offensively toward her/him and when s/he responded with intolerance and rage to these others and the remarks that they made. These too can be examined, in a more detached way, in the presence of the therapist, and understood as being less offensive.

Anger is a problem for the upper client both in and outside therapy. Often, the therapist is aware that the client is harboring intense anger, toward either the therapist or someone in her/his present or past life. Whereas the therapist would not think twice about encouraging or permitting the client to weep during the therapy session, s/he will be more cautious about allowing the client to give expression to anger. However, if it is reasonable to permit the client to weep, it should be equally reasonable to allow her/him to be angry. Such anger when released can be extremely frightening, because the client may shout and scream and hit and throw objects. It is better contained within a group setting, where there are people who might be able to restrain the client if the anger should get out of hand. However, it would not be right to avoid the expression of anger in the individual session, if such expression is what is required.

I have sometimes suggested to clients that they might find some way of giving expression to their anger either at home, by hitting cushions against a wall, or by going to some isolated place where they can shout without disturbing other people, but they very rarely manage this. The expression of anger seems to be much easier in the presence of a therapist. Even in a state of rage, the client is usually respectful of the therapist and does not want to harm her/him. It is important to deflect the anger away from the therapist onto a cushion or toward a drawing of the hated person.

Resisting the behavior of external lower others

Negatively upper people either enter into relationships with negatively lower people or they coerce those with whom they form relationships into adopting a lower role in relation to them. This has the effect of maintaining them in their upperness. Upper distant people enjoy throwing their weight around and bullying others into submission. They derive enormous gratification from this. Narcissistic people require sycophants to sustain them in their grandiose posturing. Upper close people need weak and helpless others whom they can take pity on. Upper distant people can be helped to understand that when they beat others into submission they actually destroy the person with whom they are trying to have a relationship. Narcissistic people can be helped to understand that by shutting out the criticisms of others they never get to learn about their deficiencies and are unable to improve themselves. Upper close people can be helped to understand that by forever involving themselves with weak and helpless people they are creating for themselves an exaggerated sense of their own importance.

As negatively upper people gain more insight into their behavior they become less able to conceal from themselves the effect that they have upon the lower people with whom they habitually relate. They are more inclined therefore to avoid them and relate more to people of equal status. One reason why controlling people control is that they are afraid of losing control to others. They should be helped to appreciate that others can be entrusted with a degree of control without the situation getting out of hand. One reason why certain upper people require everything to be done their way is that they are afraid of the otherness of other people. They should be helped to appreciate that letting other people sometimes have a say in how things should be done does not necessarily mean getting lost in the identity of these other people.

Particularly in marital therapy, the weaker person with whom the negatively upper person relates is given the opportunity to complain and even to threaten to leave the relationship if the negatively upper person continues to relate in this way.

Summary

Therapists vary in the extent to which they adopt an overtly upper attitude toward their clients. Hypnotherapists are the most obviously upper, and behavioral-cognitive therapists, with their emphasis on education, come a close second. While some humanistic therapists are dictatorial, many try to present themselves as coexplorers. Interpersonal therapists, because they are concerned with correcting the rigidly upper or lower attitudes of their clients, try to remain neutral. When they are narcissistic, sadistic, compulsively caring or seductive, therapists are being negatively upper. Negatively upper clients should be helped to be positively upper, and negatively lower clients should be helped to be positively lower. Negatively upper clients are afraid of being lower. They should be helped to entrust themselves to others. Negatively lower clients are afraid of being upper. They should be helped to teach, lead and take responsibility for others. Clients should be helped to resist the pressure exerted from significant others to keep them as they are.

Chapter 7

Interrelating

Up until now in this book, relating and being related to have, somewhat artificially, been considered in isolation. This has been done in order to clarify the mechanisms involved. In this chapter and the next, an attempt will be made to integrate relating and being related to, and to view the integration as a single entity called interrelating. An analogy may be drawn with a beginner learning to play a new piece on the piano. S/he first learns the left-hand part, and then learns the right-hand part, and then proceeds to play both parts together. Even in these two chapters, the integration will not be complete, for in describing an interaction it still remains necessary to consider separately what is happening on either side of it.

The process of interrelating was briefly described in Chapter 1. While it was defined there in the simplest of terms as that process by which two people relate to each other, it can, in practice, be anything but simple. During an episode of interrelating, each person both relates to and is related to by the other and, in turn, each person responds to and is responded to by the other. During these interactions, each person, from minute to minute, day to day, week to week, or month to month, is attempting to define her/his own relating needs, in order to monitor how successful s/he is being in attaining and maintaining them and to what extent the relating of the other is assisting or hampering her/him in doing so. At the same time, s/he is attempting to determine what the other needs/wants and by what means s/he is trying to get it. At every stage of this process s/he needs to be determining to what extent her/his objectives and the other's are compatible, who is being the more successful in attaining and maintaining her/his needs, whether different tactics might be more effective or, in the end, whether the interaction is worth pursuing. All of this is happening very fast and quite automatically. It is, therefore, inner brain activity. Thus, the inner brain is the principal operator in the interrelating process.

The outcome attained by each relater during a period of interrelating has been described as a *state of relatedness*. The term *outcome*, rather than *objective*, is used here because a person can attain a state of relatedness either by the active process of relating to someone or by the passive process of being related to by someone. On the horizontal axis, a person can attain closeness or distance either by attempting to get close or distant in relation to someone else or by someone else attempting to get close or distant in relation to her/him. On the vertical axis, a person can attain upperness either by relating in an upper way toward someone or by being related to in a lower way by someone, or can attain lowerness either by relating in a lower way toward someone or by being related to in an upper way by someone. If this is the case, then that state of relatedness may or may not be that which the person wants, for it may simply have been imposed upon her/him by the relating of the other.

The period of interrelating can be arbitrarily demarcated by the nature of the *occasion*, like a psychotherapy session or two people spending an evening out together. The interrelating that takes place in a shop is different from that which takes place at a party. That which takes place between a doctor and patient is different from that which takes place between a husband and wife. Thus, before there is any interrelating at all, the participants will have certain expectations of what is normal in that situation.

Interrelating can occur over an entire range of time spans. It can be only a brief interaction lasting a few seconds, or it can extend over an hour, a day, a number of hours, days, weeks, months or even years. When interrelating extends over a period of time—and this need only be an hour-long conversation—one or both participants may be consistently striving for one particular relating objective throughout that period, or one or the other may be striving for different objectives at different times during that period. In order to analyze what is happening during a lengthy period of interrelating, it may be necessary to divide it into *episodes* of variable duration, or even to divide each episode into brief *interactions*.

Much interrelating must occur so rapidly that it can only take place by way of automatic processes, that is, it must be an inner brain activity (Chapter 2). The participants cannot have time to think out their respective actions and reactions and need to rely upon the specialized centers within the inner brain that make rapid assessments of relating needs and devise appropriate strategies for meeting them (Chapter 1). Such strategies must need constant revision in the light of successes or failures in meeting these needs and the incoming information concerning the relating strategies of the other. As in all relating, the higher (*primary*) specialized centers for determining the general directions of relating are able to call upon lower (*secondary*) specialized centers for selecting appropriate actions and reactions, which, in turn, recruit lower centers still (called *tertiary*), such as those for movement and speech, in order that these actions and reactions can be brought into play.

Adaptability versus rigidity

Up to this stage, attention has been directed to the relating of an individual. The principle has been laid down that the individual relates best if s/he is competent in all eight positions of the octagon. If s/he is, she is described as versatile. In this chapter and the next, attention is directed to the interrelating between two or more individuals. Interrelation works best if all members of a group or a family are versatile. If they are, the group or family can be described as *adaptable*. There are degrees of adaptability, depending upon the number of members who are versatile. If the group or family is large and the majority of the members are versatile, then the few who are not can be accommodated, and the level of adaptability still remains high. If the number of members who are versatile is small, then certain fixed patterns of interrelating become established and the group or family is called *rigid*.

Relating compatibilities

When two interrelating individuals are versatile, the question of compatibility does not arise, since they are each able to play different parts in relation to the other. When this is not the case, the relating of one may or may not be *compatible* with the relating of the other. On the horizontal axis, forms of relating are compatible if they are from the same pole. If two people both want closeness or both want distance, their relating is compatible. If one wants closeness and the other wants distance, it is incompatible. On the vertical axis, forms of relating are compatible if they are from opposite poles. If one wants upperness and the other wants lowerness, it is compatible; but if both want upperness or both want lowerness, it is incompatible. The issue of compatibility can be more complicated, because within each of the general objectives, there are specific subsidiary ones, and while there may be agreement at the general level there may be disagreement at the more specific level. Two partners may both want closeness, but one may want to talk and the other may want to make love; or they may agree to an upper to lower interaction but one may want to give advice and the other may want to be reassured.

Donative and receptive relating

In each position, it is possible either to give or to receive a state of relatedness. A form of giving closeness is being kind and understanding; a form of being given closeness is having the experience of the other being kind and understanding. A form of giving distance is respecting the other's need for personal space and privacy; a form of being given distance is having that personal space and privacy respected by the other. On the horizontal axis, when a person gives a state of relatedness, it almost inevitably provides that same state of relatedness to the giver. The person who gives closeness is, by so doing, also providing her/himself with closeness; the person who gives distance is, in the process, also providing her/himself with distance. A form of giving upperness is praising, admiring and worshipping the other; a form of being given upperness is being praised, admired and worshipped by the other. A form of giving lowerness is providing protection or care; a form of receiving lowerness is being protected or cared for by the other.

On the vertical axis, when a person gives a state of relatedness it most usually provides the opposite state of relatedness to the giver. Apart from the process of promotion—in which an upper person promotes someone who is lower than her/himself to a position that is upper in relation to certain other people, though still lower than her/himself—giving upperness to the other most usually involves adopting a position that is lower to that person (i.e., acknowledging a need for that which the other has to offer). Similarly, giving lowerness to the other most usually involves adopting a position that is upper to that person and conveying a willingness to make available that which the other appears to need.

Donative or receptive relating can be of either a positive or negative kind. A state of relatedness may be given irrespective of whether it is what is wanted. A person may be given (or, more precisely, forced to have) closeness even though s/he may want distance, or vice versa. A person may be given (or, more precisely, forced to have) lowerness even though s/he may want upperness, or vice versa. This may be because the giver thinks that that is what is wanted, or because that is what the giver wants and the giver does not care that it is not what the recipient wants. This would be called *negative donative relating* for the giver and *negative receptive relating* for the recipient.

One-way and two-way interrelating

A person may relate predominantly by a donative or predominantly by a receptive form of relating. S/he may, for example, be keen to give closeness but reluctant to receive it. Either way, the relationship will be a close one and both participants will experience closeness, but the direction of the flow of closeness within the relationship will be predominantly one way. Alternatively, s/he may be keen to give lowerness (from a position of upperness) but reluctant to receive it; so in all upper to lower interactions s/he will coerce the other into adopting a receptive position. S/he will try predominantly to direct, lead, instruct, protect or care for the other and not allow the other to direct, lead, instruct, protect or care for her/him. In some forms of interrelating it would be appropriate for the direction to be predominantly one way (e.g., a parent would predominantly give both closeness and lowerness to a child). In other forms of interrelating (e.g., between marital partners), it would be more appropriate for each participant to relate sometimes in one direction and sometimes in the other.

Active and reactive relating

Active relating is making a direct move or gesture in a particular direction (e.g., attempting to become close). *Reactive* relating is responding to that move or gesture. The reactive relater may respond in one of five ways: (1) ignore the active move or gesture; (2) *passively* allow the action to take place, for example, not object to the person getting close; (3) positively acknowledge the move or gesture and respond *reciprocally*, for example, appreciate and welcome it and actively participate in the interaction; (4) resist or object to the move or gesture, for example, push the other away or back away; or (5) adopt a *retaliatory* response by taking offense at the move or gesture and getting back at, or turning the tables on, the initiator of the action. This set of responses can apply to interrelating of any duration. In a long-term relationship one person may persistently act in a particular way (such as always wanting to get closer) and the other may consistently respond in a particular way (such as always wanting to become more distant).

Active relating can be either donative or receptive. Being actively donative is called *proposing*, and being actively receptive is called *inviting*. An actively donative act would be to offer help; an actively receptive act would be at ask for help. Reactive relating can also be either donative or receptive. A reactively donative act would be to respond to an expression of distress by being consoling; a reactively receptive act would be to accept the help that is on offer.

It is often useful, and sometimes essential, to determine whether a person is actively relating, that is, behaving in a particular way because s/he is striving to attain a particular state of relatedness, or reactively relating, that is, responding to the relating behavior of another. Is a person moving toward another because that is what s/he positively wants to do, or because the other is showing signs of moving away? If the active relater stops, the reactive relater may stop reacting, so the reactive relater's action is determined by the action of the active relater. The active relater may decide to stop because the reactive relater objects, so the active relater still wants to act in a particular way, but decides to give way to the reactive relater's objection. In this case, the reactive relater is controlling the nature of the interaction. The reactive relater's reaction may continue long after the active relater has stopped. The reactive relater may continue to respond over a period of minutes, hours, weeks, months or years to a momentary action of the active relater. In such a case, the reactive relater's behavior can be understood only in terms of the active relater's original act.

When a person makes an active gesture toward another, s/he is in effect offering the other a particular state of relatedness. Because states of relatedness are placed at opposite ends of axes, offering one state of relatedness has the effect of taking away from or denying the person the opposite state of relatedness; when someone is offering closeness, s/he is at the same time denying distance. If distance is what the other wants, then the offer of close-ness may represent a threat, which may be why the other responds reactively.

People respond to any threat to an existing store of a particular state of relatedness first by experiencing anxiety, second by attempting to protect that which they have, third by developing an increased desire for what they want and fourth by intensifying their striving for what they want. These appear to be automatic, protective responses. They may occur even though the threat is not great and their store has not been seriously depleted. Responding to the threatened loss of at least a degree of a particular state of relatedness is a common stimulus to relating behavior, and threatening to deprive a person of a particular state of relatedness is a common way of provoking her/him into action. On the horizontal axis, threatening to get too close can provoke someone into withdrawing, and threatening to leave can provoke someone into wanting to get closer. On the vertical axis, challenging a person's author-ity (what Price [1988] would call an up-hierarchy catathetic signal) can pro-voke someone into reasserting her/his position and attempting to push the challenger down (with a down-hierarchy catathetic signal), and threatening to withdraw help or assistance can provoke someone into behaving more helplessly.

Negotiated and forced interrelating

Interrelating is most successful when it takes place between willing partici-pants. This is most likely to occur when the participants are versatile. Then, like two good dancers, they can switch positions within the octagon as and when they need to, and each can switch in tune, or in time, with the other in order to permit the interaction to continue. Over the course of a period of interrelating, both can move back and forth along the horizontal axis, some-times being close, sometimes being distant; and both can change places within the vertical axis, so that sometimes one is upper and sometimes the other is.

Interrelating is less successful when one or the other participant tries to force the other into a form of relating that s/he does not want or is not capable of. This is most likely to occur when one or the other participant lacks versatility, because s/he is incompetent in one or more forms of relating. A person who is frightened of, or has a limited capacity for, closeness has no option but to try to keep the other at a distance at all times. A person who is frightened of, or has limited capacity for, distance has no option but to try to keep the other close at all times. If the other is relatively versatile, s/he can indulge the more rigid relater over quite long periods, but the time will come when s/he will begin to yearn for the form of relating that she has been denied for so long.

Reasonably successful interrelating can take place between two less than perfect relaters, sometimes for quite long periods, provided that they are adequately *matched*. Two every clinging people, or two very remote people, can remain reasonably compatible, just as a person who needs to dominate and a person who needs to be dominated can. Such relaters have to stay within a fairly rigid and unchanging relationship, and in it, they are compelled to play out the same interactions over and over, but this can be better than having no relationship at all. The matching may not be as complete as it may seem, and one relater may be making concessions to the other to keep the relationship going. Rigid relationships of this kind run into difficulties when one participant begins to become more capable of the opposite form of relating. If the other participant remains the same, s/he will attempt to suppress the first participant's new style of relating.

The interrelating encounter

The set of actions that *initiate* a process of interrelating is called the *interrelating encounter*. A person may enter into such an encounter in an *egocentric* manner, with little regard for the needs of the other, and simply grab, unilaterally, as much of a particular state of relatedness as s/he can. The egocentric relater will force her/his attention upon someone even though the person does not want it, or walk away from someone even though she knows the person wants her/him to stay. At the other extreme, a person may enter into the encounter in an *altruistic* manner, with little regard for her/his own relating needs, and simply be concerned, again unilaterally, with providing that which s/he believes the other needs. The altruistic relater will visit a lonely person even though s/he does not feel like it, or refrain from disturbing someone who wants to be left alone, even though s/he wants to spend time with the other. Between these two extremes falls the entire range of forms of interrelating in which each participant derives some degree of benefit from the interaction, though the benefits may not necessarily be evenly divided.

The most friendly and cooperative form of initiation is when, by one means or another, the potential participants make it clear what they (1) need, (2) have to offer and (3) are prepared to give. The *opening gesture* may take the form of an *offer* or *proposal* that is offering or proposing to relate to the other in a particular way ("Can I show you how to do it?") or an *invitation* that is inviting the other to relate in a particular way ("Will you show me how to do it?"). The offer, or proposal, is a more *active* gesture and the invitation is a more *passive* one (like the flower inviting the bee). There then follows, usually very quickly and at an automatic level, something equivalent to a *negotiating* or *bargaining* process in which each (mainly at the inner brain level) decides whether what s/he is likely to gain from the interaction is an adequate return on what s/he is in a position, or willing, to give. If each decides that there will be a reasonable return on her/his investment in the exchange of actions, then (again, mainly at an inner brain level) a "deal is struck" and the interrelating begins.

Inner-outer brain conflict in the interrelating encounter

Because interrelating is happening continuously, in most instances, neither the negotiating/bargaining process nor the striking of the deal can be a consciously thought-out act. It is simply something that takes place, quickly and automatically, usually between the inner brains of the two participants. Since the inner and the outer brains operate independently, they might be making their own, separate decisions about what to say or do, but the outer brain is sometimes aware of the inner brain's intention and may choose to override it. The inner brain is direct and naive, but the outer brain is shrewd and devious. What the inner brain may want to say or do might be modified by the outer brain to increase the individual's chance of achieving her/his objective. The inner brain might want to say, "Can we have sex?" but the outer brain might modify this to, "Would you like to come up for coffee?" Something of this kind was depicted in a brief sequence in the film *Annie Hall*. As Annie Hall (played by Diane Keaton) and Alvie Singer (played by Woody Allen), on their first encounter, were politely exchanging remarks, their more basic thoughts were being printed on the screen as subtitles.

Sometimes what is proposed by the initiator does not appeal to the other, and yet, for some reason, the other is prepared to go along with it. A child may invite its mother to play, but its mother may be feeling tired. A wife may suggest to her husband that they go to a party, but the husband may prefer a quiet evening at home. Neither the mother nor the husband wants what is on offer, but they may agree because they can see how much the other wants what is being proposed and they are prepared to make the sacrifice. The decision is perhaps more an outer brain than an inner brain one, because the outer brain is more inclined to take a longer-term view ("If I play with the child now, I might get some peace later," or "If I don't go to the party, she'll think I'm an unsociable bore".). The inner brain, rather like the psychoanalytic id, is more selfish and would not see the point of indulging in closeness when distance is what is wanted. This conflict may reveal itself when the action proceeds. In the playing, and at the party, the mother's and the husband's lack of enthusiasm may be all too apparent, because their hearts are not really in what they are doing.

It is also true that the inner brain *cannot be fooled*, just as the penis does not lie. The inner brain can see *through* the wiles of the outer brain. The inner brain of the respondent may really know what the proposer is getting at when s/he says, "Would you like to come up for coffee?" and this may affect how s/he responds. Similarly, the inner brains of the child and the wife may have perceived the mother's and the husband's lack of enthusiasm, which may be reflected in their lack of pleasure in getting what they asked for. This kind of knowing is what people sometimes call intuitive.

Forced interrelating

Sometimes there is not a proposal at all. The initiator simply starts relating in a particular way. The other may object, but the circumstances may be such that s/he can do nothing about it. In such a situation the initiator is using her/his upperness to force (egocentrically or disrespectfully) a particular form of relating upon the other. A mother may insist that her daughter tells her all her secrets. A husband may demand that his wife always have a meal ready for him when he gets home. The interaction proceeds, but resentment builds up in the recipient and may eventually get expressed.

Extended interrelating

The term *extended interrelating* is used to describe any sequence of interrelating extending over a given time span. The unit of interrelating is the *interaction*, during which each of two people has related to the other and been related to by the other at least once. An *episode* of interrelating is when a sequence of interactions is strung together as part of a definable event, as for instance when a couple are having a row. Beyond this, one might be thinking in terms of an entire *relationship*.

A period of interrelating can comprise one particular pattern of interrelating extending consistently over time, like two people, living together in the same house, but scarcely speaking to each other (both being distant), or a tennis player and her/his coach working together (one being lower and the other being upper); one particular pattern of interrelating can predominate, but there can be occasional variations within it, like two people who normally get on well together, hitting a bad patch when they are both trying to avoid each other (closeness interspersed with distance); or there can be no particular pattern, like two versatile people who frequently vary the way they interrelate, sometimes being close, sometimes being distant, sometimes one being upper, sometimes the other being upper.

As a general rule, positive relating in one participant evokes a positive response in the other, and negative relating in one evokes a negative response in the other. A person who acts in a friendly way is likely to induce the other to relate back in a friendly way, but a person who relates in a hostile way is likely to induce a hostile response in the other. Gibb (1961) observed how a *defensive communication* can evoke a *defensive response*, which in turn can evoke a further defensive communication, leading to a spiral of interactions of increasing destructiveness. Gibb called the opposite of a defensive communication a *supportive communication* and proposed that a supportive response can dispel the anxiety of a defensive communicator and de-escalate the destructive spiral. Replacing defensive with negative and supportive with positive, it is probable that, over time, a positive relater will dispel the negativity of a negative relater. Children become competent (positive) relaters through exposure to other competent relaters. Clients in psychotherapy become competent relaters through exposure to the competent relating of the therapist.

Set patterns of interrelating

Both within society and within relationships, people slip into set and conventional patterns of interrelating. These are like dance steps that, once learned, get passed down to the inner brain, to be drawn upon automatically when required. There are conventional interaction patterns when people stop and talk in the street, visit friends, go to parties, or buy articles in shops. These interaction patterns are usually understood in advance to be of limited duration, and there are conventional ways of starting and stopping them. As with other learned inner brain sequences (e.g., the learned sequence of actions of the gymnast), they greatly facilitate interrelating behavior by avoiding the necessity for thinking out each stage of the interrelating sequence. In a sense, they are like instincts; like instincts, they work well as long as there is no deviation from the usual set of circumstances. The interrelating will continue beyond such an exchange only if the participants wish to continue to indulge in their attained, respective states of relatedness, such as two people wishing to continue to indulge in their attained closeness by converting a brief exchange of greetings into a long conversation.

Often, when two people meet, the conversation follows a predictable sequence, in fact the same sequence that it always follows. Certain pairs of people have almost the same conversation every time they meet, adopting the same stances, using the same phrases, covering the same topics and expressing the same opinions. Long-term friends, or people who live together, have set sequences of behavior and conversation that get repeated over meals or when they are out walking together. Such behavior and conversations serve the function of maintaining a status quo within the relationship, whether it be a good one or a bad one, and of providing the opportunity to express shared long-standing anxieties, disappointments, grievances or hatreds, or of providing mutual reassurance or consolation. Whenever certain couples have a row, it follows the same sequence as in all previous rows. They make the same accusations and counter-accusations, recall the same resentments about present and past behavior, and offer the same excuses and defenses. They seem to follow a well-written script. Each accusation by one partner prompts the same counter-accusation by the other. These rows are not so pointless as they may seem, for they allow chronic frustrations to be ventilated. What they do not do is allow interpersonal conflicts to be resolved. Even in psychotherapy sessions, it is all too easy for therapists and clients to slip into the same kinds of repetitive interaction, so that the therapy makes no progress.

Set patterns of interrelating occur within the more complex structure of families. Gorell Barnes and Cooklin (1994) wrote of an *interactional sequence* in which it is possible to predict more or less accurately which family members would say what, roughly in what order, and in what sort of tone each would speak. Such a sequence, they claimed, is likely to be repeated with a similar shape and similar attitudes taken by the various members, despite the fact that the subject of conflict may differ markedly. They referred to family members as the players in a drama, reacting to each other in a self-regulatory fashion.

Interrelating within the horizontal axis

Extremely distant people do not become involved in relationships at all, but such people are rare. Almost everyone enters into relationships of some kind. A relationship of any kind is bound to create a degree of closeness for the participants, but within any relationship there need to be opportunities for distance.

Matching for closeness and distance

People who find closeness disturbing lead solitary existences and contact people only out of absolute necessity. Quite often they relate to objects, machines, computers, landscapes, plants and animals. They may derive vicarious closeness from cine films, video and audiotapes, television, radio, books, music and works of art. They work at solitary occupations, live in solitary places and indulge in solitary pursuits, like walking and sailing alone. They create barriers around themselves, like high walls, hedges and fences. They keep themselves well covered. They say little and reveal little about themselves. Solitary people like other solitary people, and they do solitary things together. It is best when solitary people marry other solitary people, so that, within their marriages, they are able to remain distant from each other, coming together occasionally, having limited conversations and pursuing their own individual interests.

People who find distance disturbing organize their lives so that they are rarely alone. They seek occupations in which they can always be working and talking with other people. They choose to live in close-knit communities where there are plenty of people to talk to. They are always visiting and telephoning their friends. People are always welcome in their homes. They like social gatherings and go on holidays to places where they know there will be lots of other people. They have no qualms about revealing personal facts about themselves, and they ask other people personal questions about themselves. They mix with, make friends with and marry other closeness-seeking people.

When two people interrelate within the horizontal axis, they get on best when they both need the same amounts of the same state of relatedness, that is, when they both need a lot of closeness or they both need a lot of distance.

However, people's tolerance of closeness or distance varies both absolutely and from time to time over long or short periods. In absolute terms, there are couples who so love closeness that they cannot get enough of it, and there are couples who find closeness so disturbing that either they avoid it altogether or they permit themselves only limited amounts of it or limited periods of it. In terms of variation over time, most couples appear to need both periods of closeness and periods of distance. Because closeness and distance are mutually exclusive, a period of closeness is, for both partners at the same time, a period of distance deprivation, and a period of distance is a period of closeness deprivation, again for both partners at the same time. After a lengthy period of closeness, the condition of *closeness fatigue* begins to be experienced (Chapter 1), and each person yearns for distance. After a lengthy period of distance, the condition of *distance fatigue* begins to be experienced, and they yearn for closeness.

Versatile people derive pleasure from both closeness and distance; they enjoy intimate exchanges with each other but they also enjoy spending periods entirely on their own. The ideal arrangement is for two versatile people to co-exist with each other. Such people may be so synchronized that, quite naturally, they enter together into periods of closeness, in which, at approximately the same time, they experience closeness fatigue, and from which, by some common understanding, mediated at an inner brain level, they move into periods of separation. Feldman (1979) described a sequence in which marital partners, supposedly at an inner brain level, use conflicts as a means of terminating periods of intimacy. The conflicts drive them into periods of separation, in which they begin to experience distance fatigue and yearn for further intimacy. They contrive a means of making up, and the cycle repeats itself.

In the normal course of daily life, people who live together pass through naturally occurring periods of closeness and distance that help to maintain the relationship on an even keel. They part in the mornings to go to their respective places of work and reunite in the evenings. They may have different social and recreational pursuits that, at different times during the week, take them away from each other. They have holidays together, when they live through more prolonged periods of closeness than usual, which sometimes imposes a strain upon the relationship. Sometimes the nature of the employment of one or both partners gives rise to prolonged periods of absence, which deprive them of adequate amounts of closeness. Sometimes unemployment or retirement brings them together for intolerable periods of closeness, and periods of separation need to be introduced to create more distance.

Disturbances of the closeness-distance balance

Versatile couples are not always synchronized in their closeness-distance needs. Sometimes one partner needs closeness when the other needs distance. It is essential in such situations for each to make her/his needs known to the other, for inevitably, one is going to be disappointed. Ideally, one will agree to make the sacrifice and the other will acknowledge that a sacrifice has been made. In a relationship between two positively close partners, who are attentive to each other's needs, over time, such sacrifices will even out.

Couples are not always evenly matched in their closeness-distance needs, or sometimes circumstances change, resulting in the closeness or distance needs of one becoming greater or less than before. When there are major disparities between the closeness-distance needs of the partners, long periods arise when at least one partner is not getting what s/he wants. This leads to tensions.

The most destructive interaction on the horizontal axis is the *vicious circle*. This develops when one partner needs more closeness and the other needs more distance. The more the one presses for closeness, the more the other flees into distance; and the more the other flees into distance; the more the first presses for closeness. The interaction may assume a number of guises depending upon the form of close or distant behavior adopted. If the close person is clinging, the distant one will be rejecting. If the close person tries to talk a lot, the distant one will go silent. If the close person is prying, the distant one will be secretive. If the close person is attention seeking, the distant one will be ignoring. A woman whose husband tried to escape from her by watching television said, "If I were to jump out of the window, he would wait for the commercial break before coming to see if I was all right".

The closeness-distance balance may be upset by the presence of others. If the couple have a child or children, one partner may become, or appear to be, so preoccupied with the child or children as to make the other feel ignored or rejected. One partner may feel that s/he has loyalties to a parent, sibling or friend who is in difficulties or is ill. One partner may become, or appear to be, pleasurably involved with work colleagues or students, which causes the other to become jealous. One partner may become excessively absorbed in her/his work or a hobby. There is a Liverpool joke about a wife who said to her husband, "I think you love Liverpool (Football Club) more than you love me". He replied, "I love Everton (a rival Liverpool football club) more than I love you".

Partners caught up in a vicious circle sometimes seek solace in a relationship with a third person. The third person is appealing because there is no tension. The distant partner finds the third person appealing because s/he is not demanding. The close partner finds the third person appealing because s/he is responsive. The situation may become further complicated by the rejected or jealous partner retaliating by doing the same thing. Each draws the third person into the conflict to serve a function. The third person simply becomes someone for the two partners to fight over.

Cohesion

Olson, Sprenkle and Russell (1979) described relationships within the horizontal axis in terms of what they called *cohesion*. Because they were concerned with describing a relationship, rather than the interrelating of two people, they tended to assume that both partners were behaving in the same way. If cohesion was very high they called the relationship *enmeshed*; if it was fairly high they called it *connected*; if it was fairly low they called it *separated*; and if it was very low they called it *disengaged*. In general terms, they considered a relationship to be dysfunctional if it was enmeshed or disengaged. By enmeshed they meant that the participants were excessively caught up in each other's life: They spent much time together, did everything together, made joint decisions, had only shared friends, and had minimal private space. By disengaged they meant that the participants led separate existences: They spent little time together, went their separate ways, made independent decisions, had mostly individual friends and kept to themselves. While the concept of cohesion is a useful one, it does not take us very far in understanding what exactly is going on between the relating participants. It fails to take account of the relating needs of the respective participants. It falls into the trap of assuming that extreme always equals bad (see discussion on classical interpersonal theory in Chapter 1). An extreme relationship can be either good or bad.

Fusion versus intimacy

When two people are in a close relationship, they can be either *fused* or *intimate*. The difference is that when they are fused their two egos (selves) have become so merged that they function almost as though they were one. Bowen (1978) called this an *undifferentiated ego mass*. When they are intimate, however close they get, their egos remain separate. In Chapter 3 it was explained that one cannot become confidently close without the assurance that one has a state of secure distance to return to. Such secure distance assumes the form of what Laing (1965) called ontological security (Chapter 3). Only two ontologically secure people can become intimate without progressing into fusion. In such a state "each has a source of strength from within and is capable of taking responsibility for her/his own person while, at the same time, being responsive to the other" (Laing et al., 1966).

In fusion it is difficult to discern where one person ends and the other begins. The ideas of the two people are almost interchangeable. One person is hardly aware of the separate existence of the other and cannot therefore perceive or be responsive to the other's needs. Fusion is not always contributed to equally by the two people. It is more common for one to be more ontologically secure than the other and for the less secure one to become ontologically dependent (Laing, 1965) or parasitic upon the other and to feel *engulfed* by the other (Laing, 1965). If the other has delusional ideas, the ontologically dependent one may have the same delusional ideas as well, a condition known as *folie à deux* (Rioux, 1963).

In intimacy, while two people may become extremely closely involved with each other, each continues to remain aware of her/his own separate identity and of the separate identity of the other. Intimate people know each other very well and are often accurately aware of what the other is thinking. This is because they are open with each other. It should not be confused with what some family therapists call *mind reading*, in which one partner claims, often quite incorrectly, to know what the other is thinking and is eager to speak on behalf of the other. More often than not this is a bid to take over the mind of the other and to try to impose an identity upon the other. Having one's mind read in this way can be an unpleasant experience, and the more ontologically insecure person will find it hard to know whether the thoughts are her/his own or the other person's.

An important feature of true intimacy is *respectfulness*. Each partner respects the other's right to be a separate individual, with separate needs, opinions and objectives. Because each partner is ontologically secure, s/he is not disturbed or threatened by the other's otherness. Neither feels that s/he owns the other, has a right to know everything about the other or has a need to enter into the private inner world of the other. Each, on the other hand, feels both sympathy and empathy for the other and likes to be kind to the other and to see the other succeed and be happy.

Intimate people do not always need to be in each other's company. They do not necessarily share the same friends or like the same things, and they are not overconcerned by the other's involvement with other people. They may lead their own separate existences, pursue their own pleasures and spend quite long periods apart. They enjoy being together and doing things together, and sometimes one is prepared to indulge the other in some activity that s/he knows the other enjoys.

The term *interdependence* is often used to describe the interrelating of intimates. It means that they depend upon each other. Sometimes one is the upper partner and sometimes the other is. Sometimes one leads, helps, advises, encourages, consoles, comforts, praises, protects and cares for and sometimes the other does. However, it may be that the most intense form of intimacy occurs when neither is upper nor lower and they interrelate, person to person, on equal terms. In fact it has been suggested (Birtchnell, 1986) that partners sometimes slip into a one up, one down position as a way of reducing the intensity of the intimacy.

Conflictual closeness

An essential feature of closeness is *involvement*, but involvement need not be harmonious. When two people are closely involved with each other they get in each other's way and inevitably there are conflicts of interest. Conflicts are unavoidable in close relationships, but such conflicts are often beneficial to the participants (Scanzoni, 1979). Interestingly, those in the most satisfied relationships report the greatest amount of conflict (Argyle and Furham, 1983). Another feature of closeness is *openness*, and openness involves being open about one's grievances. It is difficult to have a row with someone without becoming closely involved with her/him. George and Martha in Edward Albee's play *Who's Afraid of Virginia Woolf?* derived obvious satisfaction from episodes of intense and vicious argument. Rows frequently lead to actual physical fighting, and it is not unusual for intimates to switch from fighting to making love. For these people, any response is better than no response, and even hatred may be better than indifference. Love and hate are sometimes disconcertingly interchangeable, and there are relationships in which the partners appear to alternate between one state and the other. People sometimes pick quarrels with their partners in order to get a response from them, and for some couples, fighting seems to be a substitute for making love.

Some women choose to stay close to men who frequently abuse them and, less commonly, some men choose to stay close to some women who frequently abuse them. Perhaps they believe they deserve the abuse, or perhaps they are prepared to tolerate the abuse in order to get the closeness, or perhaps the only closeness they have ever known is that which was linked with abuse. In sadomasochistic relationships agreed levels of hurting and being hurt form an integral part of the closeness, and Stoller (1979) expressed the extreme view that there is a sadistic element to all sexual excitement.

Distant interrelating

Distant interrelating may seem a contradiction in terms, but many relationships are formed by people who remain relatively distant from each other. These include relationships between work colleagues, neighbors and friends, but they also include relationships between committed cohabitees and marital partners. Distant relationships often last longer than close relationships because the participants do not get close enough to cause each other difficulties. The participants remain safely within their respective personal spaces and communicate at a fairly limited level. Close relationships sometimes progress to distant relationships as the participants get older. This may be a consequence of repeated conflicts, the participants deciding that a distant relationship that works is better than a close one that does not work. The term *distant closeness* may be applied to some of these relationships, implying that a degree of closeness is maintained from the safety of distance.

Interrelating within the vertical axis

The vertical axis differs from the horizontal axis in that, for most successful interactions to occur, one person has to operate at one end of the axis (upper) and the other has to operate at the other (lower). Ideally, over time, relaters should have opportunities for being both upper and lower. Situations do arise when two predominantly upper or two predominantly lower people try to interrelate. In such situations each person tries to induce the other to adopt the reciprocal position. The result is that neither gets what s/he wants. In situations including two upper people, each tries to run the show, and the two end up at loggerheads. One way two upper people can work together is to provide a united upper front in relation to one or more people who are relatively lower, such as for instance, when two parents relate in an upper way toward their children. In situations including two lower people, each is wanting the other to take the lead or provide care or advice, and they end up being lost, uncared for and directionless. Again, two lower people can work together if they provide a united lower front in relation to one or more people who are relatively upper, such as when a couple together seek help or advice from someone whom they both acknowledge as upper to them.

Rigidity versus versatility

Rigid relationships on the vertical axis, in which each of two people adopts the same mode of relating toward the other, in more or less every situation, function well under certain restricted circumstances. A parent's relationship toward a young child or an employer's relationship toward an employee are examples of this. It is a characteristic of rigid relationships that the longer they exist the more entrenched the participants become in them and the more difficult it is to alter them. There comes a time when it is inappropriate for the parent to remain exclusively upper in relation to the child, which might also apply to the employer and the employee. The child needs to practice showing the parent how to do things, or to be consoling and reassuring toward the parent. Sometimes, it is useful for the employee to be able to behave in these ways toward the employer.

In a relationship in which one person repeatedly and consistently adopts an upper position in relation to another, there is a danger of the upper person becoming more and more used to being upper and the lower person becoming more and more used to being lower. When the upper person elects always to be the helper and the lower person elects always to be the one who is helped, the upper person becomes ever more capable and the lower person becomes ever more incapable. The upper person acquires an inflated opinion of how capable s/he is and the lower person acquires an inflated opinion of how incapable s/he is. Furthermore, the upper person becomes forever deprived of the (pleasurable) experience of being lower and the lower person becomes forever deprived of the (pleasurable) experience of being upper. The upper person may tire of always being upper and the lower person may tire of always being lower, but because the relationship is so rigidly set this way neither is capable of making the change.

Close upper to lower/lower to upper relating

Because there are so many different ways of being helpful, two people, particularly when they are in a close, long-term relationship, may indulge in the practice of exchanging one form of help for another. Such exchanges are called *reciprocal*. They happen frequently, spontaneously and informally, and the partners do not normally tot up points to determine who owes whom a favor. Each partner tries to be helpful to the other whenever it seems appropriate, and it is assumed that, over time, the favors will balance out. In such exchanges it is not possible, in general terms, to call one partner the upper one and the other the lower one. This is an example of mutually advantageous interdependence. Obviously if a marked imbalance does become apparent to one partner, s/he will start to feel put-upon and will begin to complain. If the other does not respond to this, the relationship will be put under serious strain.

At a more distant (professional) level, an upper person helps another in exchange for money, as when an expert charges a fee for giving advice. There are many kinds of professional helpers (psychotherapists being one) who make a living out of helping people, though receiving a financial reward is not the only incentive for doing it; the work is rewarding in itself. The act of being upper, just like an act of any of the other main positions, is gratifying in itself.

Lower people, particularly when in psychotherapy, come to learn that any sign of helplessness, hopelessness or desperation evokes a sympathetic response in those who care for them. It is tempting therefore to feign or exaggerate such signs. Ironically, therapists frequently find such behavior gratifying. As a result, at some level, a deal gets struck such that the client continues to behave needfully and the therapist encourages it because s/he finds such needfulness gratifying. In marital or other family situations, one person may come to realize that behaving in a helpless or hopeless way can be an effective means of maintaining the interest and concern of the other. They make remarks such as, "I am a poor old thing, aren't I? You are so good to me. I don't know what I would do without you". Those who get drawn into the reciprocal upper position justify their behavior by remarks such as, "I could never leave her/him. S/he can't do anything on her own. S/he would be lost without me".

The power of a lower close person to influence an upper close person rests upon three factors: the conscience of the upper person, the capacity of people to feel sorry for those who are in difficulties or distress and the satisfying experience of upperness that feeling sorry for and helping lower people generates. Weeping is a particularly effective means of evoking sympathy in an upper close person. Witnessing another person weeping hurts and sometimes causes the upper person to weep as well, out of a process of identification with the suffering other, which is why the upper person frequently pleads, "Please don't cry". Conscience is a mixture of what might be called *common decency*, a personal conviction that decent people do not leave other people to suffer and the social coercion that makes a person feel ashamed of not responding to the expressed needfulness of others. These feelings are reinforced by the internalized upper other (See Chapters 5 and 6). The lower person takes advantage of them. The good beggar, quite unashamedly, looks appealingly and helplessly into the face of the upper person, with an expression that the upper person finds hard to resist.

Distant upper to lower/lower to upper relating

Distant relating on the vertical axis is a common feature of the relating of animals, determining which animal dominates and which submits. It can assume a similar form in humans, but it usually involves a more subtle interaction. It can be of a positive or a negative kind. In positive distant upper-to-lower relating, the upper person imposes rules, restrictions and boundaries upon the lower person, who has little option but to accept them. Such relating occurs between judges and those they pass judgment upon; military officers and those under their command; the police and the public; managers and their staff; teachers and their pupils; referees and the participants in sporting events; and, at times when there is a need to impose discipline, parents and their children. Why do lower distant people allow upper distant people to exert control over them? Frequently, upper people can draw upon backup forces to enforce their control, but this is not the whole explanation. Most people willingly adopt the lower position because they know that ultimately this will be for their benefit or for the benefit of the organization to which they belong.

People understand that societies would disintegrate into chaos if limits were not set and order were not maintained. People obey the law and accept penalties because they know that others, who might otherwise do them harm, are also going to be kept within the limit of the law and restrained or punished if they transgress. People competing in sporting events prefer to have a neutral, objective person to impose the rules. Positive distant upper-to-lower relating works only because the lower people respect the upper people and regard their impositions as fair, reasonable and responsible. When lower people believe that the upper people are being unfair, unreasonable and irresponsible, they may revolt, defy them and even overthrow them.

Upper to lower relating in families

It is normal in families for the parents to be upper and the children to be lower. When parents are positively upper close, they are protective, caring, encouraging, consoling and praising; when they are positively upper distant they assume responsibility, provide controls, impose restrictions and maintain justice; when they are negatively upper close they are overprotective, overindulgent, possessive and smothering; and when they are negatively upper distant they are exploitative, punitive, intimidating, abusive and suppressive. Sometimes one parent adopts one form of upper behavior and another parent adopts another. Sometimes one parent, most usually the father, adopts a dictatorial attitude toward the entire family and the family live in fear of him. Family power differentials can be reversed, sometimes advantageously, as when parents are infirm or disabled or cannot speak or write the language, and sometimes disadvantageously, as when children become strong enough to tyrannize their parents or when parents behave helplessly toward their children, seeking comfort and consolation from them. Upper to lower interactions also occur between siblings, and responsible parents oversee these and ensure that they are not abused.

Comparison with other theories of interrelating

Systems theory

General systems theory was introduced by Bertalanffy (1950). A system is any organization of objects that interact one with another (e.g., the solar system). Certain rules of systems are the same, irrespective of what these objects may be. From the point of view of interrelating, these are two important characteristics of certain kinds of systems which are called *circularity* and *feedback*. Circularity is important because it represents a break from the traditional scientific principle of linearity, which is concerned with simple cause-and-effect relationships, for example, grief follows when somebody close dies. In circularity, one event follows another event, which in turn affects the original event. A husband returned home one morning and told his wife that he had spent the night with another woman. His wife flew into a rage and destroyed some of his valued possessions. He left because, as he put it, he could not tolerate living with such a jealous and aggressive woman. In feedback, the event that follows one event has a modifying effect upon the original event. For example, the wife's anger following the husband's infidelity modifies the husband's extramarital behaviour. In *positive feedback*, the husband resolves to have even more extramarital relationships. In *negative feedback*, he resolves to desist from further extramarital relationships.

At the outset it should be stressed that systems theory and relating theory differ in that the focus of study in systems theory is the *system*, namely, a group of people interacting together, and the focus of study in relating theory, even when one is examining interrelating, is the two individual relaters. In systemic thinking (Bateson, 1973; Jones, 1993) when two people relate to each other they do so in one of two ways, which are called *symmetry* and *complementarity*. In symmetry, the partners mirror each other's behaviour; symmetrical interaction is characterized by *equality*. In complementarity, the behaviour of one is the opposite of that of the other; complementary interaction is characterized by *difference*. An example is given of one partner occupying a one-up position and the other occupying a one-down position. In systems theory the partner in the one-up position is considered to *dictate the nature of the interaction*, through there seems to be no reason that the partner in the one-down position should not do this also. From the descriptions provided, it would appear that both forms of relating take place on what, in relating theory, would be called the vertical axis, though there seems to be no reasons that they should not also take place on the horizontal axis.

Watzlawick, Beavin and Jackson (1967) maintained that one partner does not impose a complementary relationship upon the other; rather there is an interlocking of dissimilar behaviors, such that each evokes the other. However, they also posit that there is a *metacomplementary* relationship in which one partner lets or forces the other to be in charge and suggest the possibility of what they would call *pseudosymmetry*, in which one lets or forces the other to be symmetrical.

It is argued that if either symmetry or complementarity persists, the relationship deteriorates by a process which is called *schismogenesis*. In symmetry, it is claimed, the deterioration is due to escalation, as when two people try to outboast each other, and in complementarity, it is claimed it is due to rigidity, as when one partner becomes progressively more assertive and the other becomes progressively more submissive. A third interaction pattern is proposed, which does not lead to schismogenesis. It is called *reciprocity*. It means that the complementarity sometimes goes one way and sometimes goes the other. Bateson (1973) considered that stability might be established by introducing small amounts of symmetry into a complementary relationship and vice versa. These are all concepts that could be accommodated within relating theory.

The similarities between systems theory and relating theory are obvious, but systems theory lacks certain essential concepts such as relating objectives, relating competencies and versatility. Because of this, it cannot adequately differentiate between positive relating and negative relating. Schismogenesis would not occur if either a symmetrical or a complementary relationship were maintained by mutual agreement. On the horizontal axis, symmetry would cause no problems because both relates would want the same thing and would both be able to have it. On the other hand, asymmetry would, because one wanted closeness while the other wanted distance. It is only on the vertical axis that symmetry would cause problems, when both wanted upperness or both wanted lowerness. Complementarity can apply only to the vertical axis, since the term makes no sense in terms of closeness and distance. Even on the vertical axis it would cause no problems if both participants agreed to it and were happy with it, even if the arrangement extended over a long period of time.

Interpersonal theory

Classical interpersonal theory dated from a paper by Freedman and colleagues (1951). Its relationship to the present theory has been discussed extensively in Birtchnell (1990, 1993/1996, 1994) and briefly in Chapter 1. It also is a biaxial theory and proposes a horizontal axis concerned with love versus hate and a vertical one concerned with dominate versus submit. Interpersonal theorists (e. g., Carson, 1969) do not use the terms *complementarity* and *reciprocity* in the same way that systems theorists do. By *complementarity* they mean that each form of relating evokes a reaction from the other that leads to a repetition and reinforcement of the original relating act. On the horizontal axis, such complementarity is called *correspondence* (love evokes love and hate evokes hate) and on the vertical axis it is called *reciprocity* (dominate evokes submit and submit evokes dominate). Unlike systems theories, interpersonal theorists (e.g., Leary, 1957) argue that a complementary interaction is mutually rewarding and enhances the security of the participants. Carson (1969) introduced the term *noncomplementary* to describe an interaction in which the response is complementary on one axis but not on the other and *anticomplementary* to describe one that is not complementary on either axis.

Interpersonal theory has been complicated by fitting segments into the spaces between the poles of the axes to create a circular arrangement. This was introduced by Freedman and colleagues (1951) and Leary (1957) and later modified by Wiggins (1979) and Kiesler (1983), mainly in order that the segments on opposite sides of the circle should be strictly bipolar. They did to ensure that it conformed to the statistical model called the circumplex (Guttman, 1954). It is questionable, however, whether forcing the segments into such a model is advantageous (Birtchnell, 1990). The idea was that Carson's rules of complementarity should apply not only to axes but also to individual segments on opposite sides of the circle. Kiesler (1983) introduced the further terms *isomorphic* and *semimorphic acomplementarity* to refer to whether the other responds from circle segments identical to or opposite to those of the initial relater.

In the light of the principles of interrelating outlined in this chapter, the rules of complementarity would appear to be simplistic, and Orford (1986) had observed that many of them are not supported by the evidence. They do not take into account the distinction between what may be termed adaptive and maladaptive forms of relating, and Wiggin's (1979) taxonomy does not even allow for such a distinction. On the horizontal axis, love would evoke love only if that is what the other wanted and hate would not inevitably evoke hate. On the vertical axis dominate would evoke submit only if the recipient were intimidated; otherwise it would evoke protestation or defiance. Submit would evoke dominance only if the recipient felt inclined to dominate.

The present theory differs from both systems theory and interpersonal theory in that it is based upon the assumption that people relate in order to attain certain interpersonal objectives. To do this they acquire competencies and develop strategies. It is also assumed that, at a neural level, there are the equivalent of hungers and feedback loops that control and monitor relating behaviour. In contrast, interpersonal theory posits that people develop certain relating styles in order to avoid or minimize anxiety (Leary, 1957).

Exchange theory

Exchange theory, first described by Thibaut and Kelley (1959) and later reviewed by Burns (1973) and Hinde (1997), is directed toward the formulation of laws of general validity in social psychology. It began with the assumption that such laws could best be established by using volunteers to create miniature situations in laboratory experiments. These experiments took as their unit of study the *interdependence* between persons and were concerned with judging the likely outcome of dyadic interactions. Such experiments were conducted around a two-by-two matrix in which each participant had a choice between two alternatives. (The term *interdependence* as used here is not the same as the relating theory concept of interdependence between intimates). A numerical value was used to express the *reward* or *cost* to each person of a particular course of action. The term *profit* was used to refer to the reward minus the cost. As the experiments progressed, each person was required to make a series of conscious (i.e., outer brain) decisions and modifications, which depended upon the choices made by the other. Difficulties arose in creating laboratory situations that adequately represented real-life situations and in making generalizations from the laboratory to the real world.

The relevance of exchange theory of relating theory depends upon what might be meant by reward and a cost. In terms of relating theory, a reward could be attaining a desired state of relatedness and cost could be losing or being denied one. Sometimes a reward is described as a pleasant stimulus, or reinforcement, and a cost as an unpleasant stimulus, or punishment. This places rewards and costs more in line with the emotional responses—of, say, elation and depression—to attaining and losing a state of relatedness (Chapter 1). Some authors (e.g., Milardo and Murstein, 1979) have tried to apply exchange theory to couple relationships.

In its more general form, exchange theory states that social interaction is an exchange of mutually rewarding activities in which the receipt of a needed valuable (a good or service) is contingent upon the supply of a favor in return. Homans (1974) used the term *distributive justice* to mean that an individual expects to receive rewards in relation to her/his costs and is angry if s/he does not. It would seem that s/he was just likely to be depressed. In order to induce another to rewards her/him, a person has to provide rewards to the other. Whether an interaction, once initiated, turns out to be rewarding depends upon whether the initiator has chosen a person capable of providing rewards and whether the actor has provided the person with the incentives to deliver them. The security of the relationship increases as each participant recognizes that the other needs her/him as much as s/he needs the other. (This is interdependence in the relational sense.) Exchange involves everything that lies between (the more positive acts of) unconditional commitment, altruism and a denial of self-interest at the other (Chadwick-Jones, 1976).

Exchange theory, with its emphasis on resources, investment, rewards, pay-offs, costs and profits, would appear to have grown out of economics, though Hinde (1997) pointed to an obvious link with classical learning theory and operant theory. It is not easily applied to interactions of a more personal nature. Also, this kind of hard-bargaining approach to relating is more appropriate to the distant side of the interpersonal octagon. Relating on the close side is less competitive and takes account of the feelings of the other. A close relater enjoys seeing the other succeed and is more inclined to make sacrifices in order to please the other.

The emphasis of exchange theory on the framing and testing of hypotheses is admirable, but one of its limitations is that it does not concern itself with the objectives of relating. It is not at all clear whether exchange choice are made at an outer brain (conscious) or an inner brain (unconscious) level, and such an issue is not usually considered. Frude (1991), as described in Chapter 2, seems to believe they are made at an unconscious level. Relating theory maintains that interrelating is predominantly an inner brain activity and that interrelating decisions are largely not made by the slower, conscious, outer brain, as commonly appears to be implicit in exchange theory. However, some of the reasoning that lies behind exchange theory decisions and relating theory decisions may be similar. It is possible that if social psychologists and relating theorists were to combine forces, a more rigorous study of personal relationships would emerge.

Summary

Whereas a relationship is an entity with particular characteristics, interrelating is a process, by which two or more people relate to and are related to by each other. In interrelating, each participant strives to attain or maintain a particular state of relatedness, which may be negotiated or forced. If it is negotiated, a "deal is struck" when the relating objectives of the respective participants are compatible and when each is able to meet her/his relating needs. If it is forced, one participant imposes her/his own style of relating on the other. On the horizontal axis, it is essential that the participants should obtain for themselves and allow each other adequate amounts of closeness and distance, though two closeness seekers or two distance seekers can sometimes coexist. A vicious circle arises when a predominantly close relater is in a relationship with a predominantly distant one. Relating on the vertical axis works best when each participant has opportunities to be both upper and lower. Rigidly upper to lower relationships result in the upper partner becoming progressively more upper and the lower partner becoming progressively more lower. Links can be made between relating theory and systems theory, classical interpersonal theory and exchange theory.

Chapter 8

Interrelating in psychotherapy

This chapter will consider interrelating between clients and others, therapists and clients and, in certain forms of psychotherapy, clients and clients. The therapist listens to clients' account of the interrelating between themselves and others and tries to help them understand what is happening. S/he points to ways by which clients might modify their relating behaviour as a means of improving the quality of their interrelating experiences. Sometimes the therapist proposes that they invite one or more others into therapy. The interrelating now takes place in the presence of the therapist. The therapist is able to observe it, make remarks that might help the participants understand what is happening between them and propose strategies that each might adopt for improving the quality of the relationship.

Groups or communities of clients may be brought together in a therapeutic setting. In this, clients are likely to reproduce with members of the group or community the interrelating patterns that occur within their normal lives. The therapist observes the interactions that take place, attempts to define what is happening and orchestrates alternative forms of interrelating that lead to more satisfactory outcomes. Interrelating difficulties may be as much to do with the relating deficiencies of those with whom the client interrelates as with the client's own relating deficiencies. Therefore, the therapy is as much to do with helping clients cope with the deficient relating of others as with improving their own relating abilities.

An alternative to working with couples, families, groups or communities is devising ways of reproducing the interactions between clients and others in some representational form (art, make-believe, sculpting, role play or drama). Apart from avoiding the complications of enlisting the cooperation of others into therapy, this has the advantage of enabling clients to say and do things to these other people that they may not find possible to do in their presence. This sometimes serves as a stepping stone, by preparing clients for actually saying and doing these things to the others in their real lives.

Interrelating characteristics of different styles of therapy

Whatever form of therapy is adopted, the therapist inevitably interrelates with the client or clients, but the degree and style of this interrelating varies according to the form of therapy adopted. It is most clear-cut in individual therapy, in which there is simply the therapist and the client, who inevitably enter into some form of interrelating with each other. Sometimes an additional person is brought into what is essentially an individual therapy situation. In these circumstances, it has to be made clear that whoever is brought in is there as a fellow client, and not as a relative or a supporter of the client.

In therapy involving the client with one or more other person or persons or in therapy involving a couple, members of a family, a group or a community, the main thrust of the interrelating takes place among a variable number of people. The kinds of interrelating that take place in situations such as this may not normally take place between these people and may only be doing so in response to the therapist's suggestions, prompts and interventions.

Once there is more than one client, the therapist has less control over what is happening. In large families, therapeutic groups and therapeutic communities, some of the interrelating is constructive (positive) and some is destructive (negative). The therapist encourages and supports the constructive interactions and discourages and intervenes in the destructive ones. Groups, communities and families contain within them the potential for self-help and self-healing, and the good therapist works with the group to enable this self-help and self-healing to happen.

With therapy in a group or therapeutic community, all of the group or community members are clients; therefore they interrelate with both themselves and the therapist or the therapists. In group therapy, there is usually one group leader, but there may be two or more. In a therapeutic community, the clients live together and interrelate as part of their daily living program. There are usually several therapists. Because they are around for long periods of time, they become part of the community and take part in the normal, everyday interrelating processes within it. There are regular, more formal and more artificial group sessions in which interrelating occurs and is examined. There are unscheduled groups that are called by the therapists to deal with interpersonal crises. The therapists have their own groups in which they interrelate with each other.

Gestalt therapy is a kind of hybrid of individual therapy and group therapy. Within the setting of the group, the therapist works with one group member at a time, while the other group members watch. The presence of the other group members powerfully influences the interrelating that takes place between the therapist and the group member, and in turn, this interrelating between the therapist and the group member powerfully influences the other group members. A prominent feature of this process is the extent to which the group members identify with the member being worked with. The accounts that they hear of the member's interrelating outside the group resonate with their own interrelating experiences.

In therapy involving the representation of a relevant other person or other people, the main thrust of the interrelating takes place between the client and that representation. To all intents and purposes, the representation *is* the other person; and by way of the representation, the client talks to the other person and experiences feelings about the other person. Additionally, the client may be encouraged to play the part of the represented person and speak her/his lines.

Individual therapy

In psychoanalytic psychotherapy the therapist tries to conceal from the client any relating needs that s/he may have and to consider only the needs of the client. This does not mean that no interrelating takes place. However, such interrelating as does take place is predominantly one way. On the horizontal axis, the therapist endeavors to give the client such closeness or distance as may be appropriate but is not inclined to allow the client to give any closeness or distance back. The therapist makes no self-revelations but encourages the client to freely make self-revelations to her/him. The therapist shows great interest in the client and may even reveal sympathy toward the client, but does not expect the client to show interest in or reveal sympathy toward her/him. Therapist and client meet frequently and over a long period of time; inevitably, the client becomes familiar with the therapist's ways and mannerisms, and most probably, despite the therapist's secrecy about her/himself, becomes quite fond of the therapist and would be concerned if s/he heard that the therapist was unwell. Equally, despite her/his strictly professional attitude toward the client, the therapist, if only because of all s/he knows about the client, is likely to become quite fond of the client.

The psychoanalytic therapist would maintain that, because s/he has revealed so little of her/himself to the client, any feelings that the client might experience toward her/him were strictly transferential, that is, they really belong to someone else in the client's life and have simply been transferred onto the therapist. While undoubtedly this does occur, it seems unlikely that this is the complete explanation for these feelings. The psychoanalytic therapist would also maintain that the therapist should not reveal to the client any emotional response that s/he may experience to what the client says. This may be one reason why s/he sits behind the client. Frustrating the client may be an integral part of the psychoanalytic approach. If the client asks the therapist, "Do you like me?" the therapist is likely to reply, "Why do you ask me that?" For some clients, particularly those with suicidal tendencies, knowing what the therapist thinks of them is important, and they may experience a reply such as this as indicating that the therapist is behaving like a robot, simply making remarks to the client as part of her/his strategy and having no real feelings of her/his own.

One thing the psychoanalytic therapist does do is enable the client to express strong emotions, either positive or negative, toward her/him. The analytic view is that these are a replay of emotions felt toward other key figures in the client's life. The therapist in no way ducks or minimizes these emotions and sometimes finds them hard to tolerate, but discounts the possibility that they could be anything to do with her/him. The object of the therapy is to identify the person toward whom the emotions really are directed and explore the client's relationship to this other person. The psychoanalyst then tries to reduce the interrelating between client and therapist to a minimum.

In contrast to the psychoanalytic view, the view of the more humanistic therapist is that interrelating with the client contributes to the therapeutic process. In Chapter 4 it was stated that therapists with close personalities adopt a more friendly, casual and chatty style. Close therapists do make emotional responses and do answer clients' questions, which leads to a greater degree of interrelating. Spinelli (1994) wrote of the need to be with and be for the client; Kohut (1984) wrote of the need for the therapist to think and feel her/himself into the client's inner world; and van Deurzen-Smith (1988) wrote of the perfect merging of therapist and client who totally identify with each other.

From the point of view of relating theory, it would seem essential that the client experience the therapist as a real person, with real opinions and real emotions. Therefore, the therapist should be prepared to make self-revelations and to respond with appropriate emotion to what the client says. If the client is going to make good her/his relating deficiencies, s/he is going to have to be exposed to genuine states of relatedness which only the therapist can provide and to practice relating in particular ways toward the therapist. Thus, in that which might be called *relating therapy*, the therapy would grow out of the interrelating of therapist and client.

When the client invites a relevant other into therapy

In individual therapy, the client may become so preoccupied with her/his relationship with another person that it seems appropriate to suggest that s/he invite this person into therapy. Apart from the invitation of a partner, which will be dealt with under couple therapy, the commonest relevant other to be invited is a parent, or sometimes, both parents. It is helpful to arrange the seating so that client and parent/s are facing each other. This conveys the message that they are expected to talk to each other rather than to the therapist.

The interrelating can be initiated by suggesting that one of them begin by telling the other what s/he thinks the problem between them might be. After a suitable time, the other is invited to do the same back. The seating arrangement should be such that, for each, it is easier to address the other than to address the therapist. Even so, more often than not, each tries to bring the therapist in by saying something like, "That's what s/he does to me all the time". The therapist needs to recreate the interrelating between client and other by inviting the person to direct this remark to the other. The speaker may resist by saying something like, "I've told her/him before". The therapist might say something like, "I want to see how s/he responds".

The therapist is able to witness client and parent acting out a typical scenario in which each is convinced of her/his own rightness, but unable to comprehend why the other cannot see things that way. The reality is that each is right in relation to her/his own position but not in relation to the other's position. The therapist's aim is to reveal more clearly to each what it feels like to be the other. This is achieved by inviting each to tell the other what any particular remark makes her/him feel like. For example, a mother might tell her son what she thinks he ought to do, and the son might tell her that this makes him feel that he has not got a mind of his own. It is essential that the therapist try to remain impartial in order that each should feel that her/his own position is being understood.

When a client invites a relevant other into therapy, although, during the session(s) with that other, the client and the other are treated with equal fairness by the therapist, at the end of the day, the client is still the client, and individual therapy has to be resumed. The client is usually appreciative of the support provided by the therapist during the session(s) and believes that the support enabled her/him to stand her/his ground with the other and to say things s/he otherwise might not have said. S/he may have a clearer understanding of why the other behaves the way s/he does and be more sympathetic toward the other. The therapist now knows what it is like for the client to be related to by the other, so both therapist and client are able to talk more easily about the experience.

Couple therapy

Couple therapy is the simplest form of therapy involving interrelating. It will be dealt with at some length to provide a template for the other interrelating therapies. There are almost as many forms of couple therapy as there are forms of individual therapy. In the more distant forms, first names are avoided and homework assignments are given. In the closer forms, first names are encouraged, and if the couple prefer or request it, the therapist volunteers her/his own first name. Psychoanalysts prefer to have two therapists, one of each gender, in order that each partner has someone of the same gender with whom to identify is called *conjoint therapy*. It resembles mixed doubles in tennis, and the two therapists and the two clients face each other. This facilitates the development of transference and countertransference between clients and therapists.

The form of couple therapy that will be focused upon here is that which is based upon relating theory. Because the therapy is directed at the interrelating between the partners, issues of transference to the therapist or countertransference by the therapist are of minimal importance. In couple therapy, most usually, from the start, the couple present themselves as a couple. They present because their relationship is not working. Therefore, the therapist's commitment is to the couple, rather than to either partner. Often the partners have been so weakened by the difficulties between them that they scarcely feel able to carry on. The therapist, as a third party, who enters into a relationship with them as a couple (and is perceived by them as "our" therapist) provides the support that gives them the hope, incentive and stamina to carry on.

Occasionally, one partner begins in individual therapy but reveals that the problem is mainly to do with her/his relationship to her/his partner. Consequently, the partner is invited to attend as well. Recently, I had the experience of starting to see a man for individual therapy and then being contacted by his wife, who also wanted to see me. He did not object to this. For some weeks I saw each of them separately, but one day they agreed to see me as a couple. The arrangement was that I should continue to see each separately and occasionally see the couple together. In one of the couple sessions, they decided to separate. I continued seeing each separately and occasionally both together.

It sometimes happens that only one partner turns up for therapy, and it is not uncommon for couple sessions to be interspersed with individual sessions with one or other partner. It also happens that, during the course of couple therapy, one partner reveals certain personal difficulties. Then it seems appropriate to spend a number of individual sessions working on these difficulties before resuming couple therapy.

When one partner has had, or is having, an extra-couple relationship, it is easier to take out some sessions to enable that partner to talk more openly about that relationship. It is also helpful to make available some sessions in which the other partner can speak more freely about her/his reactions to the extra-couple relationship. Often the other partner feels hurt and demoralized by the experience, though reluctant to allow this to be witnessed by the transgressor. It helps to build up this partner's confidence in order that s/he can hold her/his own in the exchanges that follow. An extra-couple relationship is often a symptom of the couple's difficulty. If the couple can be kept in therapy and the difficulty resolved, the need for the extra-couple relationship may subside.

Less frequently than in individual therapy, extra others are brought into couple therapy. Sometimes, one or more of the couple's children can usefully be invited to attend. Sometimes, one partner and one or more of the children attend. In both couple and family therapy, whenever a different combination of family members attends the family dynamics are seen by the therapist in a different light, and different forms of interrelating within the family system can be focused upon. On one occasion, the parents of one of the partners appeared to be driving a wedge between the couple, and they were invited to attend. During the session, the couple presented a united front to the parents, which had the effect of diminishing the parents' influence.

The opening sessions

Couple therapy is conducted in much the same way as therapy with an invited other. The partners are placed opposite each other, close enough for one or other to reach across and touch or hold the other; occasionally, when things get difficult, this happens. The therapist places her/himself centrally, equidistant from the partners, but slightly removed from them. This emphasizes that it is the interrelating between the partners that matters. The therapist should be close enough to each partner to be able to speak quietly to her/him. Frequently, s/he pitches her/his remarks directly between the partners so that neither can tell to whom they are addressed.

Therapy begins in a way that is similar to that with an invited other. Each partner is given time to say to the other what s/he thinks is wrong and to give expression to any feelings s/he might be experiencing toward the other. It is suggested that this might last from ten to fifteen minutes, but the partner is told to go on until s/he has said what s/he thinks is necessary. The other is forbidden to respond until s/he has finished. This may seem artificial, but (1) it is important for each partner to be free to speak without fear of interruption, and (2) it provides for the therapist a clear picture of how each views the other.

When the relationship is under strain, as it is at the beginning of therapy, the partners are inclined to turn to tell the therapist about the other, instead of talking to the other, even though, because of the placing of the chairs, this is difficult to do. The therapist may try to persuade the partner to address her/his remarks to the other, by saying, "Tell her/him". The partner may try this for a time but will quickly revert to talking to the therapist. In these early stages, it is acceptable to allow the partners to communicate with each other via the therapist in this way.

If the partners can allow it, it is most effective if the therapist can work on the relationship from the inside. To do this, she needs to become an honorary member of it, so to speak. This is called becoming *triangled in*. S/he cannot force her/his way in, and can only move in at the pace the couple can allow it. Evidence that s/he has been accepted in is that the couple begin to behave in an unselfconscious manner and to use the kind of language (e.g., swearing freely, or using intimate terms) that they would use if they were on their own. The therapist should never abuse this privilege and should always respect, and even remind the partners of, their special privacy.

The functions of the therapist

The therapist performs a number of functions. One is to control the flow of talk. It sometimes happens that one partner dominates the talking and does not give the other a chance to speak. A variant of this is that one partner speaks more freely than the other; while the other struggles to get her/his words out, the more fluent partner breaks in. Rather like the conductor of an orchestra, the therapist may need to halt the flow of one partner or bring in the other by making appropriate gestures. When one partner tries to dominate the interaction, or breaks in, s/he is revealing that s/he is not interested in what the other is saying. A partner often hovers in mid-sentence. One might say, for example, "I sometimes feel that he. . . ." At this point, the other may start to speak. The therapist should hold her/him off and say, "Yes, that he. . . ." This conveys that s/he cares about what the first person is trying to say. It also forces the other to hear what the first person is trying to say. Sometimes both partners talk at the same time, so that neither can hear or even wants to hear, what the other is saying. Sometimes they each shout the other down. Again, the therapist must insist that they speak one at a time.

In a discordant relationship, the partners spend a lot of time talking about the other, or telling the therapist or the other what s/he is like, what s/he is feeling, or what s/he is doing wrong. Instead of this, they should be invited to tell each other what it feels like to be themselves. The therapist should prohibit them from talking about or accusing the other, and only permit them to say what it feels like to be themselves or what they each personally want. In effect, this creates an interrelating encounter in which each conveys to the other what state of relatedness s/he needs and permits them to do a deal.

The therapist needs to act like a referee in a boxing match, ensuring fair play and ensuring that neither gets too badly hurt by the other. Partners can make extremely cruel and destructive remarks to each other, without realizing the damage they are doing. The therapist may have to step in and hold the more aggressive partner off and, more important, reveal the extent to which that partner is hurting the other. There are things that one partner will only dare say during couple therapy, knowing that s/he will be protected from retaliation by the other. Sometimes a partner is inhibited by fear of retaliation when they get home.

The main function of the therapist is to observe the couple in action and try to make sense, initially to her/himself, but later to the partners themselves, of what is going on between them. Commonly what is happening is that the partners are striving for incompatible states of relatedness. The harder each strives for his/her state of relatedness the more the other feels that her/his state of relatedness is being denied her/him. S/he therefore strives even harder to get it. This is a contest that neither can win.

The row

In this section, difficulties will be divided into the horizontal and the vertical, though sometimes, the two are totally interwoven. The phenomenon called the *row* is often so compounded. A row breaks out when each partner fears that s/he is losing out in terms of a desired or needed state of relatedness. On the horizontal axis, the row may occur because one partner is feeling either crowded in (imposed closeness) or ignored (imposed distance) by the other. The crowded in partner is trying to drive the other away; the ignored partner is trying to get taken notice of. Another horizontal conflict is over identity (i.e., distance), who is going to get her/his choice, her/his opinion heard or her/his point across. On the vertical axis, the row may be because each is afraid that the other is having too much influence (upperness). Each tries to put the other down by revealing weaknesses or deficiencies in the other or by being insulting, intimidating or violent. A less common vertical conflict is to do with who is going to be looked after by the other (lowerness).

Rows have an appallingly repetitive quality. Couples have the same row over and over, when exactly the same words get said, exactly the same responses get made and exactly the same moments of hurt from the past get recalled. Each reasserts her/his position, and each is afraid of losing ground to the other. The partners are like actors in a long-running play. They each know their own lines and the other's lines perfectly. Rows do not lead to progress, they only serve to maintain the status quo, yet the partners cannot stop having them.

Rows are reported upon in therapy, and sometimes they break out in therapy. It is sometimes useful for the therapist to precipitate a row. Partners feel easier about rowing in therapy, because they know that the therapist is there to see fair play and can prevent things getting out of hand. In the course of the row, each hopes to convince the therapist of the rightness of her/his position. In fact, because each partner is arguing from her/his own point of view, each is right, and it is important that the therapist should point this out to them. The row frequently takes the form of a vicious circle, and the therapist can perform an important function by explaining to the partners the structure of their particular vicious circle. In a recent session, the woman was screaming at the man because he was ignoring her, and the man was demanding that the woman stop screaming at him. I told the woman that the more she screamed the more he would ignore her, and I told the man that the more he demanded that she stop screaming, the more she would believe he was ignoring her. The man started to show the woman more concern and the woman stopped screaming. It is important that the row be resolved before the end of the session. To this end it may be necessary for the therapist to curtail it by shouting "Stop". This then gives the therapist time to provide an explanation for what is happening.

The separation

Sometimes a separation has occurred before the commencement of therapy and sometimes it occurs during the course of therapy. One partner decides that s/he cannot live with the other any longer. It can occur either out of the home or within the home. Out of the home the partner may go to parents, married children, a married sibling or a friend. Within the home s/he may retreat to part of the house or one room or may simply go silent. The separation can last for hours, days, weeks or even months. Even within the home, partners are capable of remaining silent for hours, days and sometimes even longer. The separation can have a number of beneficial effects. The person who initiates it has reached a breaking point and needs to go into retreat to heal the pain. The person who remains is left thinking about what s/he may have said or done to cause the separation. If the therapist sees each partner during the separation, s/he can help each understand how the separation came about, which may form the basis of a bid for reconciliation. The resolution of the separation is similar to the resolution of a row, and amounts to one promising to not to do one thing in return for the other promising not to do another.

Even if a reconciliation does not take place, much can be gained from the therapist continuing to see one or both partners separately. The partner seen may continue, for some time, to maintain that s/he was right and the other was wrong. The therapeutic breakthrough occurs when s/he is able to acknowledge her/his part in the breakdown and to appreciate why the other behaved the way that s/he did.

Sometimes a separation will occur during the course of a session. One partner will get up and leave. The usual strategy is for the therapist to continue working with the remaining partner. Frequently the partner will return and the therapy continues.

Horizontal difficulties

The vicious circle is particularly clear-cut on the horizontal axis. It is more usual for the woman to be pressing for more closeness and for the man to be pressing for more distance, but sometimes it happens the other way around. The chasing partner is in a state of constant anxiety that the other has no interest in her/him or is more interested in other people. Therefore s/he is forever checking up on the other's activities, listening in on the other's telephone conversations and watching her/him in the presence of other people. S/he may indulge in all manner of behaviors to gain or maintain the other's attention and try to interrupt or spoil the other's interactions with others. The fleeing partner feels constantly under scrutiny and attack. S/he feels stifled by the other and trapped in the relationship. S/he is preoccupied with trying to find ways of escaping from the other's attentions and interrogations and of getting time or space for her/himself. S/he may even seek solace in a relationship with a less demanding other person.

Another horizontal difficulty is the need that each partner has to continue to develop and maintain his/her own separateness, in terms of both space and identity. When two people share the same living space and spend long periods in each other's company, there is the risk that one or the other will begin to experience closeness fatigue. Each will start finding excuses to spend time alone or away from the other, and each will start pressing to have more of her/his own way. Fights about what color the curtains should be, what pictures should be on the wall, what ornaments should be on the mantlepiece, what television programs they should watch and where they should go on holiday are not unimportant, because they are fights about whose identity should prevail. The therapist plays a part in stressing how necessary it is that each should feel that her/his views and preferences are adequately represented, that each can recognize her/himself in the way the home is and the experiences they have. Intimacy may be about sharing, but sometimes it is necessary for each to feel that certain things are *my* things and certain choices are *my* choices.

Vertical difficulties

Vertical issues involve one partner trying to hold on to one particular position. The partner who holds on to upperness is afraid that the other will have too much influence, and so tries to reduce the influence of the other. S/he will insist upon everything being done her/his way and will interpret any effort on the part of the other to have some say in the decision making as the other trying to gain control. The persistently upper partner may truly believe that the other would only make a mess of things if s/he were to have more say and that the only way to ensure that things are done properly is to assume control of everything. This causes the lower partner to feel squashed and useless. When s/he expresses an opinion it is contradicted. When s/he makes a suggestion it is overruled.

The upper partner does not benefit from this strategy because, in her attempts to maintain control, s/he has reduced the other to an unconfident, uninteresting, non-entity, whom s/he experiences as an embarrassment. The other will have adopted an attitude of defeat and resignation, is probably depressed and no longer seeing the point in carrying on. During a recent marital therapy session, a dominating husband said to me, in front of his wife, "I look at her and I think, did I do that?"

The partner who tries to hold on to lowerness runs into similar problems. By presenting her/himself as weak or helpless s/he forces the other to be the responsible one. Initially, s/he finds it gratifying to be helped, just as the helping one finds it gratifying to do the helping. The more helpless the helpless one becomes, the more helpful the helper becomes in response to her/his helplessness; and the more the helper tries to help, the more helpless the helpless one becomes. Consequently, the helpless one gets weaker and weaker and more and more incapable, until the helper finds s/he has to devote more and more of her/his time to helping. The helper begins to complain about the demands the helpless one now makes upon her/him and does not seem to realize that it is her/his own enthusiasm for the role of helper that has rendered the helpless one so helpless. Each believes that the helpless one could not survive without the helper, which by this extreme stage is probably true, but the situation is not irreversible.

Resolution of the difficulties

By the time they come to therapy, the partners have settled into a fixed pattern in which neither experiences any real satisfaction from the other, and each has organized her/his life in order to exist without that state of relatedness of which s/he is being deprived. The therapist's message to them is that it does not have to be like this. First, the therapist must try to discover why the active partner has started the pattern. Why is the controller so afraid of the other being in control? Why is the helpless one so afraid of doing things for herself? This must be explored and worked upon. It is important for the other to witness this, since it makes her/his behavior more comprehensible.

When this has been done, it may be possible to start breaking the pattern. The active partner should be invited to try cautiously reducing her/his predominant style of relating. This will have the effect of reducing the other's reaction. Consequently, this results in a doubling of the degree of change. The reactive partner should be given the responsibility of pointing out to the active partner each time s/he lapses into her/his old style of relating.

The changes take place both outside and within the therapy session. Outside the session the partners continue their normal lives, and in each session, they report upon interactions that have happened. The therapist comments upon what each has done right and what each has done wrong. S/he observes them as they talk to each other about the interactions and tries to continue the dialogue into the session. In the session, under the therapist's supervision, the partners practice their new ways of relating. Acting like the director of a play or the conductor of a master class, the therapist suggests particular positions that each might adopt in relation to the other, correcting them when they make unhelpful remarks and praising them when they make helpful ones. S/he throws in little prompts to keep the interaction going. Keeping the prompts brief causes least interference to the flow of the interaction.

When the relationship is starting to work better, the partners interrelate more freely, more effectively and more pleasurably. The therapist interrupts less and lets them carry on alone for longer stretches, as when someone learning to ride a bicycle finally gets the hang of it, and goes cycling off on her/his own. At this point the therapist may have to force her/himself not to speak. As the couple become more confident, they become less tolerant of the therapist's presence and start triangling her/him out. This is the time to let them go.

Family therapy

Family therapy differs from marital therapy in that the members of more than one generation are involved. A couple may attend with their children or with their parents, or even with their grandparents. Combinations of family members can vary from session to session, according to who are invited or who decide to attend. Quite small children, or even babies, sometimes attend. The children or babies serve the purpose of enabling the therapist to observe the effects they have upon the other family members or the way that the other family members relate to them. Sometimes the children can understand quite clearly what is going on and make useful contributions to the therapy.

Because every family member has a relationship with every other family member, the interrelating within a family can be extremely complex. In a family of three, there are three separate relationships; in a family of four, there are six; in a family of five, there are ten; and in a family of six, there are fifteen; even in quite a small family, it is impossible for the therapist to be aware of, let alone be in control of, everything that is going on. While there is no specifically interpersonal form of family therapy, the interpersonal principles discussed under couple therapy are readily applicable to family therapy.

The family as a system

A commonly adopted solution is to treat the family as though it were a single entity. For this reason many family therapists have been inclined to think in terms of systems (Gorell Barnes, 1985). The family is a system insofar as what happens to any part of the system, that is, to any individual family member, will affect all other parts of the system, that is, all other family members. The family therapist considers it necessary, at least for some of the sessions, to have the entire family present in order to observe the system functioning. Systems, over time, reach a stable state, or equilibrium, in order that all parts of the system can coexist. A therapy group is also a system, but the family system, unlike the system in a therapy group, continues to exist and function outside of the therapy session. All families attain a state of equilibrium, whether they be functional or dysfunctional, but in dysfunctional families, the equilibrium is attained at the expense of the discomfort of some of the family members.

A family is often referred for therapy because of the disruptive behaviour of one of its members, but the strategy of the family therapist is normally not to single out this member for special attention. The assumption is that the disruptive behavior of one member is a symptom of the dysfunctioning of the entire family. This approach has the advantage that it runs counter to the commonly held psychiatric assumption that there is one ill family member, with whom the remaining members have to cope. One member may opt to be ill to keep the others well or serve as a scapegoat for the others to blame for the family's ills. Laing once used the analogy that an ill member functions as a lightning conductor for the family. The sacrificial member expresses the family's anger or despair. If s/he stops performing this function, someone else has to. Therapists commonly observe that when one member gets better, another gets worse.

Family structure

What appears to happen in much family therapy theory is that the axes normally used to define the relating characteristics of an individual are used to define the relating characteristics of the family. On the proximity axis, family therapists write of the *cohesion dimension* (Olson, Sprenkle and Russell, 1979) and of the desirability of an optimum balance within a family of *togetherness* and *apartness* (Rosenblatt and Titus, 1976). They also write of the *coalition structure* (Lange and van der Hart, 1983). They describe certain relationships within it as being strong (close) and others as being weak (distant). It is considered that, within a three-generation family system, relationships within the generations should be stronger (closer) than those between them. If a cross-generational relationship is stronger than the two within-generation relationships, for example, if a grandmother's relationship with a mother is stronger than her relationship with the grandfather or than the mother's relationship with the father, then there must be difficulties in one or both of the within-generation relationships.

It is more difficult for family therapists to describe an entire family on the power axis. Consequently, they are inclined to determine which family members hold the power. They write of the *power structure* (Lange and van der Hart, 1983), within which they consider it appropriate that the parents should be more powerful than the children. If a child is able to get into a position in which s/he can dictate to the parents, the family system is put under strain. More commonly, one child, perceiving a rift in the parental relationship, sides with one parent against the other. This has the effect of increasing the rift between the parents. Structural family therapists consider it necessary to redress the power balance, in order that the parents are once more in control of the children and are united in their position of authority over the children.

Adaptability and rigidity

A theme of this book is that ideally the individual should have versatility, that is, be competent in every form of relating, in order to relate however s/he needs to in any particular situation. In the family situation, such versatility is called *adaptability*. Presumably, a family is adaptable if the majority of its members are versatile. When an individual lacks competence in any particular form of relating, s/he has to restrict her/his relating to those areas in which s/he has competence. That leads to rigidity. A rigid relater forces those with whom s/he relates to adopt forms of relating that are compatible with her/his rigid style of relating. A family that is not adaptable is also called rigid. Such a family may contain a number of non-versatile, that is, rigid, members. Gorell Barnes and Cooklin (1994) observed that in situations of threat families become *rigidified*, which makes them incapable of adapting. What may happen in a rigidified family is that the rigidity of certain of its members becomes more apparent than usual, and that blocks the behavior of the other family members. For example, a mother's fear of distance may cause her to stop her son from leaving home.

Family therapists seek methods for dislodging what they call *stuck* families. One approach is pushing the family toward crisis, so that something has to give. This is reminiscent of those individual therapists who try punitive methods for breaking down clients' resistance. A more constructive approach is identifying the family member or members who is/are contributing to the stuckness, and trying to understand what his/her or their relating difficulty might be. The woman may be stopping her son from leaving home because, for example, he is protecting her from a tyrannical husband. Thus the cause of the stuckness is not the son or the mother, but the husband.

Asking questions

Family therapists, much more than other psychotherapists, ask questions. They do this to provoke family members into thinking about each other. Sometimes they address the question to the entire family; other times they single out a specific family member. A technique developed by Palazzoli and her team (Palazzoli, Boscolo, Cecchin and Prata, 1980) is called *circular questioning*. It involves asking one family member about one or more other family members. The kind of question that might be asked is, "If your father were to leave home, who do you think would be the most upset?" The effectiveness of circular questioning is that it avoids directly questioning someone, and it informs the therapist about the person asked, the person asked about and the other family members. The same question might be put to more than one member and, if there are different answers, the reasons are explored.

The one-way screen and the intervention

It is common for family therapists to use a one-way screen, with a number of observers sitting behind it. The family are told of the existence of the observers, but they never get to meet them. The observers sometimes telephone the therapist to make suggestions. The one-way screen is not without its critics

(Efran and Clarfield, 1992). Many families do not like being watched in this way. At the end of the session, the therapist leaves the family to consult the observers, and the therapist and the observers prepare a statement that is delivered to the family. This is called the *intervention*. It always informs the family of its strengths and achievements, then provides advice about what should and should not be done between sessions. Because it is presented as a joint statement, the family members cannot identify who was responsible for it. This permits shocking and sometimes hurtful statements to be made. The therapist presents the intervention, then leaves, providing the family no opportunity to respond to it. Such shock tactics are intended to create the maximum impact on the family.

Group therapy

Group therapy differs from marital and family therapy in that the group members are neither related to each other nor in a relationship with each other outside of therapy; in fact, group members are discouraged from having involvement with each other outside of therapy. They have all presented themselves to a therapist because of some personal difficulty, and the therapist has recommended that they join a therapy group. The group usually comprises six to twelve people and there is usually one therapist, though sometimes there are two.

As with individual and marital therapy, group therapy assumes many different forms, depending upon the theoretical orientation of the therapist. There are *closed groups*, with a set number of members meeting over a predetermined duration, and *slow open groups*, which have an indeterminate duration, which members can leave when they appear to be ready to and which new members can join when a vacancy occurs. Groups may be of single gender or of mixed gender and may have a restricted age range or an unrestricted age range. Group members sometimes share a common problem (such as anorexia) or sometimes present with a diversity of problems.

The psychoanalytic group

A psychoanalytic therapist will take no action at the start of a group, but will wait for the group to start itself. If no one speaks, the group may remain silent for an entire session. Even when people do speak, the therapist may simply sit and observe the actions and reactions occurring among group members. Her/his objective is to maintain an *impersonal presence* to which group members can attribute feelings, thoughts and behavior they find intolerable in themselves. Occasionally, the therapist will make interpretive remarks. The purest group therapist (Bion, 1961) will make general statements about the group as a whole, but Bar-Levav (1980) objected that this overlooks the individual as a separate being. He considered the term *group psychotherapy* to be a misnomer, since it is the psychotherapy of the individual group members, and not of the group itself. The less pure therapist (Ezriel, 1950) is prepared to comment upon how each individual member contributes to the pattern presented by the group, but will still consider the essential interaction to be one between the group members and the therapist. More liberal therapists (Whitaker and Lieberman, 1964), while still offering interpretations of the group as a whole, are prepared to respond to individual group members, ask direct questions, express opinions and consider conflicts arising between group members.

The power of the group

The general understanding of groups is that members reproduce habitual styles of relating in the group. Their real-life affiliations and conflicts become acted out within the group. When the group is working well, members feel it is safe to be open about themselves and express honest opinions about each other. As group members reveal their acceptance and sympathy, other members become prepared to make personal revelations. Group members may be more prepared to accept observations about themselves from fellow members than from the therapist. When they describe situations and events in their current or earlier lives, others who are living through or have lived through similar experiences identify with them. When two or more group members share similar experiences or opinions, these get confirmed or reinforced, which intensifies the associated emotion.

Group members respond to others' accounts with emotions such as shock, disgust, amusement and admiration. Members are affected by these responses, sometimes with dismay and sometimes with relief, sometimes accepting them and sometimes rejecting them. When members perceive that others are trying to deceive themselves or deny their true feelings, they may exert pressure upon them to reconsider what they have said. When a majority of the group express the view that someone is denying some aspect of her/himself, s/he may be persuaded to acknowledge that it might be true.

An interpersonal approach to group therapy

An interpersonal therapist would consider that it is through the interrelating of the group members that the therapy happens. Experienced group members are probably capable of interrelating therapeutically between themselves, but a skilled therapist can greatly enhance a group's therapeutic potential. Every member of a therapy group has some form of relating incompetence, but not every member has the same form. The therapist who selected the members for the group will have some initial idea of the relating incompetencies of individual members, but these will become more apparent as the group proceeds. Also, as the group proceeds, the group members themselves become familiar with the relating incompetencies of each other, which may determine who relates to whom and in what way. Close group members may find it easiest to relate to other close group members and may find distant group members unfriendly and frustrating. Distant group members may find it easiest to relate to other distant members and may find close group members clinging and intrusive. Upper group members and lower group members may become drawn to each other. Two upper members may compete for supremacy within the group, and two lower group members may compete for nurturance within the group.

The function of the group leader is to try to make sense of what people are saying about themselves and others, and of what is going on between various group members. S/he may need to intervene if s/he perceives that one group member is being victimized or scapegoated. S/he may invite group members to consider what might be happening in this situation. Are they, for example, projecting some unappealing aspect of themselves onto this person? Are they retaliating for some hurtful accusation that has been made about themselves? Expressing a possible explanation as a question rather than a statement allows group members to make up their own minds about its correctness.

An important function of groups is the opportunity they provide for experimentation. A group is a microcosm of the world outside it, but it can also serve as a training ground for the world outside it. A person who is afraid of closeness may be encouraged to risk allowing her/himself to become close to another group member. A person who is afraid of lowerness may be encouraged to risk putting her/himself in a lower position in relation to another group member. Not all of the relating in a group is negative relating. Some group members may be particularly adept at certain forms of positive relating. Such members can expose other group member to specific forms of positive relating and enable them to be accepting of it. One member may be particularly good at being consoling, encouraging and supportive. S/he may be able to behave in this way toward another group member who has never before been treated in this way.

A great deal of evidence exists to show that changes achieved during group therapy sessions do not necessarily transfer to situations in clients' lives outside the group (Goldstein and Kanfer, 1979). It is necessary for the group therapist to set each client specific interpersonal tasks to carry out in specific situations, pointing out to her/him deficiencies in the way s/he has related up to now and suggesting alternative ways of relating that might be more effective. However, the client may be incapable of adopting these new relating styles unless certain incompetencies have been worked upon and corrected within the group, in order that s/he has the confidence to try them out. Within the group, group members are likely to give her/him an easier time than will significant others outside the group who are experienced at playing upon her/his weaknesses. Clients should be warned to expect failures, in order that they not be disheartened by them and are not afraid to report them back to the group.

The therapeutic community

The therapeutic community is a therapy group in residence, though sometimes a day-hospital is run on therapeutic community lines. The group members live together, in the same residential setting, usually over a period of months or years. Sometimes the members are of comparable age, but unrelated. Sometimes the group members share a common problem, such as an antisocial personality disorder or an addiction to drugs. Other times, there are a number of discrete families living within the same community (Kennedy, 1986). The community usually has a number of therapists, some of whom may sleep in the community some of the time. Rapoport (1960) defined the characteristics of the therapeutic community as *communalism*, an emphasis on shared community experience; *democratization*, a reduction or flattening of a hierarchical structure and the involvement of all staff and patients in decision making; *permissiveness*, the increased tolerance by community members of each other's deviant behavior; and *reality confrontation*, the repeated and frank examination of each member's problems in living with and relating to others. The therapeutic team includes a range of professionals who, ideally, share their expertise with one another for a common purpose (Vinokur-Kaplan, 1995). This is called the *interdisciplinary model* (Yurkovich, 1989).

Certainly originally (Clark, 1965; Jones, 1968), all therapeutic communities were intended to be run on democratic lines, with therapists and members having equal say in what happens in the community; this includes who is admitted, what the rules should be, what sanctions should be imposed upon those who break the rules and who is discharged. Almond (1974) however, would wish to impose a limit upon the degree of democratization, believing that some form of hierarchy should be maintained. For the greater part of their time, the members of a therapeutic community are caught up in the general activity of living together. This is called a *living and learning* experience and is considered to be therapeutic in itself (Van der Linden, 1988). Since the therapy staff opt out of making practical decisions, community members are compelled to organize themselves in such a way that their accommodation is kept clean and orderly, and their food is bought and prepared. This too can have a therapeutic effect. As Millard and Oakley (1994) observed, it is impossible to differentiate entirely between ordinary daily living, the running of the place and the psychotherapeutic input.

Within the setting of the community, various therapeutic events occur, the single most important of which is the regular *community meeting*. It is attended by the majority of staff and members. In it, the rules of the community that regulate the behavior of both staff and members are set down, and recent infringements of them are examined. Disputes and conflicts occurring within the community are reported upon and discussed. Members express opinions about who did what to whom, and what went wrong and why. Staff may offer opinions and provide explanations, but so far as possible, they will not pull rank. They may intervene if a member is being hurt, unfairly treated or pushed beyond her/his limits. An important difference between the community meeting and a conventional therapy group is that group members continue to interrelate in the gaps between the meetings.

Another feature of the therapeutic community is the *staff group*, which commonly follows the community meeting. In this, the staff members give expression to their anxieties and frustrations about what is occurring in the community as a whole and what occurred in the community meeting. They examine tensions that arise both within the community and between themselves. The flattening of staff hierarchies in therapeutic communities generates insecurities that must be compensated for by staff solidarity (Millard and Oakley, 1994). There may be disagreements about how situations have been handled, and unless these are rapidly resolved, they may have serious repercussions on the running of the community.

Other therapeutic events that occur within the community are small therapy groups, the formal individual psychotherapy of individual members and art therapy and psychodrama sessions involving selected members. There are also many impromptu, brief therapeutic encounters between staff and members, or groups of members, which over time have a cumulative therapeutic input.

Therapy involving a representation of a relevant other

It is the humanistic therapies that most frequently involve introducing a representation of a relevant other. An important feature of introducing such a representative is that the so-called transference is directed not at the therapist, as in psychoanalysis, but at the representation. The humanistic therapies form a bridge between individual therapy and group therapy. They are conducted in a group setting, but the therapist works with one group member at a time. While the therapist is working with one member, the other members watch attentively. Their presence has a powerful effect upon the therapy. Both the therapist and the member being worked with derive strength from the presence of the group. Some group members identify with the person being worked with and are helped vicariously from this identification. The characters in her/his story could be characters in their story. Her/his emotion brings out emotion in them. Toward the end of the session, the therapist invites other group members to speak to the person being worked with; it is at this time that the similarities in the stories emerge and the emotions of different group members flow together. The group member most affected by the session becomes the next member to be worked with.

The advantage of using a representation of the other is that it is sometimes easier to say and do things to a representation of another than to say or do them to the actual person. In practicing saying and doing them in a make-believe situation, in the security of a group and in the presence of a reassuring and supportive therapist, the client becomes more familiar with the new form of behavior and gains the courage to try doing it in a real-life situation. This is sometimes referred to as *almost-but-not-quiteness* (Birtchnell, 1989).

Humanistic therapies involve a degree of *risk taking*. This pushes group members into areas of self-revelation or interrelating with others that otherwise they would avoid. Clients are often required to do unusual and difficult things. Therefore, more so than in other forms of group therapy, the therapist has to be directive. It is essential, from an early stage, for her/him to become accepted by the group as a trustworthy person, who knows what s/he is doing. It is also essential that the group members believe in what s/he is doing and are willing to go along with what s/he suggests. Even one dissenter can undermine the group's confidence and prevent things from happening.

Most humanistic therapies incorporate some degree of enactment of interpersonal situations. It is not easy to do this from cold, so group members are usually invited to begin the therapy session by participating in activities that involve getting close to, if not actually touching, other group members and interacting with them. During such activity they may become embarrassed, get out of breath or start to laugh, which puts them in the right state of mind to be spontaneous and emotional and to make personal revelations (all aspects of closeness). This is called a *warm-up* period.

Humanistic therapies adhere to what is called the *here-and-now* principle. This means that it is therapeutically advantageous to re-enact in the here and now experiences that belong to other places and other times. Bringing them into the here and now has the effect of increasing their vividness in the mind of the client and reviving the emotions that were felt in the other place, at the other time. However, because the here and now is not the there and then, it is safer to take a closer look at these experiences and re-evaluate them.

A number of techniques have been developed for bringing experiences into the here and now (Fagan and Shepard, 1970). The client is invited to try to imagine her/himself in the original situation, to picture the room and the people present and to recall certain specific details, like the shape and color of the furniture and the clothes that the people were wearing. S/he is then invited to speak in the present tense, using the pronouns I, you and we, and not he, she or they, and to reproduce verbatim the words that were said. When the therapist has become sufficiently familiar with the circumstances described, s/he may try to speak the words of one of the other people to the client, roughly as they might have been said at the time. S/he might also introduce new words, which were not actually said, which might bring out more strongly what appeared to be going on between the client and the other person.

A particularly effective technique is called the *empty chair*. The client is invited to imagine that a particularly important figure is sitting in the chair opposite her/him and is invited to speak to this person, again in the present tense, and using only the pronouns I, you and we. The therapist can prompt the client (in a quiet voice) to discuss certain issues with this person or to say certain things to her/him, with remarks like, "Tell her what you think of her for doing that" or "Tell her what that did to you". The therapist might even suggest that the client uses certain phrases that might bring out the feelings more strongly, like, "I hated you for that". An extension of the empty chair technique is inviting the client to sit in the empty chair, imagining her/himself to be the other person and speaking her/his lines to the chair s/he has vacated. By this means the therapist can enable the client to have a clearer idea of what it feels like to be the other person. The client can be encouraged to conduct a conversation with this other person by playing the parts of both her/himself and the other and switching chairs appropriately. The client can even be encouraged to have a conversation with her/himself by asking her/himself questions in one chair and moving on to the other chair to answer them.

Most Gestalt therapy-based approaches inevitably lead to the release of strong emotion (Perls, Hefferline and Goodman, (1951). While there may be some therapeutic benefit to such catharsis, the release of strong emotion is not an end in itself. It is simply that whenever areas of interpersonal difficulty are entered into, the client becomes extremely emotional. This is why the process of *picking up and following a scent* (described in Chapter 2) is so essential. Only the client knows where these areas of interpersonal difficulty are; or more precisely, only the client's inner brain knows where they are. The therapist is dependent upon the client, or the client's inner brain, to take her/him to them. S/he listens for those words, or watches for those actions, that appear to be emotion-laden and tries to show greater interest in them. S/he may even suggest alternative words or actions that may carry more emotion, because they have closer links with these areas of difficulty. Actually entering into these fraught areas is often accompanied by intense emotional release, but such release is only a by-product of the work that therapist and client are doing in exposing and resolving the interpersonal difficulties.

Gestalt art therapy

In Gestalt art therapy (Birtchnell, 1998), the client is invited to draw or paint a picture of the experience to be recalled. In this kind of work, no particular artistic ability is required, for even the crudest drawing is sufficient to provide the representation of key figures. Actively trying to draw or paint people or scenes helps to bring them into consciousness, and even the most inartistic client is capable, under these conditions, of creating striking representations.

This form of art therapy differs from art in that the object of the exercise is to externalize inner imagery so that it can be looked at and talked about. Clients are made to work quickly in order that they should avoid any temptation to add aesthetic embellishments. As soon as something approximating to the person or scene to be depicted has emerged, the therapy has already begun. As in straight Gestalt therapy, the therapy is carried out in a group setting, but the therapist works with only one client at a time. Talking and creating the pictures is a continuous and interconnected procedure. The sheet of paper is the work surface, which is shared by both therapist and client, and either is permitted to make use of it.

Although it is the client's picture, the therapist is entitled to make additions to it, like drawing in someone the client has omitted, but who seems to be important. The therapist can also draw circles around important parts of the picture, draw lines to indicate possible connections and, most important of all, write down verbatim, so that they do not get lost, remarks that the client makes that represent strong feelings. Again, as in straight Gestalt therapy, the therapist can write down a phrase that the client has not used, but which appears to encapsulate something the client is trying to say, like "I want my mummy". Sometimes, if the phrase is right, it can induce a strong reaction in the client. The therapist listens and makes quiet, brief prompts, or even suggests a change of direction, if it appears that the client is drifting away from an area of difficulty.

Therapist and client sit together on the floor with a sheet of paper between them and more paper and an accumulation of art materials to one side of them. The client begins to talk about a particularly fraught interpersonal situation, and as s/he talks, s/he makes representations of this situation on the paper. S/he might say, "This is my dad. He's a brute. He always has dishevelled hair (drawing the hair as s/he speaks). This is my mom. She's scared of my dad. She tries to keep out of his way. (She draws her rather small, and at a safe distance from her dad.) This is me. I'm always caught in the middle of it all. (She puts herself between her dad and her mom.) When the fighting starts I try to hide". (She draws some lines around herself for protection.) The therapist asks quietly, "How does it start?" The client continues, "My mom's usually come in from doing some shopping, and my dad asks her where she's been, who did she meet, who did she talk to". The therapist writes in big letters, over her dad, "Where have you been? Who did you meet? Who did you talk to?" (Using the present tense brings the action into the present.)

The therapy proceeds in much the same way as in straight Gestalt therapy. The client is invited to imagine herself into the scene she has depicted and to feel the feelings she would be feeling. Now she is no longer telling the therapist about what is happening; she is actually in the scene, experiencing it. She thus speaks in the present tense. She is invited to address her father or her mother, but instead of using the less emotional reported pronouns (he, him, she and her) she uses direct ones (I and you). She may invert roles and actually speak the part of her mother or her father. This may provoke a cathartic outburst. The therapist's aim is to rework the scene, with the client in it, more constructively. She may be encouraged to let go of someone she is needlessly clinging to or to stand up to someone who is intimidating or humiliating her.

Psychodrama and dramatherapy

Psychodrama and dramatherapy differ from other forms of group therapy in that the *participants*, as they are called, do not stay in one place; they move about. For this reason, these therapies are sometimes called *action therapies*. Heisey (1982) proposed that action therapies are effective because memories are not simply cognitive, but also have anatomical and physiological components, which are reawakened during re-enactment. Of the two therapies, psychodrama (Moreno, 1972) comes closer to Gestalt therapy and bears a striking resemblance to Gestalt art therapy. Just as Gestalt art therapy has little to do with art and requires no artistic ability, psychodrama has little to do with drama and requires no acting ability. The psychodramatist, sometimes called the *director*, aims to find someone within the group who will be called the *protagonist* and who will become the focus of the action. The remaining group members, more so than in Gestalt therapy and Gestalt art therapy, are called upon to serve as *auxiliary egos* to the protagonist, playing roles that represent important people in her/his life. The protagonist is required to describe, in detail, the setting in which a particular interpersonal difficulty has arisen and to describe the relevant others who were involved. Group members are selected to play the supporting roles in the drama and need to be briefed about the kinds of things that they might say and do. As the drama unfolds, the protagonist may need to stop the action to correct the words or actions of one of the players in order that they represent more correctly the person s/he is playing. The protagonist may also stop because s/he perceives a similarity between the scene that is being enacted and some earlier experience in her/his life. The director may suggest that s/he change to enacting this experience, with the group members adopting the new roles. Sometimes another group member may be invited to take the part of the protagonist to show him/her an alternative way of behaving in that particular situation.

If psychodrama is like Gestalt art therapy, drama therapy is like the more conventional forms of art therapy. Where these forms of art therapy concern themselves with the therapeutic value of art, dramatherapy concerns itself with the therapeutic value of drama. Where conventional art therapists say the art is the therapy (Schaverien, 1989), dramatherapists say the drama is the therapy (Jones, 1996). In dramatherapy clients shed real tears and express real anger, but within a fictional context. Both conventional art therapy and dramatherapy address issues obliquely and gradually. In dramatherapy there is no need for a protagonist, and the whole group may work together without focusing upon a particular individual. They work through metaphor, role or story, remaining a safe distance from their own personal issues.

Summary

Interrelating is described as it occurs in different psychotherapeutic settings. In psychoanalytic individual therapy, the therapist intends to serve only as a representative of some other person in the client's life. In the more inter-personal forms of individual therapy, the therapist learns about the client's interrelating difficulties outside of therapy and enables the client to relate more effectively by interrelating with her/him during the therapy session. In couple therapy, the therapist encourages the partners to interrelate during the course of therapy and observes and comments upon their respective relating strategies. S/he also aims to improve their interrelating outside of therapy. In family therapy, the therapist observes the interrelating within the family and proposes ways in which family members might interrelate more effectively both in and outside of therapy. In group therapy group members reveal their various relating deficiencies through their interactions within the group and practice alternative ways of relating within the group. In therapeutic communities, members improve their relating competence through living together over long periods, attending community groups and interrelating with staff. In the humanistic therapies individuals work with the therapist in the setting of a group, where they re-enact relating experiences. They relate to representatives of significant others through the empty chair, artistic representation or dramatization with other group members.

Chapter 9

Measuring relating and interrelating in psychotherapy

The earlier book (Birtchnell, 1993/1996) was written to introduce the theory that in this book is called relating theory. A theory is like a tool: It is invented to make a particular task easier. Tools and theories survive only as long as they do this, or until newer and better tools and theories come along that do it even better. Initially, tools and theories are useful only to the person who invented them; but if they are any good, they get taken up, used, and even modified by others. For me at least, relating theory has made the task of making sense of what goes on between people easier. It has also made psychotherapy and marital therapy easier.

Another kind of tool is a measuring instrument. The best kind of measuring instrument is one that is derived from, and fashioned upon, a theory. Thus, the one kind of tool (the instrument) grows out of the other kind of tool (the theory). Once a theory has become established, it is useful to develop an instrument based upon it. The theory proposes that certain attributes exist and defines their characteristics. The measuring instrument incorporates scales based upon these definitions and characteristics. If the instrument is successful in measuring them, it is an endorsement, or confirmation, of the theory upon which the scales are based. If the instrument is not successful in measuring them, either the scales are defective and need to be reconstructed, or the theory is defective and needs to be revised. Thus the theory and the instrument, while having independent existences, depend upon each other for their survival.

The theme of the present chapter will be the development of instruments, based upon two successive theories of relating. It will explain how concern with certain theoretical issues generated a need to develop certain kinds of questionnaire. It will be shown how one generation of questionnaires gave way to a second, as one theory grew out of another. The circumstances that gave rise to the theories and led to the development of the questionnaires, the questionnaires themselves and the use to which they have been put will be described.

Both theories and both generations of questionnaires arose initially within a research setting. It was only later that their application to psychotherapy and marital therapy became apparent. This is particularly so for the second generation, which now can be used either as a straightforward clinical measure for demonstrating the existence, and degree, of certain forms of defective (negative) relating, or as part of a more formal psychotherapy research program. I must apologize in advance to the psychotherapist reader for the technical nature of some of the parts of this chapter. These can easily be skipped, and I must emphasize that the questionnaires can be used by the clinician without any technical knowledge and can provide easily understandable and clinically relevant information. The questionnaires are scored by an easy-to-use computer program, with which the clinician may or may not wish to become involved. The computer print-out can be entirely non-numerical, easy to understand and visually appealing.

The self-rating and the partner-rating questionnaires

The original theory has its origins in a preoccupation with the nature of psychological dependence. At a time when I was interested in the long-term consequences of early parent death, I encountered a paper (Barry, Barry and Lindemann, 1965) that suggested that one of the consequences of early parent death was psychological dependence. One of the few measures of this available at that time was the dependence scale of the MMPI (Navran, 1954). I used this in a community study of early-bereaved women 40–49 years old. The study did not confirm the dependence hypothesis, but it did reveal a high correlation between dependence, as measured by the Navran scale, and depression, as measured by the Zung (1965) Depression Rating Scale (Birtchnell and Kennard, 1983). This overlap between dependence and depression became increasingly apparent, and increasingly interesting, to me (Birtchnell, 1984; Birtchnell, Deahl and Falkowski, 1991). From that point on, I became less concerned with depression and more concerned with the nature and measurement of psychological dependence (Birtchnell, 1988a, 1991a, 1991b).

When I began a study of 25–34-year-old depressed and non-depressed married women and their husbands, I decided to create my own questionnaire measure of dependence, which was, as far as I could make it, distinctly different from depression. Within the same questionnaire, I decided to include two other relating measures, which, in their respective ways, represented the opposite of dependence. The first was called *detachment*, the tendency to draw away from others. (In present terminology, that would be distance, as opposed to closeness.) The second was called *directiveness*, the tendency to dominate and take control of others. (In present terminology, that would be upperness, as opposed to lowerness.) Together, the three measures became the *Self-Rating Questionnaire*, and both the women and their husbands were invited to complete it.

Finally, I decided to construct a questionnaire by which both women and their husbands were able to rate each other in terms of these three qualities. This became the *Partner-Rating Questionnaire*. Thus for each couple, there were twelve measures, representing a self and a partner rating of the three forms of relating. Besides inviting the partners to complete the questionnaires, I arranged to interview the women alone, the men alone, and the couples together. On the basis of the three interviews, I computed a score for the overall quality of the marriage.

There arose the problem of how to enable the two partners to complete the questionnaires without either knowing how the other had answered; for obviously, it would not feel safe to respond honestly to the questionnaire items if either thought that the other would know how s/he had answered. At the time, the method I adopted was to ask one partner to complete the questionnaires while I was interviewing the other, but the problem recurred in other situations. A practical solution was to hand the couple a large envelope that contained two smaller envelopes, one containing the man's two questionnaires and one containing the woman's. Each was invited to complete the questionnaires in a private place, then seal them in the small envelope. The two small envelopes could then be sealed into the larger one and handed back to me. When the questionnaires were used in this way it was no longer necessary to keep the partners apart while the questionnaires were being completed.

The study revealed that the depressed women had much worse marriages than the non-depressed women (Birtchnell, 1988b) and that both the depressed women and their husbands rated themselves and each other highly on all three measures (Birtchnell, 1991c).

Because couples who were rated as having poor marriages on the basis of my three interviews also had high scores on the Self-Rating and the Partner-Rating Questionnaires, it seemed a useful idea to use the combination of four questionnaires as a means of assessing marital quality. A series of couples seen by marriage guidance counselors and judged to have bad marriages was compared with a series of couples who were seen as part of a community survey and judged to have good marriages. The mean scores in the two series were strikingly different. The difference was most marked with the Partner-Rating Questionnaire, and with this questionnaire, the difference was most marked on the directiveness scale. Thus, when marriages are failing, the partners are inclined to accuse each other of trying to dominate and to take control, which, in terms of present terminology, is being negatively upper (Birtchnell, 1988c).

The Person's Relating to Others Questionnaire

The more I thought about it, the more convinced I became "that psychological dependence was compounded of the twin motives of seeking closeness to another person and needing to be the recipient of something which is offered by that other person" (Birtchnell, 1987, p. 17). Livesley, Schroeder and Jackson (1990) extracted two similar components by a principal components analysis of psychiatrists' ratings. They called the need for closeness *insecure attachment*, and the need to be a recipient *dependency*. In this earlier writing, I called seeking closeness attachment, and needing to be a recipient receptiveness. I considered attachment to be the opposite of detachment and receptiveness to be the opposite of directiveness. Splitting dependence into these two components led to the creation of the biaxial system, from which the present relating theory emerged. Attachment versus detachment became the horizontal axis, and directiveness versus receptiveness became the vertical axis (Birtchnell, 1987).

Once the two axes were decided upon, the interpersonal octagon and its accompanying relating theory, as set out in Chapter 1, quickly fell into place (Birtchnell, 1990). The octants of the octagon (see Figure 1 of Chapter 1) were named according to the following plan: Each octant was given a two-word name, the first word referring to the vertical axis and the second to the horizontal axis. Where an octant defining the pole of one axis had no connection with the other axis, the word *neutral* was inserted where the word for the other axis would be. For example, the purely upper octant was called *Upper Neutral*, and the purely close octant was called *Neutral Close*. The intermediate octant, located between the upper end of the vertical axis and the close end of the horizontal axis, was called *Upper Close*. An octant could also be referred to by its initial letters, such as UC.

Out of this new theoretical structure emerged the successors to the Self-Rating Questionnaire and the Partner-Rating Questionnaire. The Self-Rating Questionnaire will be described first. Constructed in 1990, it came to be called the *Person's Relating to Others Questionnaire (PROQ)*. It has eight scales, corresponding to the eight octants of the octagon, with ten items per octant, distributed randomly throughout the questionnaire. At the time of the construction of the Self-Rating Scales, the distinction between positive and negative relating had not been clearly thought out, but in fact, the items of the Self-Rating Scales were predominantly negative items. With the PROQ, the decision was made that all ten items of each octant should be negative items, but in order to relieve the overall negative tone of the questionnaire and to give respondents something good to say about themselves, two additional, usually unscored, positive items were included for each octant. Thus, with eight octants and twelve items per octant, the questionnaire had 96 items. For each item there were four possible responses, *Mostly yes, Quite often, Sometimes* and *Mostly no*, and each item yielded a score of 3, 2, 1 or 0. Thus, the maximum score per octant was 30. Since the questionnaire measured only negative relating, a person who related competently would obtain a low score for every octant.

Because hand scoring of the eight scales would be time consuming, a computer program was written that, once loaded onto an IBM-compatible personal computer with a Windows facility, was easy to use. It projected onto the screen a replica of each of the questionnaire's four pages. As the scorer depressed one of four keys, to indicate the column in which the respondent's tick was made, a red tick appeared in the appropriate place on the replicated page on the screen. As each page was completed, the next page appeared on the screen. When all of the ticks for all four pages had been entered, the program projected onto the screen the negative and positive scores for each octant, the subtotal scores for closeness, distance, upperness and lowerness, and the total negative score. An additional and visually appealing feature of the program was the projection onto the screen of an octagon, on which the score for each octant was represented as a shaded area spreading outward from the center. With a maximum score, the entire octant was shaded. The scores and graphic representations could then be printed out. The completely non-numerical, visual representation of the scores had considerable appeal for the non-technical psychotherapist, who was able to see, from the shading of the octants alone, the nature and extent of the client's negative relating.

The relationship between the PROQ and relating theory

Nunally (1978) maintained that a measure should spring from a hypothesis regarding the existence and nature of an attribute. Thus it was necessary to propose the hypothesis that the attributes of the eight octants of the inter-personal octagon existed and to define their characteristics before sets of items could be selected that should contribute to their measurement. Thus, the successful design and use of the PROQ would be a test of the existence and nature of the proposed attributes upon which it was based. If people could recognize the items of the PROQ as referring to typical ways of relating to others, and if they could select those items that described the particular ways that they related to them, they would be confirming the existence and relevance of the attributes enshrined within the theory.

What if this did not happen? Would it mean that relating theory would have to be abandoned? Not necessarily, for if the theory has proved its use-fulness as an explanatory framework, it does not necessarily have to be con-firmed by empirical means. This having been said, any failure of the PROQ to confirm the theory would have to be examined most carefully, and pos-sible explanations for this failure sought. It may be, for example, that the items that were selected as descriptors of a particular octant were not inter-preted as such by the majority of people, in which case they would need to be revised. Alternatively, it may be that the majority of people are unable to differentiate between the attributes of neighboring octants, even though a minority of people are. This would mean that in samples of subjects who were not sophisticated in interpersonal matters, for example, motor mechan-ics, the items would appear not to be discriminating; but in samples of subjects who were so sophisticated, for example, social workers, they would appear to be.

Since the PROQ is designed to be a measure of a person's negative relating, the totally well-adjusted individual, who never relates negatively, would score zero on every scale and the graphic representation of the scores would be a complete blank. It is unlikely that anyone would respond in this way, and so far no one ever has. However, it would be expected that the best-adjusted people would have the lowest scores, and the worst-adjusted would have the highest scores. Since the object of psychotherapy is to minimize negative relating and to maximize positive relating, it would be expected that, with the exception of those people who, with therapy, become better able to recognize their negative relating (see the next section), the PROQ scores would drop during the course of psychotherapy.

Since the axes of the octagon are made up of opposites, it might be expected that the scales of the PROQ are bipolar. If this were the case, there would be a high negative correlation between the scales at each end of an axis, such as between closeness and distance. In fact, this does not appear to be the case. The correlation matrices produced from various samples show low positive correlations between the poles of axes. There is a reasonably convincing explanation for this. Because all the scales are negative scales, it cannot be assumed that someone who has a high score at one end of an axis would necessarily have a low score at the other. For example, a person who has a high closeness score would not necessarily have a low distance score, or vice versa. One reason is that as the items do not refer to a person's relating at any one moment in time, a person may on some occasions relate in a negatively close way and on other occasions relate in a negatively distant way; and her/his responses may reflect this variation. Therefore, it is quite possible for a person to have both a high closeness score and a high distance score, which sometimes does happen. However, one would expect a tendency for people who have negative close scores not to have high negative distant scores, and vice versa, which is generally the case.

Some limitations of the PROQ

It has to be stressed that the PROQ is only a questionnaire, and questionnaires have many limitations. People have to be able to read them, understand what the words mean, apply what they think they mean to themselves and make correct judgments about themselves. It is generally accepted that questionnaires are unacceptable to people unless they can be kept short and simple. They have to contain the smallest possible number of items for describing each particular attribute, and the items themselves have to consist of brief, unambiguous statements. Constructing the PROQ was an ambitious and risky enterprise. It was intended to be a global measure of all the major ways by which one person can relate (negatively) to another. Because it needed to contain eight separate scales, it had to be long, but the number of items for each scale had to be kept small.

If the octagon represents all possible ways of relating, then each of the eight octants must be an extremely complex attribute, containing many sub-components which overlap to varying extents. The entire range of subcomponents cannot adequately be represented by a mere ten items. In order to make the items of each scale reasonably consistent, it was decided to focus upon one particular aspect of each attribute (octant), which meant that the other aspects of that attribute had to be left out. The alternative would have been to include one item to represent each subcomponent. This would have generated a rather diffuse set of items that had fairly low intercorrelations.

It was decided that the PROQ would be most useful if it were predominantly a measure of negative relating, for negative relating is the form of relating that links with psychopathology. This led to certain problems. Negative relating is not something that people are normally proud of or prepared to readily admit to. Therefore, terms for the items had to be selected that alluded in a rather oblique way to forms of negative relating, without being too open about them. For example, a person would be unlikely to admit to being domineering, but may admit to an item such as "I try to arrange things so that people do what I want". A person would be unlikely to admit to being helpless, but may admit to an item such as "I appreciate it when others tell me what to do". There will always be those who can see through the camouflage and who are unwilling to admit to characteristics that they undoubtedly have, but that put them in an unfavorable light. In practice, the system appeared to work well.

Those of us who work within the field of relating are not always aware that many people do not normally think in these terms. They do not know how they relate to others because they do not normally think about it. When faced with an item like "I tend to keep my feelings to myself", they cannot respond to it with any conviction because it has never occurred to them that this is something that they might do. Others might find it hard to say whether what they do with their feelings is any different from what others do with their feelings. What people say about themselves may be completely at variance with what others might say about them. Some may simply choose to lie about themselves.

There are difficulties to using this questionnaire to assess change in psychotherapy because sometimes in the course of psychotherapy, people come to think *more* about the issue of relating. They become more aware of how they relate to others and are better prepared to admit to certain negative forms of relating in themselves. If this is the case, their negative scores at the end of therapy will be higher than they were at the beginning, which will give the impression that they have gotten worse. Others will reach this stage in therapy and then go on to work upon and improve their negative relating, so that by the end of therapy their negative score will have dropped back to its pre-therapy level. This will give the misleading impression that nothing has changed. For such reasons, the ideal arrangement is to administer the questionnaire at different stages throughout the course of therapy.

The PROQ was intended as a measure of a person's general relating tendencies, and it was designed, quite intentionally, not to specify the other person, or persons, to whom the relating was directed. Some respondents find this a problem, and sometimes they will write on the questionnaire a remark such as, "It depends to whom I am relating". Or again, they might write, "At work, yes. At home, no". Of course, people do relate differently to different others, and even relate differently, at different times, to the same other. This is more the case with versatile people. People who are negative relaters more often than not relate rigidly, in one particular way in almost all situations and toward almost all people, which is what the PROQ is designed to detect. This is the kind of relating that the more interpersonal forms of psychotherapy are directed toward remedying.

Finally, it should be stressed that the psychotherapist who is well versed in relating theory is able to make her/his own clinical assessment of the relating tendencies of her/his clients, which may or may not correspond with those indicated by the scores of the PROQ. If there is a marked discrepancy between the therapist's assessment and the PROQ scores, the therapist may wish to consider why this might be so. S/he may try to determine which is right or simply accept them as two separate points of view.

Some early analyses of PROQ data

In all samples examined, there were differences between the mean scores of men and women. Men tended to score higher on the neutral distant, upper distant and upper neutral octants, and women tended to score higher on the three close octants. These are in accordance with the proposed gender differences described in chapters 3 and 5.

The eight scales of the questionnaire showed a high degree of internal consistency. The alpha coefficients were: UN .75, UC .81, NC .83, LC .85, LN .82, LD .74, ND .81 and UD .70.

Since there is no clear demarcation between the characteristics of one octant and those of its neighbors, there is bound to be some overlap between octants, particularly between neighboring ones. Therefore, in a correlation matrix in which each octant is correlated with each other octant, positive correlations are expected to be highest between neighboring octants and lowest between octants most separated from each other around the octagon. Generally, this was so, with certain exceptions. There was a high correlation between upper neutral and upper distant (.69) but a much lower correlation between upper distant and neutral distant (.21) and between upper neutral and upper close (.11). There were high correlations between all three lower octants (LN/LC = .62, LN/LD = .72 and LC/LD = .70). There was a high correlation between neutral close and lower close (.59) but a lower correlation between neutral close and upper close (.34). Similarly, there was a high correlation between neutral distant and lower distant (.52) but a lower correlation between neutral distant and upper distant (.21). As expected, the correlation between lower neutral and upper neutral was low (− .08), and the correlation between neutral close and neutral distant was low (.06).

Since the octagon is, statistically speaking, a circle, a statistician might have expected the octants on opposite sides of the octagon to be highly negatively correlated, that is, they would be demonstrating bipolarity. In fact, they are not, because all of the octants are measures of negative relating. Others, working with measures derived from the interpersonal circle (e.g., Alden, Wiggins and Pincus, 1990), have found more clear-cut evidence of bipolarity. This is because these workers have failed to clearly differentiate between positive relating and negative relating. Obviously, a form of positive relating, such as love, is more likely to correlate negatively with a form of negative relating, such as hate. Love and hate are the horizontal extremes on the interpersonal circle.

Some of the higher inter-octant correlations, such as between the three lower octants, between upper distant and upper neutral and between neutral close and lower close, are disconcerting. Either the items do not clearly distinguish between these closely related constructs, or people have difficulty distinguishing between them.

The PROQ in psychotherapy research

Normal scores for the questionnaire were obtained from three samples of students. The questionnaire was then administered to patients with major depressive disorder who were taking part in a drug trial. Before treatment, the depressed patients scored significantly higher than the normals on negative closeness, negative distance and negative lowerness, but not on negative upperness. By the end of the treatment period, the PROQ scores of those patients whose depressive symptoms appeared to be in complete remission had dropped to within normal limits, but those of the patients who showed only a partial remission of depressive symptoms remained high (Birtchnell, Falkowski and Steffert, 1992). This is similar to the finding reported at the beginning of the chapter, that dependence and depression appear to go hand in hand.

Since the PROQ was shown to register significant changes in patients recovering from depression, it was decided to try administering it to clients before and after a course of psychotherapy. Two samples of clients were selected, those receiving cognitive analytic therapy (CAT), a pragmatic form of psychotherapy developed by Ryle (1995), with both cognitive and psycho-analytic features, which was usually administered in a course of sixteen weekly sessions; and those receiving standard psychodynamic psychotherapy, with the duration of therapy determined by the level of improvement. Both series were National Health Service referrals. The first attended the CAT Clinic at Guy's Hospital in London, and the second attended a psychodynamic psychotherapy clinic in Northampton. For both samples, the pre-therapy scores were significantly higher than the scores for the students, and this was particularly so for the lower and distant octants. While both therapy samples included clients who showed reductions in the total PROQ score of 20 or more points (39 % of the CAT sample and 52 % of the psychodynamic sample), only the psychodynamic sample showed a significant drop in the mean total score (129 to 103, compared with 115 to 105 for the CAT sample). The degree of improvement in the psychodynamic sample was not related to the number of sessions, which ranged from less than 20 to over 60, and the degree of improvement was not uniform around all octants; it was greatest in the three lower ones, though it was apparent also in the neutral close and the neutral distant ones.

While the numbers in this study were relatively small, it may be tentatively concluded that the PROQ is able to distinguish between students and psychotherapy clients, both in absolute terms (in terms of the total score) and in more particular terms (in terms of the separate octant scores). This would imply that psychotherapy clients do tend generally to be more negative relaters; in particular, they tend to be more lower and more distant than students. Again, it may only be tentatively concluded that, while both forms of psychotherapy can bring about changes in relating, psychodynamic psychotherapy can bring about more changes and greater changes. The changes that psychodynamic psychotherapy can bring about are more in the direction of reducing negative lowerness, though it can also reduce negative closeness and negative distance.

The relationship of the PROQ to the IIP

The instrument that most closely resembles the PROQ is the *Inventory of Interpersonal Problems* (IIP). It was developed by Horowitz (1979), following his observation that the problems of clients entering psychotherapy are primarily interpersonal ones. In recent years, it has become the questionnaire most frequently used in psychotherapy research. It comprises 127 statements made by psychotherapy clients. They are expressed in the form of problems and are grouped under two headings: "It is hard for me to . . ." and "I do . . . too much". Unlike the PROQ, the IIP is not based upon any assumptions about classes of problem, and it has been left to others to extract clusters from the pool of statements. This is completely at variance with Nunally's (1978) principle that a measure should spring from a hypothesis regarding the existence and nature of an attribute.

By a principal components factor analysis, Horowitz, Rosenberg, Baer and colleagues (1988), using only 83 of the items, generated six scales, which they called: Hard to be Intimate, Hard to be Sociable, Hard to be Submissive, Too Responsible, and Too Assertive. In a small series of psychotherapy clients who had completed both the PROQ and the IIP, a high level of intercorrelation between these scales was observed, particularly between Hard to be Sociable and Hard to be Intimate (.76), Hard to be Sociable and Hard to be Assertive (.80) and Hard to be Assertive and Too Responsible (.76). There were also high correlations between some of these scales and some of the PROQ scales. These were between Hard to be Assertive and the three lower scales (LC .79, LN .71 and LD .65), Hard to be Submissive and two of the upper scales (UD .63 and UN .54), Hard to be Sociable and two of the lower scales (LD .68 and LC .67) and the distant scale (ND .66).

Alden, Wiggins and Pincus (1990), using a principal components procedure, generated a set of 8 eight-item scales, which appeared to correspond with the eight octants of the classical interpersonal circle (see Chapter 1). There was a reasonable degree of correspondence between these scales and the scales of the PROQ. In a series of psychotherapy patients who had completed both the questionnaires, the Domineering scale showed high correlations with UD (.63) and UN (.62); the Nurturant scale showed high correlations with the three close scales (LC .58, UC .56 and NC .53); the Intrusive scale showed moderate correlations with NC (.47), LC (.39) and LN (.47); the Exploitable scale showed high correlations with the three lower scales (LC .69, LN .65 and LD .57); as did the Non-Assertive scale (LC .78, LN .65 and LD .67); the Socially Avoidant scale showed high correlations with LD (.68), ND (.68) and LC (.61); the Cold scale showed moderate correlations with the three distant scales (ND .57, UD .47 and LD .37), as did the vindictive scale (ND .57, UD .48 and LD .43).

Two attempts were made, by me, one month apart, to classify the items of the IIP in terms of relating theory. Of the 94 items that were classified the same on both occasions, only 9 were classified as close, but 34 were classified as distant, 16 were classified as upper, and 25 were classified as lower. A high proportion of the upper items were strictly aggressive items. The remaining ten items were distributed among the four intermediate positions. It is a serious disadvantage of the IIP that its items are not evenly distributed around the octagon, for if there is a deficiency of items in particular parts of the octagon, it is not possible to measure adequately all forms of relating.

In two recent British studies (Barkham, Hardy and Startup, 1994; Savournin, Evans, Hirst and Watson, 1995), the IIP responses of psychotherapy clients were factor analyzed and eight factors were extracted. These were characterized by me according to the classification of IIP items of relating theory. In both studies the large, first factor was predominantly lower. Both studies produced a small, aggressive factor. The Barkham and colleagues study produced an upper distant and an upper close factor. Both produced a lower close factor. Both produced two separate distant factors, one concerned with avoiding social involvement and one concerning fear of intimacy. That the two studies produced factors that correspond so closely to the positions of the octagon confirms that these positions are the main categories of relating.

Another British researcher (Riding, 1996), who had accumulated IIP data from a series of 150 clients receiving psychodynamic psychotherapy, learned the characteristics of the eight octants of relating theory and constructed, so far as was possible, 8 five-item IIP scales that represented the eight octants. They had good internal consistency. He used this measure, which he called the *IIP-40*, to study therapeutic engagement and change in psychotherapy.

To summarize, the evidence suggests that, though the IIP was developed quite independently of the PROQ and though it is not theory driven, there is a considerable degree of overlap between the item content of the two instruments. The IIP is intended to be a measure of stated interpersonal problems and, as such, is not strictly a measure of relating. Because of the IIP's lack of theoretical underpinning, its item distribution is uneven and there are gaps in its item content. It is less than satisfactory that researchers have been left to seek out factors and scales from its item pool and that in this process, large numbers of its items have been found to be redundant.

The PROQ2

A revised version of the PROQ was constructed in 1995. It was called the *PROQ2*. From this point on, the original PROQ will be called the *PROQ1*. Ambiguous items, items with low response rates and items with low factor loadings were modified or replaced; and items that loaded more heavily on neighboring octants were transferred. The items of the Upper Distant octant were revised to make them more internally consistent and more distinct from the Upper Neutral octant, and the items of the Lower Distant octant were revised to make them more internally consistent and more distinct from the Lower Neutral octant. Because with the PROQ1 some respondents had been confused about how to respond to certain items, the four possible responses to the items were changed to *Nearly always true, Quite often true, Sometimes true*, and *Rarely true*. The scoring program was revised and the presentation of results was improved. A typical computer print-out of the scores and their graphic representation are shown in Figure 3.

The PROQ2 was administered to a number of new samples, including students, and new psychometric and research data were obtained.

Some early analyses of the PROQ2

The gender differences were less apparent in the PROQ2 than in the PROQ1, particularly in student samples. Men continued to show higher mean scores on the neutral distant, upper distant and upper neutral octants, but only in

UN–	18	/ 30	60%	UN+	4	/ 6	67%
UC–	10	/ 30	33%	UC+	4	/ 6	67%
NC–	3	/ 30	10%	NC+	3	/ 6	50%
LC–	20	/ 30	67%	LC+	2	/ 6	33%
LN–	7	/ 30	23%	LN+	4	/ 6	67%
LD–	6	/ 30	20%	LD+	1	/ 6	17%
ND–	23	/ 30	77%	ND+	5	/ 6	83%
UD–	22	/ 30	73%	UD+	6	/ 6	100%
U–	34	/ 60	57%	U+	9	/ 12	75%
C–	18	/ 60	30%	C+	6	/ 12	50%
L–	20	/ 60	33%	L+	6	/ 12	50%
D–	37	/ 60	62%	D+	8	/ 12	67%
TOT–	109	/ 240	45%	TOT+	29	/ 48	60%

Not answered   0   / 96   0%

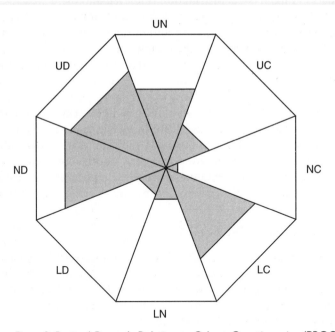

Figure 3 Revised Person's Relating to Others Questionnaire (PROQ2): numeric and graphic computer print-outs.

In the numeric print-out, the negative scores are shown on the left, and the positive scores are shown on the right. The top eight scores are the octant scores. The next four scores provide an estimate of the total upperness, closeness, lowerness and distance; to get this estimate, the intermediate scores are halved. The bottom score is the sum of the octant scores. In the graphic print-out, the eight octant scores are represented as shaded areas of the octants.

samples of psychotherapy patients did women show higher scores on the three close octants (Figure 4).

The test-retest reliability on a small sample of nursing students was encouraging.

The eight scales again showed a high degree of internal consistency. The alpha coefficients were: UN .80, UC .77, NC .81, LC .81, LN .83, LD .86, ND .82 and UD .83. In contrast, the coefficient for ten randomly selected items was only .46.

Despite the substantial revision of items, the correlation matrix of the PROQ2 (in which each scale is correlated with each other scale) was remarkably similar to that of the PROQ1. Therefore, it may be that it is not so much that the items do not differentiate clearly between certain neighboring octants as that many people are not capable of this degree of discrimination.

Some typical mean PROQ2 scores

As with the PROQ1, nobody ever gets zero on the PROQ2. In a student sample, the mean total score is around 100, and the mean octant scores range from 9 to 15, the exception being the upper close octant, for which it is 21. The items of the upper close scale are still not sufficently extreme and still not sufficiently negative, and will have to be further revised. The mean scores for psychotherapists are lower even than those for students, particularly on the lower octants. They have a mean total score of around 80. The mean scores for psychotherapy patients are very significantly higher than those for students. They have a mean total score of around 130. The octant scores that differentiate most markedly between students and psychotherapy patients are those of the three lower octants, particularly the lower close octant, and also the neutral distant octant (Figure 4).

The PROQ2 in psychotherapy research

The comparison between clients receiving CAT and those receiving psychodynamic psychotherapy was repeated, and the difference between the findings for the two forms of treatment was even more marked than before. Only 19 percent of the CAT sample showed a reduction in the PROQ2 score of 20 or more points, compared with 82 percent of the psychodynamic sample. Whereas the drop in the mean total score for the CAT sample was minimal (135 to 132), that for the psychodynamic sample was greater even than in the PROQ1 study (140 to 97). Again, the degree of improvement was not related to the number of sessions, but the improvement was spread over a broader range of octants, only the upper close octant showing no significant change.

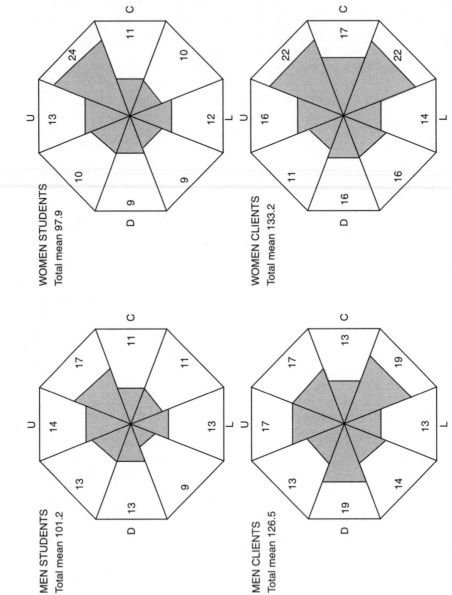

WOMEN STUDENTS
Total mean 97.9

WOMEN CLIENTS
Total mean 133.2

MEN STUDENTS
Total mean 101.2

MEN CLIENTS
Total mean 126.5

Figure 4 Mean PROQ2 scores for students and psychotherapy clients, by gender.

The clinical usefulness of the PROQ2

Ideally, psychotherapists who work with the PROQ2 should be familiar with the meanings and characteristics of the octants, as described in Birtchnell (1993/1996), and their clinical theory and practice should be orientated around them. The staff of a small number of psychotherapy departments have started to administer the PROQ2 routinely at the beginning and the end of therapy. They send me their questionnaires to be scored. I send back the scores and graphic representations and add a short note, indicating what they appear to show in terms of my understanding of the characteristics of the octants. They often remark how well my comments correspond with their clinical observations. It should shortly be possible, both before and at the end of therapy, to ask these psychotherapists to make clinical assessments of their clients in terms of the octants before they see the PROQ2 scores and to determine to what extent their descriptions correspond with the scores. This would be a step in the direction of their beginning to think and work within a relating theory framework.

In the pre-therapy assessment of the client, the graphic representation of the scores is often more useful than the actual scores. At a glance, it is possible to see where the client's major areas of difficulty lie. On the basis of this assessment, the relating psychotherapist would be able to devise a set of therapeutic strategies that are aimed at correcting specific areas of relating incompetence. Such strategies have been described in various parts of this book. At stages throughout the course of therapy, the PROQ2 can be repeated in order to determine whether the desired changes are taking place. Figure 5 shows an example of a client's pre- and post-therapy print-out.

It is not unusual for a client to have high scores in more than one zone of the octagon. Sometimes, when the PROQ2 is repeated after a particular period of therapy, a major improvement is revealed in one zone but not in others. At this point, the relating therapist would devise a new strategy that was directed toward the unimproved zones and, after a further period of therapy, repeat the PROQ2 in order to determine whether this new strategy has been effective.

The psychotherapists who are presently working with the PROQ2 are not relating therapists. They simply send me the completed PROQ2 at a time when they consider the therapy to have finished. Often I find that improvements have been made in some zones but not in others. This may reflect the fact that certain zones of negative relating are more responsive to therapy than others. The lower close octant appears to be particularly responsive. On the other hand, it may be that the particular form of therapy being used is more effective or that the psychotherapists themselves are more effective in treating certain forms of negative relating than others. Continuing work with the PROQ2 should show whether one or both of these possibilities is the case, which may lead to the development of new psychotherapeutic techniques that

BEFORE

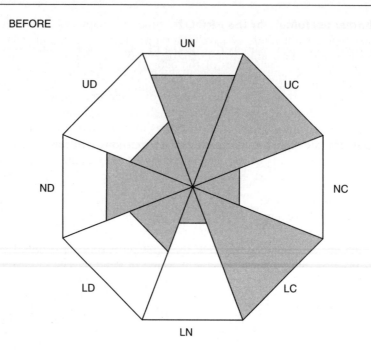

AFTER

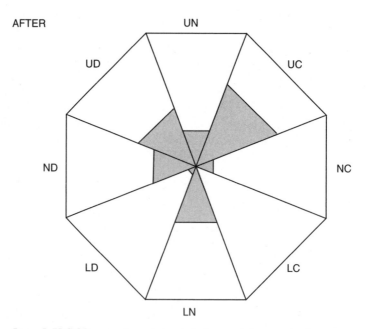

Figure 5 PROQ2 computer print-outs before and after psychotherapy.

could be directed toward the less responsive zones. In chapters 4 and 6, it was proposed that certain kinds of psychotherapists may have certain relating tendencies. These conceivably would make them good at treating some conditions and bad at treating others. Encouraging psychotherapists to complete the PROQ2 would reveal any such tendencies and make it possible to explore this possibility.

The couple's relating to each other questionnaires

There has not been a direct successor to the combined Self-Rating Questionnaire and Partner-Rating Questionnaire, because these two earlier questionnaires were both measures of general relating tendencies. It was considered inappropriate to have a measure of the interrelating between two people that did not refer specifically to what went on between these two people. The new questionnaires represented an important departure from the PROQ1 and PROQ2 because they were not general measures of relating. The successor to the old Self-Rating Questionnaire was a questionnaire that measured a person's relating to a specified other person. In the first instance, this was a measure of the way that an individual related to an adult partner, marital or otherwise. The general style of the items was "I do this to her/him". The successor to the old Partner-Rating Questionnaire was a questionnaire that measured how the individual believed that a specified other person related to her/him. In the first instance, this was a measure of the way that an individual believed that an adult partner, marital or otherwise, related to her/him. The general style of the items was "S/he does this to me". As with the old Self-Rating and Partner Rating Questionnaires, each partner completed two questionnaires, one concerning relating and one concerning being related to. Also, as with the old system, each person's two questionnaires were kept in a separate envelope, and each person was asked to complete them in private and return them to the envelope and then seal the envelope.

The four questionnaires were constructed along the same lines as the PROQ, each questionnaire having eight scales, corresponding to the eight octants of the octagon, and each scale containing ten negative items. Again, two usually unscored positive items per octant were included to relieve the overall negative tone of the items. As with the PROQ, there were four possible responses to each item: *Mostly Yes, Quite Often, Sometimes* and *Mostly No*, which yielded a score of 3, 2, 1 or 0. The four questionnaires were called MS (man's rating of self), MP (man's rating of partner), WS (woman's rating of self), and WP (woman's rating of partner). Together the questionnaires were called the *Couple's Relating to Each Other Questionnaires (CREOQ)*.

At an early stage it became clear that although the questionnaires provided a lot of useful information about what went on between the two partners, they could not of themselves be an indication of how well the partners actually got on together. Whereas the MS and WS questionnaires comprised mainly "I" items and the MP and WP questionnaires comprised mainly "s/he" items, what seemed needed was an additional questionnaire that comprised mainly "we" items. In this, each partner would be required to answer on behalf of both of them. Because the items of this questionnaire were not organized according to the eight octants, there could be fewer of them. In the end it was decided to settle for a 20-item questionnaire, with each item requiring a *True* or *False* response. Good items (e.g., "We are always pleased to see each other") alternated with bad ones (e.g., "We rub each other the wrong way"). The questionnaire produces a single score, ranging from zero to 20, zero being good and 20 being bad. It is called the US, because it refers to "the two of us".

A computer program was written that, when loaded onto an IBM-compatible computer, is as easy to use as the PROQ program. It reproduces the four questionnaires on the screen, and as with the PROQ, a red tick appears in the appropriate column when one of four computer keys is pressed. The scores of the four questionnaires are printed in a block, and the four graphic representations of the scores are printed together on one sheet to facilitate comparison. A typical print-out of the four sets of scores and their graphic representations is shown in Figure 6.

Because of the sensitive and private nature of the marital relationship, obtaining normal data for the CREOQ has not been easy. A number of organizations were invited to offer the package of questionnaires to their employees, but they declined to do so. A headmistress refused to allow the packages to be handed out at a parents' social evening. A general practitioner tried to persuade a sample of his patients to complete the questionnaires and return them anonymously, but so few agreed to do so that the exercise was abandoned. So far, only a small sample has been accumulated by inviting friends to offer the packages to other friends who appeared to have good relationships and asking them to return them anonymously.

A clinical sample of 92 couples was accumulated by sending out the questionnaires routinely to couples applying to a private couple therapy clinic.

Some early analyses of CREOQ and US data

The alpha reliabilities of the octant scales of the four CREOQ questionnaires were above .7 for 27 of the 32 scales (i.e., four sets of eight).

As with the PROQ, for each of the four questionnaires of the CREOQ, in a correlation matrix in which the scores of each octant were correlated against the scores of each other octant, the highest positive correlations were with the octants that were closest around the octagon.

As with the PROQ, on the CREOQ, even couples with good marriages do not produce scores of zero. On the self-rating questionnaires, the mean total negative score was 60 for men and 70 for women, with the mean octant scores ranging from 3 (ND) to 14 (LN). On the partner-rating questionnaires, the

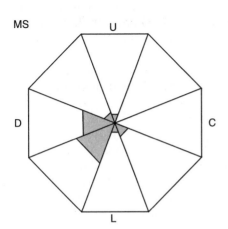

	MS	MP	WS	WP
US	19		15	
–UN	3	21	16	21
–UC	0	9	1	3
–NC	0	19	15	3
–LC	5	9	27	6
–LN	4	1	11	0
–LD	14	2	11	12
–ND	12	8	15	27
–UD	4	23	13	12
–TU	7	53	30	36
–TL	23	12	49	18
–TC	5	37	43	12
–TD	30	33	39	51
–T	42	92	109	84

	MS	MP	WS	WP
+UN	4	6	3	6
+UC	0	0	1	3
+NC	1	0	0	3
+LC	1	2	0	0
+LN	2	4	3	0
+LD	4	0	3	6
+ND	6	0	6	6
+UD	0	2	6	3
+TU	4	8	10	12
+TL	7	6	6	6
+TC	2	2	1	6
+TD	10	2	15	15
+T	18	14	22	27
NA	0	0	0	0

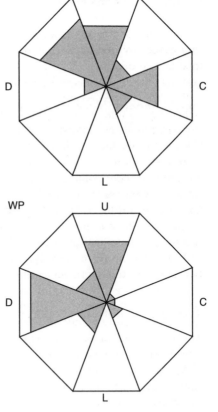

Figure 6 Couple's Relating to Each Other Questionnaires (CREOQ): numeric and graphic computer print-outs.

For negative scores only: MS is man's view of self, MP is man's view of partner, WS is woman's view of self, and WP is woman's view of partner.

mean total negative score was 40 for men and 50 for women, with the mean octant scores ranging from 2 (UD) to 8 (LC). On the US, the good marriage scores came very close to zero, the mean score being 1.4 for men and 1.7 for women.

The mean total negative scores and the mean scores on almost all octant scales were much higher in the clinical sample than in the friends of friends sample. On the self-rating questionnaires, the mean total negative scores were 85 for men and 93 for women, with the mean octant scores ranging from 7 (UC) to 15 (LC). On the partner rating questionnaires, the mean total negative scores were 80 for men and 100 for women, with the mean octant scores ranging from 5 (LD) to 16 (ND). On the US, the mean score was 8.8 for men and 10.5 for women.

To conclude, in both the good and the bad relationships there was a tendency for women to score higher than men. In the good relationships, people tended to be more critical of themselves than of their partners, but in the bad relationships, the reverse was the case. In the bad relationships, the women were especially critical of the men, particularly in terms of distance and upperness.

Some comparable measures of marital relating

The instrument that most closely resembles the CREOQ is Ryle's (1966) *Marital Patterns Test*, subsequently modified to the *Ryle/Scott-Heyes Marital Patterns Questionnaire* (Scott-Heyes, 1982). Each partner completes only one questionnaire, which consists of 24 paired items, one concerning the subject's behaviour toward the partner, the other concerning the partner's behavior toward the subject. The items belong to two classes, called affection and dominance; roughly speaking, they refer to the horizontal and the vertical axes. As the affection items are all positive and cover a wide range, they really are a measure of positive general disposition. They cannot measure such negative characteristics as clinging. In contrast, the dominance items are all negative. A complication of the dominance items is that as they are relative, the subject can only record which partner is the more dominant. Because there is no absolute measure of dominance, it is not possible to record whether both partners are either very dominant or very un-dominant.

Another instrument of relevance is the *Family Adaptability and Cohesion Evaluation Scales III, Couples Version* (Olson, 1985), a 20-item questionnaire, and the theory underlying it was described in Chapter 7. Like the US, it comprises mainly "we" items and is completed by both partners.

The clinical usefulness of the CREOQ

There is rarely any difficulty persuading couples attending for marital therapy to complete the CREOQ, and they are usually keen to see and discuss the printouts. With a little explanation, they are able to understand the graphic representation of the scores. Up until now, only a small number of couple therapists routinely administer the CREOQ to their clients and send me the questionnaires for scoring. As with the PROQ, I always send, with the printout, a brief summary of what I think is wrong with the relationship on the basis of my knowledge of the characteristics of the octants. As with the PROQ, the therapists are often impressed by the correctness of these summaries. In their latest book, Scharff and Scharff (1998), two acknowledged authorities on couple therapy, demonstrate the usefulness of the CREOQ in exploring the relationship of a couple in therapy.

The US, with a maximum score of 20, provides a useful indicator of the state of the relationship. On the basis of the data so far, a score of between 5 and 10 would be some cause for concern, but a score between 10 and 15 should set off alarm bells, and a score of over 15 would point to a relationship that is close to the breaking point. Usually the US scores for the men and the women are in reasonably close agreement. Occasionally they are widely divergent, which would suggest that one partner is denying the seriousness of the problem.

When the US scores are high, usually the CREOQ scores are also high. Occasionally, the US scores are low but the octagonal scores are high. This suggests a good prognosis, for if the couple continue to get on together, they should be able to work at and resolve their difficulties.

Having the four octagonal representations on the same sheet of paper is useful, since it often indicates with some clarity what appears to be happening between the partners. Six aspects of these representations should be taken into consideration: (1) the overall magnitude of the negative scores, as high scores indicate a poor relationship; (2) the disparity between the magnitude of the negative scores of the two partners, suggesting that one partner is relating more negatively than the other; (3) for each partner, the disparity between the magnitude of the person's self-account and that of the partner's account, the difficulty here being deciding whether one partner is denying the extent of her/his negative relating or the other is exaggerating it; (4) the location of the negative scores of the two partners; (5) the relationship between the locations of the two partners' negative scores, some combinations making more sense than others; and (6) the level of agreement between one partner's self-assessment and the other partner's partner-assessment. It is usually a hopeful sign if there is good agreement, for this is likely to mean that one partner is correctly perceiving how the other is relating. If there is poor agreement, how one partner perceives her/himself is different from how the other perceives her/him. Who is wrong and who is right may emerge in the course of therapy, but it may not be as simple as this. As with the PROQ, there is a third point of view, that of the therapist. The therapist's view may correspond more with the view of one than with the view of the other, but this may not mean that the therapist is right.

All of these points may be borne in mind by the therapist or even discussed with the partners. As with individual psychotherapy, the interpersonal marital therapist is able to formulate, on the basis of the octagonal distribution of scores, what each partner appears to be doing to the other and how the other appears to be responding to this. The therapist may formulate hypotheses about why this might be happening and use these hypotheses as a guide to the kind of therapeutic work that needs to be embarked upon.

The measurement of other forms of interrelating

What might be called the four-questionnaire approach provides a basis for measuring the interrelating between any two specified people. It is not difficult to modify the wording of some of the items to create four questionnaires that would measure the interrelating between any two people, such as two siblings, a child and a parent or even a therapist and a client. The tense of the items can be modified in order to measure interrelating at a specified time. They can be used to measure the recalled early interrelating between a parent and child, or a couple's recalled interrelating at an earlier stage of the marriage, for example, before they had children.

The Family Members Interrelating Questionnaires (FMIQ)

In Chapter 8 it was observed that, as family size increases, the number of relationships between family members increases to an even greater extent. This makes it extremely difficult to measure interrelating within a family. Since four questionnaires are required to measure the interrelating between any specified pair of family members, the number of questionnaires required to measure the interrelating within a given family is four times the number of two-person relationships within it. In a family of three, two parents and a child, there are three two-person relationships (father-mother, father-child and mother-child); so twelve questionnaires are required, four for each family member. In a family of four there are six two-person relationships; so 24 questionnaires are required, six for each family member. With a computer, the scoring of such large numbers of questionnaires and even the presentation of results pose no great problem. The greater constraint is tolerance of the family members for completing so many questionnaires. Compromises are possible, for it may not be necessary to measure all pairings within a family, and only certain pairs may be selected for measurement.

A generic term for all such intrafamilial measures is the *Family Members Interrelating Questionnaires (FMIQ)*, but different terms may be adopted for describing specific combinations of family members. A set of twelve questionnaires was recently constructed for measuring the interrelating between a young adult and two parents. This was called the *Father, Mother and Child Interrelating Questionnaires (FMCIQ)*. A computer program for presenting the results in graphical form was also produced, and an example is shown in Figure 7. For completeness, it should be stated that the four-questionnaire approach can be applied to groups of individuals who are not members of a family. An occupational psychologist may wish to use it as a means of assessing the interactions among people who work together.

The clinical usefulness of the FMIQ

If a family therapist were asked how many relationships there were within a family of four, s/he would probably have to stop and think, yet family therapists frequently treat families of four. It is highly likely that family therapists deny the true complexity of the families they treat because, if they thought about it, they would be put off by the enormity of their task. The appeal of systems theory to family therapists is that, by working with the system, they can avoid focusing upon the individual relationships within it. This is not necessarily wrong, because families, like groups and communities, have their own inner strengths, and members are able to help each other.

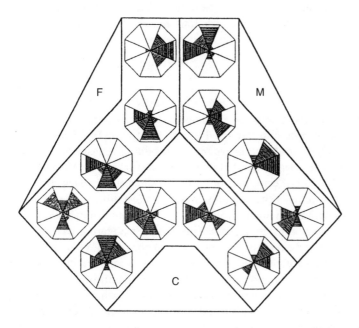

Figure 7 Father, Mother and Child Interrelating Questionnaires (FMCIQ): graphic computer print-out.

The four octagons between the letters F and M are like the four octagons of Figure 6, though the positions are different. The four octagons between F and C represent the interrelating between the father and the (adult) child. The four octagons between M and C represent the interrelating between the mother and the (adult) child. The inner six octagons represent the relating of self to the other. The outer six octagons represent the subject's view of the relating of the other to the self.

At times, however, it can be useful to have a plan of the interrelating of all the pairs within the family system. Taking the family of three as the simplest system, it can be of interest to observe whether one member considers that s/he relates in the same way or in a different way toward each of the other two members, or whether s/he considers that the other two members relate in the same way or in a different way toward her/him. Equally, it can be of interest to observe whether any two members agree about the way that they relate to the third member or the way that the third member relates to them. For example, does a daughter consider that both parents are dominating toward her, do both the mother and the daughter consider the father to be distant, or do both parents consider the daughter to be clinging toward them?

As with both the PROQ and the CREOQ, the family therapist can, at the outset of therapy, use the FMIQ to observe and record the major interrelating deficiencies within the family and can direct her/his therapeutic strategy toward rectifying these. At stages through the therapy and at the end of therapy, s/he can repeat the FMIQ to determine whether the therapy has been successful. A possible scenario is that the father clings to the daughter because he perceives the mother to be cold and remote. If the therapy were directed toward reducing the mother's remoteness, the father would become more positively involved with her and less negatively involved with the daughter.

Summary

Concern with the structure of psychological dependence led to the development of the Self-Rating and Partner-Rating Questionnaires. These each had three scales called dependence, detachment and directiveness. With the development of relating theory the Self-Rating Questionnaire gave way to the Person's Relating to Others Questionnaire. This has eight scales corresponding to the eight octants of the octagon. It was the first of the computer-scored questionnaires with a graphic representation of scores. It may be used for the assessment of psychotherapy clients. The Couple's Relating to Each Other Questionnaires represented a new departure in that the four questionnaires that they comprise are each directed toward a specified other person, and they measure both the relating of one person toward another and that person's conception of the other's relating toward her/him. They are supplemented by a short, single-scale questionnaire called the US, by which each member of a couple rates the quality of the relationship. This set of five questionnaires may be used in couple therapy. The four-questionnaire approach was extended to families of three, four or more members by the development of the Family Members Interrelating Questionnaires. These may be used in family therapy.

Chapter 10

The emergence of a new approach to psychotherapy

It is clear from the contents of Chapters 4, 6 and 8 that the ideas that have been developed in this book can have application across a broad range of psychotherapies. In fact, there is probably no form of psychotherapy to which they cannot be applied. Therefore, a major theme of the book is that it is both unwise and undesirable for psychotherapists to restrict their attention or their mode of practice to any one clinical style. The central focus of the book is essentially the same as that of the previous book, namely, that humans relate within certain circumscribed parameters and that, within these parameters, there are certain relating objectives that are called states of relatedness. They need to acquire competence in attaining these states of relatedness. They need to do this because certain states of relatedness are beneficial to them, and they feel good only when they have attained and retained such states of relatedness.

People seek psychotherapy because they feel bad. Though this may not be the way that they perceive it, they feel bad because either they have an impaired capacity to attain certain states of relatedness, that is, they lack competence in certain areas of relating, or they are being deprived of certain states of relatedness by the restrictive relating behavior of others. The word bad, as used here, has no moral implications: It simply means feeling that all is not well. The argument put forward in the book is that it can be helpful for psychotherapists to view humans in this way, to formulate their theories about what is wrong with their clients within this framework, and to plan their therapeutic strategies on the basis of these assumptions.

At present, the majority of psychotherapists do not do these things. They have their own tried and tested frames of reference and are unlikely to be motivated to take on a new set of ideas that may seem strange to them. They would be more inclined to translate the theoretical formulations put forward here back into schemata that are more familiar to them, or to argue that nothing has been proposed here that has not been expressed more clearly or more completely within existing theories. Such a reaction is only to be expected and is completely understandable. A suitable response would be that what is offered here is not so much a new form of psychotherapy as a new way of viewing what goes on within any form of psychotherapy.

This having been said, a particular orientation toward psychotherapy does appear to have emerged in the writing of this book, a style of working that might even be identifiable as a particular approach. If so, it might warrant the name *relating therapy*. The theory I have assembled here has changed the way I view and interpret the difficulties that clients present to me and the way I plan and execute my therapy. I have noticed that I actually use the words close, distant, upper and lower when talking to clients about their problems and that clients use the words back to me. More and more, I find myself adopting the concepts of the inner and the outer brain when trying to clarify clients' difficulties, and I find, with some satisfaction, that in subsequent sessions, they incorporate them into the framing of their own self-descriptions.

The link with evolution

It may have been disconcerting to the reader to be confronted, at the beginning of the first chapter, with ideas about evolution. In fact, the link with evolution is central to the theory upon which the book is based and also to the aims of psychotherapy described. It places psychotherapy upon a sound footing. It is important that psychotherapists should have, somewhere in their minds, a clear understanding of what being human is all about and what the ultimate goals of humans might be. It is disconcerting that most schools of psychotherapy pay no attention to this. How can psychotherapists help their clients on their way when they have no conceptualization of where their clients are aiming to get? Our goals are the goals that have evolved in us. The human psyche has evolved in exactly the same way as the human body. Just like the body, the psyche has evolved in order that we should be optimally equipped to attain our evolved goals. The brain has evolved in order to enable the psyche to do this. When thinking in this way, it is impossible to separate the brain from the psyche.

The brain as a computer

The brain is not a random collection of neurons. Just like any other organ, it contains many separate, though interconnected, departments, each with its own specific function. The psyche is simply a manifestation of the functioning of these departments. Psychotherapists may be reluctant to acknowledge that, in working on people's psyches, they are working on their brains; though the way that they do so is not the same as the way that neurosurgeons do. The relationship of the psyche to the brain is like that of the software of a computer to the hardware of a computer; but unlike a computer, the brain comes with a great deal of its software already in place. This in-place software is sometimes referred to as *hard-wired*. In addition to the hard-wired software, non-hard-wired software is continually being added and modified. This is the equivalent of writing and rewriting programs. The general dispositions toward the four major relating objectives, and the neural mechanisms for monitoring them, have got to be part of the hard-wired software, but the detailed strategies that we acquire for their attainment and maintenance, promoted by the experiences that we gain within our particular life circumstances, constitute the software that is added and modified. This is an ideal arrangement, for it permits the maximum degree of flexibility within a set of fixed guidelines.

The role of the psychotherapist is to assist us in the process of adding to and modifying the software. Our software may require additions or modifications either because the experiences that promoted its original instillation were imperfect, for example, our parents were not good at introducing us to secure and pleasurable closeness, or because we now live under circumstances in which the original strategies are no longer advantageous to us, for example, the untrustworthy people we once lived with have been replaced by trustworthy people, but we continue to treat the trustworthy people as though they were untrustworthy.

To carry the computer analogy a little further, neurosurgeons and psychopharmacists are like electronics engineers, who can influence the psyche by changing the structure of the brain or by introducing drugs that affect the working of the brain. The time may not be too far off when relating behavior can be modified by direct action on the brain. In a condition called *Aspberger's syndrome*, (Attwood, 1997), which is related to autism, the person avoids closeness and manifests many of the characteristics of distance. In another condition, called *Williams' syndrome* (Davies, Udwin and Howlin, 1998), the person is over-friendly, attention-seeking and, some would say, adept at gauging what is going on in the mind of another, all of which are forms of closeness. Researchers claim to have located areas of the brain that are associated with these two conditions. The neurosurgeon may soon be able to influence a person's closeness- or distance-seeking tendencies by modifying one of these.

Certain psychopharmacological agents may modify our closeness- or distance-seeking behavior. Alcohol may be taken to increase sociability. The drug Ecstasy is considered by some to have a similar effect, though it is difficult to separate the drug from the circumstances under which it is taken. At the end of an allnight rave, people feel friendly toward their fellow ravers and talk freely to them. Opium may have the opposite effect, making people more solitary and introspective. Certain mood-elevating drugs sometimes push people into a manic state, in which they adopt an upper, grandiose form of behavior. Nesse and Berridge (1997) made the point that psychoactive drugs bypass adaptive information-processing systems and act directly on ancient brain mechanisms that control emotion and behavior. The effect can be to disconnect the emotion from the circumstances that promote it, so a person may be happy under circumstances in which it would be more appropriate to be unhappy. When a person is seeking to attain relating object- ives, this can be confusing and unhelpful, since the emotion is no longer linked with success or failure in attaining them.

The relevance of the inner/outer brain distinction

The inner/outer brain distinction is very much a part of the evolutionary orientation. It has to be emphasized that the concept of the inner and the outer brain was introduced as a way of making sense of how the brain appears to operate. In evolutionary time, the inner brain must have come first, but this is not to say that the outer brain evolved out of the inner brain. It is more likely that it became an additional structure, wrapped around it. The arrival of the outer brain appears to have had little effect upon the inner brain, which has continued to function as it always has done. For much of the time, the inner brain operates as though it is not aware of the existence of the outer brain. No attempt has been made (nor has needed to be made) to identify the anatomical locations of the brain that might correspond to the inner and the outer brain, though it is assumed that the outer brain roughly corresponds to what MacLean (1973) has called the neomammalian cortex.

The concept of an inner and an outer brain became necessary out of the consideration that there appears to be a part of the brain, the inner brain, that is acutely aware of our successes and failures in attaining each state of relatedness and that triggers emotions that indicate to us whether we have succeeded or failed or whether we are in danger of failing. The striking thing about the inner brain is that it appears to operate quite independently of that which we would normally call ourselves (the outer brain). In this respect it resembles more the heart or the liver. Just like the heart or the liver, it seems to know what it is doing and operates perfectly efficiently, and yet we, ourselves that is, play no part in its decision making. This is a strange state of affairs. What is even stranger is that few people ever notice or comment upon it. The inner brain, to me, feels as though there is another person inside me. When something new happens to me, I find myself thinking, "I wonder how my inner brain is going to take that?" I then wait for the emotional response. If I start to feel happy, I conclude that the inner brain must have liked it. This may seem a passive way to behave. My counter to this is that people are deluding themselves if they believe that it was *they* who made the decision that caused them to feel happy and it was *they* who decided to feel happy. This can only be rationalization after the event.

The interplay between the inner and the outer brain

That part of us that we call ourselves, which it is convenient to call the outer brain, does seem to be aware, in some way or another, of our relating objectives, for it does appear to act purposively too. Its main advantage is that it has a clearer idea of changing circumstances, so where the inner brain continues to behave as though things will always be the same, the outer brain is able to observe that they are not and to modify our relating strategies accordingly. The inner brain, having once experienced the untrustworthiness of a certain person, will prompt us to behave as though that person cannot be trusted or even as though no one can be trusted. The outer brain, having observed the continuing behavior of that person, may decide that s/he has changed her/his ways and is probably now trustworthy; or, having observed the behavior of people in general, may have concluded that, in general, people are trustworthy. It may, however, need to labor long and hard to get across to the inner brain that that person has changed or that s/he may not be someone from whom generalizations can be made.

Another important way in which the inner and the outer brain can advantageously work together is in the division between old routines and new adaptations. Once the inner brain has learned a routine, it can be trusted to carry it through, over and over, the same way every time, efficiently and automatically, without the individual (the outer brain) needing to pay attention to what it is doing. This is what is commonly referred to as going onto *automatic pilot*. Susan Greenfield, of Lincoln College, Oxford, recently observed that in such instances that which starts as a function of the cerebral cortex becomes taken over by the cerebellum. She also observed that athletes are capable of astonishing performances when in this mode, providing they are able to force themselves to pay minimal attention to the event in which they are participating and to function almost as though they are in a dream. In other words, they are keeping their outer brains well out of the picture.

Where the outer brain comes into its own is in trying to find a way through a totally unfamiliar, or changed, situation. It needs to size up the situation, decide what has to be done, determine what might be possible, try out a number of different alternatives and come to a conclusion. Most situations come midway between these two extremes. There are some familiar features, for which some old and well-tried strategies are effective, and here the inner brain can play its part, and there are some new and unexpected ones, which will require the inventiveness of the outer brain.

The inner/outer brain conflict in art, sex and drama

A striking feature of the inner brain is its automatic response to certain cues. When we look at a representation of an object, the representation is sufficiently like the object to provoke the inner brain to respond to it as though it were the object. A great deal of art depends upon this. The inner brain responds to artificial flowers as though they were real flowers. It responds to a nude statue as though it were a nude woman. It responds to paintings and photographs as though they were the real thing. Women in particular are able to do things to their bodies, by applying cosmetics or having cosmetic surgery, that evoke sexual responses by the inner brain of the observer. Women can deceive the inner brain by wearing particular garments. Wearing nylon tights, for example, deceives the inner brain into believing that the man is looking at smooth brown skin. Wearing pants over tights evokes a response in the man that would be more appropriate if the woman were wearing only pants, but the inner brain cannot tell itself that the woman is wearing tights as well.

The outer brain is only partially successful in modifying these responses. Discovering that artificial flowers are not real only partially reduces our appreciation of them. In art, though to a lesser extent in photography, the aesthetic effect is largely due to the conflicting responses of the inner and the outer brain. Knowing that a nude statue is only stone, or a portrait is only paint on canvas, confuses us, but somehow we like the feeling of being confused. We know that it is not real, yet we cannot stop ourselves responding to it as though it were. This is intriguing to us. The effectiveness of many works of art depend upon getting the balance right between what we experience as real and what we know not to be real, between the message and the medium. If the representation is too close to the real thing we do not experience enough of the representing material to create a conflict in us. In terms of sexual responsiveness, men (their inner brains) are aroused by women who wear lipstick, even though they (their outer brains) know the women's lips are not really red. Knowing that a woman has silicone implants reduces, but certainly does not eliminate, a man's responsiveness to her apparently large breasts. Nylon tights are stimulating to men, even though they know that the woman's legs do not really look like this.

In novels, plays and films, the inner brain is responding to the fictitious incidents that we are reading about and experiencing them as though they were real. We (our outer brains) know that they are fictitious experiences, but we allow ourselves to be deceived by them. When engrossed in a novel, play or film, we are suspending our knowledge that it is not real because we want it to be real. We experience, vicariously, the emotions of the characters who are depicted without actually being these characters or doing the things they are doing.

The inner/outer brain distinction in psychotherapy

The inner/outer brain distinction brings a brain-functioning component into the psychotherapeutic process. In psychotherapy there are issues to do with the inner and outer brain functioning of both client and therapist. At an inner brain level, the client's old and redundant relating strategies need to be identified and then modified by the outer brain's interventions. The therapist needs sometimes to put her/himself on automatic pilot, an inner brain way of functioning, allowing her/himself to respond automatically and intuitively to what the client is saying. S/he also sometimes needs to be recognizing, at an outer brain level, an unusual and unexpected twist to the client's story that appears not to correspond with what s/he might have been expecting. Sometimes, again at an outer brain level, the therapist needs to lift her/himself above the interaction between her/himself and the client and observe objectively what they appear to be doing to each other.

Central to psychotherapy is the generation of emotion by the inner brain. It is by the emotions that the inner brain causes us to feel, by which we get the clearest indication of how the inner brain is responding to what we are doing and, more important, what others are doing to us. In Chapter 2 the idea of *picking up a scent* was introduced. This is of immense importance in psychotherapy. The therapist sits listening to the client's flow of talk until s/he hears a phrase, or even just a word, that seems to carry emotion. The client cannot speak the phrase or word without revealing a quiver in the voice. If s/he is asked to repeat it, the same quiver emerges at exactly the same point. The therapist now knows that the client has moved on to a topic of some importance to her/him. The therapist notes what is being said and what the accompanying emotion is, and this will reveal to the therapist the nature of the client's preoccupation. It is essential at this point not to lose the scent, but instead to keep track of the phrases or words that carry the emotion, in order to move in closer to the epicenter of the client's preoccupation.

The therapist has to note (1) who is being talked about, (2) what is happening between the client and this other person, and (3) what emotion the client is experiencing when talking about this person and the event that involves her/him. A young woman who had recently split up with her husband began to talk about a man she had started going out with. Each time she mentioned the man's name a smile appeared on her face. In fact, she could not speak his name without smiling. From this it was clear that she had fallen in love with this man, a point that she herself did not seem to be clear about.

The implications of the art, sex and drama experiences for psychotherapy

We gather from our reactions to art, sex, novels, plays and films that the inner brain, unlike the outer brain, responds to everything it experiences as though it were the real thing. These reactions also teach us that the outer brain's capacity to modify the inner brain's naive responses is limited. At the same time, although the outer brain knows that it is being deceived, it does not object, because it likes the emotions that the inner brain releases in response to what it is perceiving as reality.

The appeal of the arts is that they enable us to feel as though we are having certain experiences without our actually having to live through them. Dreams are similar in this respect. Sometimes we might wish we were living through them, as with passionate love scenes, and sometimes we are glad we are not, as with scenes in which we would be exposed to great danger. We seem to enjoy experiencing the emotion of fear (as generated by the inner brain) so long as we (the outer brain) know that we are not really in any danger.

In the arts, by acting certain roles, identifying with others who are acting certain roles, or seeing representations of, or reading about, others in certain roles, we can enable ourselves to feel as though we are indulging in certain kinds of behavior that normally would be forbidden or unacceptable to us, but that nevertheless we would find gratifying (that is, would satisfy certain relating objectives). This includes acts of murder, rape or extreme violence, perverse sexual acts or criminality.

In Chapter 8, forms of therapy, such as art therapy, drama therapy and psychodrama, were described in which participants are encouraged to depict actual scenes (like being raped) or imagined scenes (like killing their fathers) from their lives, as a means of getting in touch with the emotions of these scenes, within the safety of the therapy session. The value of this exercise is that the depictions have the quality of almost-but-not-quiteness. That is, they are sufficiently like the real thing to evoke the emotions, but because they are not the real thing, they can be talked about constructively. The person can allow the inner brain to stay in the scenes, because the outer brain knows the scenes are not real.

In real life, a person can live out what might be called an *encapsulated experience* that may serve a similar function. The extramarital affair could be such an experience, particularly when it is lived out in circumstances that are different from, and detached from, the person's normal life situation. A client who lived with his mother in a large city and held a responsible post in a respectable institution was unable to admit to, or give expression to, his homosexual feelings. He accumulated a secret store of clothes, into which he changed after work. He travelled to a distant part of the city, where he assumed a different identity and freely indulged in his homosexual behavior.

Because of their detachment and because the person cannot talk to other people about them, encapsulated experiences can feel as though they are not really happening. Talking to a therapist about them can provide confirmation that they are happening and that they are important. The therapist can acknowledge that certain of the client's relating needs are not being satisfied, can agree that they need to be satisfied and can be pleased for the client that they are being satisfied, even in an encapsulated way. The therapist may be able to help the client seek a way of integrating their encapsulated experiences into their normal lives.

Comparing the inner/outer brain distinction with the more conventional unconscious/conscious distinction

Typical of how psychotherapists are inclined to translate the formulations put forward in this book back into more familiar schemata is the contention of some psychotherapists that the inner/outer brain distinction is simply a reworking of the well-established unconscious/conscious distinction. Obviously, there are similarities between the two kinds of distinction, and in some respects they are describing the same phenomena. The concept of the unconscious, just like the concept of the inner brain, must have started as an attempt to explain the experience that decisions are made and mental events occur without conscious initiation, but the psychoanalytic elaboration of the unconscious/conscious distinction has followed a different route from that of the inner/outer brain distinction.

Freud defined psychoanalysis as the science of unconscious mental processes, but the psychoanalytic descriptions of the unconscious do not correspond with those of the inner brain. Frosh (1997) described Freud as a person who "might know what people are really like, who might see through the surface appearance to the messy reality underneath" (p. 4) and as "judging us in terms of our inner nature, seeing through the veneer of civilised conduct to the beast below" (p. 5). He considered one of the aims of psychoanalysis to be "the taming of the unconscious" (p. 91). He described psychoanalysis as "a discipline and practice of uncovering latent meanings, of reaching below the surface of action and consciousness to reveal the disturbing elements of unconscious life" (p. 112). He considered Freud to be "relentless in his pursuit of the unconscious sprites responsible for fooling about with everyday life" (p. 88). He wrote that "when Freud introduced the notion of a dynamic unconscious, he brought a demon into the modern world which will not let anything alone, but which continually disrupts the things we take for granted and subverts the things we assume to be true" (p. 242). He referred to "the symptom-producing unconscious" (p. 90). He wrote that "What really troubles us are those chopped-off pieces of impulse and passion" that "continue to create havoc" (p. 90). His solution was "Calling them forth from the depth . . . to interrogate them . . . to argue them out of the excess of their demand and then to find them a place in consciousness" (p. 90). He likened the process to that of exorcising a ghost. All of these descriptions imply that we (presumably the conscious) are threatened by the unconscious, that the unconscious is interfering with what we (the conscious) are trying to do and that we have to bring the unconscious under control.

The inner brain is not conceived of as some sinister place where disruptive forces lurk. It is simply an early version of the brain, or of ourselves, in which the mental mechanisms essential for our survival were first set down. It continues to be the only part of the brain that really knows what we want and where we are going. The outer brain is an added refinement that provides for us some additional, useful functions, but it would be lost without the direction of the inner brain.

It is interesting that the psychoanalyst regards the unconscious as the place the animal within us resides. Admittedly, in terms of relating theory, the inner brain is more directly linked (in terms of evolutionary time) with earlier animal forms than the outer brain is. For the psychoanalyst, the animal within us is experienced as something wild that needs to be tamed. Having an unconscious is like keeping a wild beast in the cellar. The psychoanalyst considers the conscious to be the domain of the civilized human, that has sound judgment, that is rational, sensible and temperate, that exercises discretion and that makes long-term plans and delays gratification. Although Freud was not a religious man, it is difficult to avoid drawing parallels between the psychoanalytic view of the conscious and the unconscious and the religious view of good and evil. There is a similarity between the beast in us and sin. Steiner (1995) wrote of walking "through the dark forest of our unconscious" (p. 444). Dark forests are where wild animals live. Walking through a dark forest is also like walking through hell.

From an evolutionary point of view, animals are neither better nor worse than humans. Animals and humans exist in continuity. Animal objectives are basically the same as human objectives, and different kinds of animal are adapted to attain these objectives in different environments. In fact, one could also include plants in this continuum. Plants are also adapted to achieve the same objectives in their environments. Humans have certain attributes that plants and animals do not have, but these are simply adaptations that benefit humans in their environment. There are many environments to which other life forms are better suited than humans. Humans cannot survive desiccation or extremes of heat or cold. They cannot swim like fish, fly like birds or jump like fleas.

In terms of relating theory, humans could not function without the inner brain. The inner brain is the seat of the mechanisms that make us aware of our relating objectives. It motivates us to attain them and controls the turning on and turning off of these motivations. It generates the emotions that keep us on course in our attainment of our relating objectives, and it controls the turning on and turning off of the emotions. It is far from clear from the psychoanalytic literature how vital a part the unconscious plays in human functioning or what exactly its contributions are to our functioning. From much of what is written it appears more of a hindrance than an advantage.

One of the difficulties with psychoanalysis is that it does not clearly specify what human objectives are, or whether the objectives of the conscious are the same as those of the unconscious. The idea that the unconscious is troublesome and interfering implies that it might be working in opposition to or in conflict with the conscious. Allied to this is the fact that the objectives of psychoanalysis are poorly defined. In contrast, the objectives of the inner brain and the outer brain are considered to be essentially the same. The problem is that, because they work independently of each other in order to attain these objectives, they sometimes appear to be working at cross-purposes. Part of therapy involves clarifying the confusion in order that they can work more harmoniously together. The confusion is due largely to the fact that once the inner brain has set up certain patterns of relating behavior, it will continue to adopt them long after the circumstances that gave rise to them have passed. The outer brain needs to be helped to recognize these outdated patterns and encouraged to set up new patterns of relating that are more appropriate to the present circumstances and that can be taken over by the inner brain in place of the old ones.

Many psychoanalysts would maintain that psychoanalytic psychotherapy is concerned almost entirely with exploring and clarifying the functioning of the client's unconscious. The relating therapist is not concerned to the same extent with exploring and clarifying the client's inner brain. The objects of relating therapy are primarily to do with identifying the client's relating difficulties and finding ways of detecting and correcting their causes.

The avoidance of the client's outer world in psychoanalytic psychotherapy

Conventional psychoanalysis and the form of psychotherapy described here differ in two distinct but related ways. The first is that psychoanalysts describe their objectives in vague and abstract terms. The second is that psychoanalytic therapy focuses entirely upon the client's *intrapsychic world*. The therapist is concerned not with objective reality but only with the world as conceived of and described by the client. It matters not to the psychoanalyst whether the client is talking about reality or fantasy. Because the analyst *takes at face value* everything the client says, s/he has no way of telling whether it is reality or fantasy. In fact, the greater preoccupation is with fantasy. Psychoanalysts maintain that they can do nothing to improve the client's social and interpersonal world outside the consulting room. All they can do is improve the client.

One of the stated objectives of psychoanalysis is improving the functioning of the ego, that is, improving the functioning of something akin to an organ. This has a medical ring to it and is analogous to improving the functioning of the heart. In relating therapy, the objective is not an internal one but an external one. It is improving the client's relating abilities, improving the client's interpersonal circumstances, or helping the client to cope with the disturbing relating of someone else. Another medical feature of psychoanalytic psychotherapy is its concern with the alleviation of that which is described as the client's *pathology or neurotic condition*. The implication here is that the client is suffering from an illness, which is giving rise to symptoms such as lethargy, anxiety or depression, and the object of therapy is to cure this illness.

For the psychoanalyst, the symptoms are considered to be the result of what are called internal *conflicts*, which must be uncovered and explained to the client. It is never very clearly spelled out what these conflicts consist of, or what is supposed to be conflicting with what. The object of relating therapy is much more straightforward. It is either the improvement of the client's relating competencies or the enablement of the client to cope with or respond to the incompetent relating of others. The emotions experienced by the client are considered to be manifestations of the client's lack of success in attaining or holding on to desirable states of relatedness. They are therefore valuable markers to what is happening in the client's life.

One of the principal psychoanalytic techniques is *interpretation*. The analyst listens to what the client says and, from time to time, makes interpretations of it. An interpretation is defined as making the client aware of some aspect of her/his psychological functioning of which s/he was not previously conscious. The interpretation is intended to convey to the client what appears to the analyst to be going on in the client's unconscious. Because, by definition, the client cannot be conscious of her/his unconscious, s/he is in no position to dispute what the analyst is saying. This places the analyst in an unassailable position. In such a situation there has to be an understanding that the analyst is always right. If the client disagrees with the analyst's interpretation, this disagreement is called *resistance*. In other words, the client is considered not to be allowing her/himself to accept the truth of what the analyst is telling her/him. Interpretations provide that which is called *insight*. By this process, there occurs what Kernberg (1994) has called a *rapprochement* between the client's experience and the therapist's understanding of it. The trouble with this form of treatment is that there is no convincing way of telling whether the analyst's interpretation is correct. This built-in upperness of the analyst would make psychoanalysis particularly appealing to the lower individual, but would have the effect of reinforcing the lower person's lowerness. It would also deter an upper person from seeking psychoanalytic treatment.

The relationship between the client and the therapist

The psychoanalytic focus upon the client's inner world is an inevitable consequence of the therapeutic process by which the client talks and the therapist listens. Because of the therapist's preoccupation with listening, s/he is not able to express shock or surprise at what the client says and has no way of checking upon its veracity. The expectation is that, providing the therapist restricts what s/he says to a minimum and discloses little about her/himself, the client is able, unwittingly, to project onto her/him representations of key figures in her/his life. Thus the things that s/he says to, and the attitudes s/he adopts toward, the therapist are assumed to be really things that s/he wishes or needs to say to, or attitudes s/he wishes to adopt toward, these key figures in her/his life. In practice, it is unlikely that the therapist can ever be so neutral a figure that nothing the client ever says or feels toward her/him actually applies to her/him. This amounts to a denial of the fact that the therapist is a real person with ideas or feelings of her/his own, actually present in the room with the client. This is not to deny that, under these very strange circumstances, the client does attribute to the therapist ideas and feelings that belong to someone else, and that as a technique this procedure actually works, but there may be other ways, such as the empty chair technique of Gestalt therapy, of achieving the same ends.

In relating therapy, the therapist presents her/himself much more like an ordinary person and converses with the client in a more natural manner. Where the psychoanalyst adopts a rigid, unchanging posture, the relating therapist is versatile. S/he may sometimes behave one way and sometimes behave another. Such relating can either represent the therapist's natural responses to what is going on in therapy (inner brain directed) or be contrived by the therapist in order to generate a particular kind of interrelating between therapist and client (outer brain directed). The therapist is not averse to expressing personal opinions, making personal disclosures or answering personal questions that the client may choose to put to her/him. However, s/he must always remember that s/he is there to help the client and that the client is not there to help her/him. The therapist's first objective is to establish a real and natural relationship with the client, for it is within the setting of this real relationship that the therapy takes place. In psychoanalysis, the transference happens because the therapist reveals so little about her/himself. Because, in relating therapy, the therapist presents her/himself as a real person, a transference is less likely to happen, and the feelings that the client experiences toward the therapist are much more likely to apply to the therapist her/himself, rather than be projections onto the therapist of feelings felt toward someone else.

The therapist comes to learn about the client's relating difficulties by (1) listening to the client's accounts of what goes on in her/his life and (2) observing the way that the client relates to or responds to her/him. The therapy takes place by (1) listening to what the client is saying about what is going on in her/his life and making constructive comments on it or (2) the actual process of relating to and being related to by the client during the course of the therapy sessions.

Part of behaving naturally is responding spontaneously to what the client says and does during the course of therapy. It is important that the therapist behave spontaneously in order that a natural process of interrelating can happen between the therapist and the client. If the therapist is working well, s/he will laugh when funny things are said, look shocked when shocking things are said, show pleasure when pleasurable things are described and show distress when distressing things are described. All this is part of a process of authenticating what the client is saying. The importance of this process cannot be overstated. The client may live with people who do not respond in this way or who even respond in ways that are quite unauthenticating. It can be immensely reassuring to the client to perceive that the therapist is amused or shocked by what s/he believed to be amusing or shocking. Over and above this natural interaction, the therapist has to work hard. The work involves concentrating upon and attending to what is being said and done, deciding which points to ignore and which to take up and in which course to direct the conversation.

The therapeutic value of the client's relationship to the therapist

To a greater extent than in most other forms of therapy, the interrelating between the client and the therapist in relating therapy becomes an important component of the therapy itself. In fact, in some respects, it could be argued that the interrelating *is* the therapy. If it is believed that people relate negatively because they have not adequately acquired competence in one or more of the four relating positions, then one of the objectives of therapy should be to enable the client to improve her/his competence in one or more defective positions. The child acquires competence in relating by being exposed to good or safe forms of each position. If this has not happened, the therapist may, over a period of time, be able to provide such exposure and, by so doing, improve the client's competence. During the course of therapy, the client describes her/his early relating experiences as a way of explaining how s/he came to lack competence in one or another position. Once the therapist has perceived the nature of the client's relating difficulties, the therapist will explain her/his perceptions to the client and ask if the client agrees about them. If the client does agree, the therapist will spell out to the client how s/he intends to proceed in the sessions that follow and seek the client's approval.

A person may lack the capacity for closeness because s/he had parents who kept her/him at arm's length and did not relate in a close way toward her/him. During the early stages of therapy, a person who has had such experiences in childhood will maintain a safe distance from the therapist and be afraid to let the therapist get close to her/him. S/he will be reluctant to make self-disclosures to the therapist and will express no interest in the personal life of the therapist. Gradually the therapist must try to allay the client's fears of closeness and encourage the client to try cautiously getting closer to her/him and to other people in her/his life. The therapist may show a cautious interest in the client's personal life and make simple self-revelations to the client. All of this must proceed within the limits of tolerance of the client. When the client shows signs of anxiety, the therapist should back off and allow the client to retreat into the safety of distance. Reverse procedures would need to be adopted toward a client who lacks the capacity for distance.

A person may lack the capacity for upperness because s/he was denied the experience of upperness by parents who kept her/him firmly under their control or who persisted in doing things for her/him instead of encouraging her/him to do things for her/himself. In Chapter 6, Kaufman's (1996) description of a young man who was hit or beaten every day by either his mother or his father and who, one day, was forced to his knees and made to proclaim that his father was God is an example of the suppressive behavior of some parents. During the early stages of therapy, a person who has lived through such experiences will be cowed, submissive, deferential, apologetic and obedient. Gradually, the therapist must try to allay the client's fears of upperness and encourage the client to try cautiously assuming an upper position in relation to the therapist and to other people in her/his life. The therapist will need to contrive ways of becoming lower in relation to the client by, for example, discovering areas in which the client is more knowledgeable than s/he and inviting the client to explain things to her/him or to give her/him advice. The therapist might invite the client to pass judgment upon her/him or to practice giving her/him instructions. Reverse procedure would need to be adopted toward a client who lacks the capacity for lowerness.

In Chapter 4, evidence was presented that showed that one of the most effective components of psychotherapy is the closeness that develops between the therapist and the client. While this may often be so, there must of course be times when a calculated degree of distance is the more therapeutic position to adopt. Notwithstanding this, it is questionable whether the closeness shown in some of the more psychoanalytic forms of psychotherapy can be construed as genuine closeness. What kind of closeness is it when the therapist reveals nothing of her/himself to the client and does not respond emotionally to what the client is saying? Could a close therapist stop the client in mid-sentence, irrespective of what the client is saying, and announce that it is time to end the session? Some psychoanalysts have shown genuine closeness toward their clients and have advocated doing so. Ferenczi, as described in Chapter 4, is a case in point (Stanton, 1990).

While it is acknowledged that psychotherapists have to make a living, charging a fee is bound to affect the client's perception of the therapist's closeness. The client may feel that just as a prostitute would not permit sex with a client without the payment of a fee, so the therapist would not show the client concern without the payment of a fee. Is sex that has to be paid for, real sex? Is concern that has to be paid for, real concern?

The question of real concern is of particular relevance in the treatment of some suicidal clients (Birtchnell, 1983). Such clients sometimes become obsessed with the question, "Do you *really* care about me?" They may say to the therapist, "Letting me talk to you is just a job, isn't it? Would you talk to me if we met somewhere else? Would you find me interesting?" They sometimes ask, "How much would it matter to you if I killed myself? Would you be upset?" The relating therapist ought to be prepared to answer such questions honestly. Probably the relating therapist does, after a fairly short time, get to find her/his client both interesting and likable and really does care about her/him. I certainly would be upset if any client of mine killed her/himself.

What the therapist might be prepared to do for her/his client or let the client do for her/him are questions of some relevance to the relating therapist. Would s/he drive a client home or accept the client's offer of a lift home? Such behavior would be reasonable in the setting of a normal relationship, but many therapists would maintain that it would break professional boundaries. What exactly does that phrase mean? To the psychoanalyst it means that, by behaving in this way, the therapist would have to reveal something of her/his real self and that this would interfere with the development of the transference. For the relating therapist, offering or accepting help might help to reinforce a form of relating that the therapist and client were working on.

Would the therapist attend the client's wedding or the client's funeral? In most instances, this would seem to be inappropriate, since it would be encroaching upon the client's personal life, but there may be occasions on which it would be appropriate. The husband of a couple I was treating committed suicide and his wife invited me to the funeral. I declined, but I sent a wreath. In retrospect, I think I should have gone. Would the therapist see or talk to a client out of hours? If the client telephoned the therapist to say that s/he was in difficulties, would the therapist drop everything and go and help the client? Under certain circumstances, s/he might.

The role of the significant other

One of the principles of relating theory is that the client's difficulties may have as much to do with the relating of others toward her/him as with her/his relating to others. In fact, it is possible that her/his own relating difficulties are being maintained by the relating of others toward her/him. What is frequently the case is that, having acquired the tendency to relate in a particular way toward others as a result of exposure to the negative relating of a significant early figure, the client unwittingly, by her/his own relating behavior, invites others to relate to her/him in a way that maintains her/him in her/his relating difficulties.

The therapist will probably have had the experience of the client relating to her/him in this kind of way and may even have found her/himself responding reciprocally. The therapist's role in this kind of situation is to reveal to the client that this is going on and to encourage the client to break this cycle of action and reaction, not only with the therapist but also with certain important others in her/his life. This is far from easy because these important others are not in therapy and are unaware that they are having this effect on the client; even if they were aware, they would have no motivation to alter the way that they relate to the client, because they find it gratifying. Furthermore, because of their own relating incompetencies, they may not be capable of relating to the client in any other way.

The client is able to develop, try out and rehearse new and better relating strategies in relation to the therapist and, when s/he feels strong enough and confident enough, to try out these strategies on the important other, whose behavior has maintained the client in her/his deficient relating style. Inevitably, the client will find her/his new strategies are not welcomed by the important other, who will continue to relate to the client in the way s/he always has done and to try to force the client back into her/his former way of relating. For some time, the client will fail to obtain any satisfaction from her/his disrupted relationship with the other and will rely on her/his relationship to the therapist to carry her/him through this difficult period. S/he will return to the therapist exhausted and disheartened and will need to be consoled and encouraged to try again. With repeated attempts, s/he may be successful in "negotiating" a modified form of interaction with the other that will enable the client to hold on to her/his new form of relating to the other and enable the other to adopt a less restricting form of relating to the client.

It has to be acknowledged that significant others are not always harmful. The client may be sustained and supported by the relating behavior of a significant other, or a significant other may serve the important function of protecting or defending the client against the negative relating of some other person. It also has to be acknowledged that a client's improvement, during the course of therapy, may be a consequence of the behavior or a change in the behavior of a significant other, rather than of what is happening during the therapy sessions. It can be helpful to the client for the therapist to recognize that this has happened in order that the client can perceive the connection between her/his improvement and the behavior of the significant other. In psychoanalytic therapy, in which the focus is upon the client's inner world, such recognition would be much more difficult.

Relating principles in marital and family therapy

The relating therapist, observing the interrelating of marital partners and family members, perceives that certain individuals appear to be behaving in ways that suggest that they lack competence in certain positions. The therapist is able to observe that such individuals tend to avoid those who push them toward that form of relating in which they are deficient and move toward those who allow them to adopt that form of relating that comes most easily to them. Thus people who lack the capacity for closeness prefer the company of distant people, and people who lack the capacity for distance prefer the company of close people; people who lack the capacity for upperness prefer the company of upper people who maintain them in their lowerness, and people who lack the capacity for lowerness prefer the company of lower people who maintain them in their position of upperness.

The effect of these kinds of alignments is to reinforce people's predominant relating tendencies and consequently reduce the likelihood of their extending their relating repertoires. In marriages (or stable couple relationships) and in families, equilibria gradually become established between negative relaters, such that the relating tendencies of each negative relater become perfectly matched by the negative relating tendencies of those with whom s/he relates. At the start of a relationship, the matchings may not be so complete, but as time passes, it becomes more so, because people in regular contact come to modify their respective forms of relating behavior in order that they might mesh in more easily with one another. These matchings become ever stronger over time, because the same interactions occur, over and over.

Even in therapy groups, or therapeutic communities, group members, probably quite unwittingly, seek out and predominantly interact with people whose relating tendencies complement their own. A dominating person will find people to dominate, a caring person will find people to care for, a submissive person will find people to submit to and a helpless person will find people who like to be helpful.

Given these conditions, why would people ever want to change, and how are therapists ever able to change them? People probably start to want to change when there is some alteration in their interpersonal circumstances or when something happens to unbalance their particular equilibrium. When there is such a change, one person in the relationship or in the family stops adopting what has been a well-established style of relating and starts to adopt a new and unfamiliar one. Examples of such changes in circumstances are a wife's mother dying, so the wife loses her main source of support; a wife having a child, so she cannot pay her husband the attention she paid him before; a child leaving home or a husband retiring, so the couple are brought into closer contact with each other.

The therapist will sometimes find her/himself being sucked into the marital or family interactions, as part of the partners' or members' attempts to establish a new equilibrium. What may be confusing for the therapist is that each partner or member will try to use the therapist to plug a different gap in that partner's or member's relating needs. It is important that the therapist allow her/himself to be used in this way, as it provides a temporary stability in an otherwise unstable situation. It is like splinting a broken bone while the bone knits together. It is useful for the therapist to try to identify the different role s/he is being coerced into performing in relation to each partner or member.

Another common phenomenon is the tendency for partners or members to find it easier to relate to the therapist than to relate to each other. They will tell the therapist either about themselves or about the other(s). Even if invited to address their remarks to the other(s), they may be willing to look at the other(s), but will still be talking to the therapist. This deflection of attention onto the therapist should be accepted by the therapist as a temporary stabilizing devise that hopefully will be abandoned when new patterns of interrelating become established. Further evidence of partners' or members' communication problems is the tendency they sometimes adopt of communicating with each other via the therapist. A husband might say, "I wish that she would come to bed when I go to bed", and she might reply, "I would if he made it worth my while". It is easier, as an interim measure, to allow them to take this option, as this may be the only way that certain things get said.

Modifying interrelating within the therapy session

In the therapy session, the therapist is able to observe how the relating of one person evokes a response in another, which leads to a repetition, or even a reinforcement, of the initial relating. This makes it clear how certain set patterns of interrelating get established and maintained. The therapist, rather like the director of a play or the teacher in a master class, has to be able to identify, and eventually to rectify, the relating restrictions that compel the participants to keep doing the same things to each other. S/he needs to be able to help and encourage them to overcome the difficulty they have in interrelating in a certain way and to cautiously try out new ways of interrelating. Such a task is not easy, because people hold on tenaciously to that which is familiar to them and are frightened of what may happen if they allow themselves to relate to others, or others to relate to them, in ways that they have not done before.

It is the awareness that people are frightened of change that enables the therapist to make change possible. A man keeps his partner at bay because he is afraid of what might happen if he were to let her get closer. Another man keeps his partner imprisoned in the house because he is afraid of where she might go, or what she might do, if he were to let her out. A woman may organize her partner's life for him because she is afraid that if she let him organize his own life he would make a mess of it. Another woman behaves helplessly toward her partner because she is afraid that if she were to behave more capably she would cease to be attractive to him.

The reality is that both or all the participants are frightened of change. The therapist's task then is to suggest a trade-off. Each has to promise the other(s) that "I won't do this if you won't do that". S/he suggests that each participant should, ever so slightly, ease off that which s/he is doing. When each perceives that the other does not do what s/he feared the other would do, there is a relaxation of tension and a preparedness to carry the change further. What makes the change easier, when it comes, is that the participants are fatigued of the roles they have been forced to perform for so long, and they experience relief at being able to relinquish them. If the transformation has worked, the participants are able to shed their relationship to the therapist and begin to relate to each other again. The stretches in which they talk to each other as though the therapist is not there become longer, and eventually the therapist becomes redundant.

This brief summary is a gross oversimplification of what actually happens in marital and family therapy. Relationships are always extremely complex, and relating patterns are always extremely difficult to modify. There are no easy solutions to the problems of interrelating, but the process of working with them is made easier when there is a theoretical framework within which to operate and a small number of procedural rules to follow.

Links with other forms of interpersonal psychotherapy

The psychotherapist whose ideas come closest to those expressed in this book is Sullivan. Many of Sullivan's principles, as laid down by Evans (1996), are fundamental to the approach adopted throughout the book. Sullivan broke away from Freud because he could not agree with the principle, which has continued within classical psychoanalysis to this day, that the focus of therapy should be the client's psychic interior. It was Sullivan's conviction that the client's problems are best understood in terms of his or her interpersonal difficulties. His effectiveness as an interpersonal therapist was limited by his lack of any theoretical schema within which to define these interpersonal difficulties.

It has to be acknowledged that not all of Sullivan's ideas are in accord with the theoretical orientation of this book. Sullivan had a profound influence upon Leary (1957), who was largely responsible for the principles upon which classical interpersonal theory is based. It was Sullivan who first proposed that social behavior is largely driven by social anxiety and threats to self-esteem. It is a principle of relating theory that social behavior is not driven by fear, but by a need to attain specific interpersonal objectives.

It was also Sullivan who argued that maladaptive behavior is simply an extreme version of adaptive behavior. Leary (1957) incorporated this idea into the classical interpersonal circle, which he designed so that the center represented normality and so that moving outward toward the exterior, along a dimension that Guttman (1954) called *intensity*, represented a movement toward abnormality. As from an evolutionary point of view all behavior is adaptive, terms like *adaptive* and *maladaptive* have no place in an evolutionary theory. Because the difference between positive and negative relating is qualitative, not quantitative (Birtchnell, 1990, 1994), there can be degrees of positive relating and degrees of negative relating, and each can be measured separately.

Among British psychotherapists the person whose ideas come closest to those of Sullivan is Hobson (1985), though strangely he makes no reference to Sullivan in his writing. Hobson has developed what he calls the *conversational model* of psychotherapy, in which "The problem is vividly revealed in the immediate relationship where it can be observed, shared and, one hopes, modified" (p. 178). "Problems may be explored, and solutions sought, in the relationship between the therapist and the patient, and learned solutions generalised to relationships outside therapy" (Goldberg, Hobson, Maguire et al., 1984). Hobson considers the most important feature of psychotherapy to be the exploration and resolution of interpersonal problems, and though he has no clear-cut theoretical framework within which to formulate the client's difficulties, he lays great emphasis upon issues of what he calls *aloneness-togetherness*. He has less to say about the power axis.

Among American psychotherapists, the person whose ideas come closest to those of Sullivan is Benjamin (1995). Aspects of her work were described in Chapter 1. She does make reference to Sullivan, and she does have a clear-cut theoretical framework within which to formulate the client's difficulties. Called the *structural analysis of social behavior*, it was first formulated in 1974. It takes as its starting point the Leary interpersonal circle, but it introduces an additional dimension, inspired by Schaefer's (1965) system, within which the child describes the parent's behavior. This enables the rater to differentiate between what is called *parentlike* and *childlike* relating. Parentlike seems to be a mixture of upper and active, and childlike to be a mixture of lower and passive. The Benjamin system is a purely descriptive one and makes no distinction between positive and negative relating. Benjamin has, however, developed ways of measuring relating within her system, both by questionnaire (Benjamin, 1974) and by coding videotapes (Benjamin, Foster, Roberto and Estroff, 1986).

In her treatment of the more rigid interpersonal positions, which in effect would be forms of negative relating, Benjamin adopts what she calls the *Shaurette principle*. This is similar to though more subtle than Kiesler's (1986) complementary/anticomplementary approach, described in Chapter 1. The therapist begins by being totally accommodating and non-confrontational toward the client. When the therapeutic relationship is secure enough, the therapist provides what Benjamin (1987b) calls *fundamentally unwelcome feedback*. Therapist and client then work collaboratively to enable the client to understand the nature of her/his defective relating, discover how s/he came to acquire it, recognize those interactions by which it is reinforced and, with the therapist's encouragement and support, undergo the difficult process of breaking away from reinforcing interactions and adopting new, reality-based ways of relating.

Integrating theory and practice with research

As most forms of psychotherapy are backed up by a body of relevant theory, simply having a theory upon which relating therapy is based does not necessarily put it in a class apart. Psychoanalysis is based upon a rich body of theory, but such theory is complex, loosely structured and difficult to condense into strictly definable terms. It is not certain that each psychoanalyst uses the terms in the same way or employs the same techniques. That psychoanalysis is considered to work indicates that it is not essential to define and measure the terms or techniques that are used, but there are disadvantages to not being able to. Being able to operationalize a form of therapy ensures that all therapists have the same objectives and use the same techniques. By making measurements before therapy, it is possible to design and quantify what needs to be done; by making measurements throughout therapy and at the end, it is possible to determine whether, and to what extent, what needs to be done is being done and has been done.

First came relating theory, then came the development of measures based upon the theory and then came the application of the theory to the practice of psychotherapy. The development of the measures confirmed the validity of the theory, for if people are able to complete the questionnaires usefully and meaningfully, they must be able to recognize the items as representing ways that they relate to people and people relate to them. A theoretical framework within which to define people's relating objectives and competencies provides a basis upon which to describe the client's interpersonal difficulties and plan a therapeutic strategy for correcting those difficulties. Questionnaires by which these difficulties can be set out and quantified provide a means of determining when and by how much the difficulties have been corrected. The fact that when clients are treated their questionnaire scores come down indicates that what the questionnaires measure has relevance for psychotherapy; and the fact that the questionnaires are based upon the theory in turn confirms the relevance of the theory for psychotherapy.

Setting the present approach apart from existing ones

Interpersonal therapy is not itself a unitary concept, and a number of different psychotherapeutic approaches already exist under this general heading. There are six reasons for separating out relating therapy as a distinct category of interpersonal therapy: first, there is no explicit evolutionary component to existing forms of interpersonal therapy, and none includes the concepts of the inner and the outer brain; second, there is no explicit understanding of relating objectives, relating competencies and the role of the emotions in other forms of interpersonal therapy; third, no other interpersonal approach carries a clear-cut distinction between positive and negative forms of relating, with a rational explanation for each; fourth, no other approach so clearly distinguishes between relating and being related to and directs therapy toward coping with the negative relating of others; fifth, although some of the more recent forms of interpersonal therapy are based upon a biaxial theoretical structure, there is none that adopts the close/distant, upper/lower axes of relating theory; and sixth, although some forms of interpersonal therapy, particularly that of Benjamin (1987a, 1995), incorporate methods of measurement within the therapy process, none so clearly integrates theory, measurement and therapy.

Summary

The principles set out in this book have application across the entire range of psychotherapies. They also form the basis of a new form of psychotherapy, called relating therapy. From an evolutionary perspective, the brain is like a computer, and the psychotherapist functions as a modifier of defective software. The inner/outer brain distinction, an integral part of relating theory, grew out of the evolutionary perspective. It differs from the psychoanalytic unconscious/conscious distinction because whereas the inner and outer brain work together, the unconscious and the conscious are in conflict. A further distinction between relating therapy and psychoanalysis is that where psychoanalysis focuses upon mental processes, relating theory focuses upon relationships. In relating therapy, unlike in psychoanalysis, the therapy takes place within a natural and interactive therapeutic relationship. The relating therapist minimizes negative relating and maximizes positive relating and helps the client resist the negative relating of others. In marital and family therapy, the relating therapist aims to disrupt reinforcing patterns of negative interrelating. Strengths of the relating approach are its basis in theory and its integration with research. Sullivan was an early exponent of the relating approach. Contemporary exponents are Hobson in Britain and Benjamin in America.

References

Abraham, K. (1924) A short study of the development of the libido. In *Selected Papers in Psychoanalysis*. London: Hogarth Press, 1949.

Adler, A. (1931) *What Life Should Mean to You*. London: Allen and Unwin.

Ainsworth, M.D. (1963) The development of infant-mother interaction among the Ganda. In B.M. Foss (Ed.), *Determinants of Infant Behavior, Vol. 2*. New York: Wiley.

Alden, L.E., Wiggins, J.S. and Pincus, A.L. (1990) Construction of circumplex scales for the Inventory of Interpersonal Problems. *Journal of Personality Assessment*, 55, 521–536.

Almond, R. (1974) *The Healing Community*. New York: Aronson.

Altman, I. (1975) *The Environment and Social Behavior: Privacy, Personal Space, Territory and Crowding*. Monterey, Calif.: Brooks/Cole.

American Psychiatric Association. (1994) *Diagnostic and Statistical Manual of Mental Disorders* (4th ed.). Washington, D.C.: American Psychiatric Association.

Anchin, J.C. and Kiesler, D.J. (1987) *Handbook of Interpersonal Psychotherapy*. New York: Pergamon.

Anzieu, D. (1989) *The Skin Ego*. New Haven, Conn.: Yale University Press.

Argyle, M. and Furham, A. (1983) Sources of satisfaction and conflict in long-term relationships. *Journal of Marriage and the Family*, 45, 481–493.

Attwood, T. (1997) *Aspberger's Syndrome: A Guide for Parents and Professionals*. London: Jessica Kingsley.

Bailey, K. (1988) Psychological kinship: Implications for the helping professions. *Psychotherapy*, 25, 132–141.

Bandura, A. (1986) *Social Foundations of Thought and Action: A Social Cognitive Theory*. Englewood Cliffs, N.J: Prentice-Hall.

Bannister, D. (1987) The psychotic disguise. In W. Dryden (Ed.), *Therapists' Dilemmas*. London: Harper and Row.

Barker, J.C. (1962) The hospital addiction syndrome (Munchausen syndrome). *Journal of Mental Science*, 108, 167–182.

Barkham, M., Hardy, G.E. and Startup, M. (1994) The structure, validity and clinical relevance of the Inventory of Interpersonal Problems. *British Journal of Medical Psychology*, 67, 171–185.

Bar-Levav, R. (1980) The group-as-a-whole approach: A critical evaluation. In L.R. Wolberg and M.L. Aronson (Eds.), *Group and Family Therapy, 1980*. New York: Brunner/Mazel.

Barnes, M. and Berke, J. (1971) *Mary Barnes: Two Accounts of a Journey through Madness*. London: McGibbon and Kee.

Baron, R.A. and Byrne, D. (1991) *Social Psychology*. London: Allyn and Bacon.

Barry, H., Jr., Barry, H., III and Lindemann, E. (1965) Dependency in adult patients following early maternal bereavement. *Journal of Nervous and Mental Diseases*, 140, 196–206.

Bartholomew, K. (1990) Avoidance of intimacy: An attachment perspective. *Journal of Social and Personal Relationships*, 7, 147–178.

Barton, R. (1959) *Institutional Neurosis*. Bristol: John Wright and Sons.

Bateson, G. (1973) *Steps to an Ecology of Mind*. St Albans, Herts.: Paladin.

Baumeister, R.F. (1993) *Self-Esteem: The Puzzle of Low Self-Regard*. New York: Plenum.

Baumeister, R.F. and Leary, M.R. (1995) The need to belong: Desire for interpersonal attachments as a fundamental human motivation. *Psychological Bulletin*, 117, 497–529.

Beck, A.T. (1967) *Depression: Clinical, Experimental and Theoretical Aspects*. New York: Harper and Row.

Beck, A.T. (1976) *Cognitive Therapy and the Emotional Disorders*. New York: International University Press.

Beck, A.T. (1983) Cognitive therapy of depression: New perspectives. In P.J. Clayton and J.E. Barrett (Eds.), *Treatment of Depression: Old Controversies and New Approaches*. New York: Raven Press.

Benedek, T. (1956) Toward the biology of the depressive constellation. *Journal of the American Psychoanalytic Association*, 4, 389–427.

Benjamin, L.S. (1974) Structural analysis of social behavior. *Psychological Review*, 81, 394–425.

Benjamin, L.S. (1987a) Use of Structural Analysis of Social Behavior (SASB) to guide intervention in psychotherapy. In J.C. Anchin and D.J. Kiesler (Eds.), *Handbook of Interpersonal Psychotherapy*. New York: Pergamon.

Benjamin, L.S. (1987b) Use of the SASB dimensional model to develop treatment plans for personality disorders. 1: Narcissism. *Journal of Personality Disorders*, 1, 43–70.

Benjamin, L.S. (1995) *Interpersonal Diagnosis and Treatment of Personality Disorders*. New York: Guilford Press.

Benjamin, L.S., Foster, S.W., Roberto, L.G. and Estroff, S.E. (1986) Breaking the family code: Analysis of videotapes of family interactions by structural analysis of social behavior (SASB). In L.S. Greenberg and W.M. Pinsoff (Eds.), *The Psychotherapeutic Process: A Research Handbook*. New York: Guilford Press.

Berne, E. (1966) *Principles of Group Treatment*. New York: Oxford University Press.

Berne, E. (1975) *What Do You Say after You Say Hello?* London: Corgi.

Bertalanffy, L. von. (1950) An outline of general systems theory. *British Journal of the Philosophy of Science*, 1, 134–165.

Binswanger, L. (1968) *Being-in-the-World*. New York: Harper Torchbooks.

Bion, W. (1961) *Experience in Groups and Other Papers*. London: Tavistock.

Birtchnell, J. (1983) Psychotherapeutic considerations in the management of the suicidal patient. *American Journal of Psychotherapy*, 37, 24–36.

Birtchnell, J. (1984) Dependence and its relationship to depression. *British Journal of Medical Psychology*, 57, 215–225.

Birtchnell, J. (1986) The imperfect attainment of intimacy: A key concept in marital therapy. *Journal of Family Therapy*, 8, 153–172.

Birtchnell, J. (1987) Attachment-detachment, Directiveness-receptiveness: A system for classifying interpersonal attitudes and behaviour. *British Journal of Medical Psychology*, 60, 17–27.

Birtchnell, J. (1988a) Defining dependence. *British Journal of Medical Psychology*, 61, 111–123.

Birtchnell, J. (1988b) Depression and family relationships. *British Journal of Psychiatry*, 153, 758–769.

Birtchnell, J. (1988c) The assessment of the marital relationship by questionnaire. *Sexual and Marital Therapy*, 3, 57–70.

Birtchnell, J. (1989) The Leeds experience: A five day experiential, art therapy workshop. *Inscape: The Journal of the British Association of Art Therapists*, Autumn, 5–9.

Birtchnell, J. (1990) Interpersonal theory: Criticism, modification and elaboration. *Human Relations*, 43, 1183–1201.

Birtchnell, J. (1991a) Redefining dependence: A reply to Cadbury's critique. *British Journal of Medical Psychology*, 64, 253–261.

Birtchnell, J. (1991b) The measurement of dependence by questionnaire. *Journal of Personality Disorders*, 5, 281–295.

Birtchnell, J. (1991c) Negative modes of relating, marital quality and depression. *British Journal of Psychiatry*, 158, 648–657.

Birtchnell, J. (1993/1996) *How Humans Relate: A New Interpersonal Theory*. Westport, Conn.: Praeger (hardback, 1993); Hove, East Sussex: Psychology Press (paperback, 1996).

Birtchnell, J. (1994) The interpersonal octagon: An alternative to the interpersonal circle. *Human Relations*, 47, 511–529.

Birtchnell, J. (1995) Exercising caution in applying animal models to humans: A response to Price and Gardner. *British Journal of Medical Psychology*, 68, 207–210.

Birtchnell, J. (1996) Detachment. In C. Costello (Ed.), *Personality Characteristics of the Personality Disordered*. New York: Wiley.

Birtchnell, J. (1997) Personality set within an octagonal model of relating. In R. Plutchik and H. Conte (Eds.), *Circumplex Models of Personality and Emotions*. Washington, D.C: American Psychological Association.

Birtchnell, J. (1998) A Gestalt art therapy approach to family and other interpersonal problems. In D. Sandle (Ed.), *Development and Diversity: New Applications in Art Therapy*. London: Free Association Books.

Birtchnell, J., Deahl, M. and Falkowski, J. (1991) Further exploration of the relationship between depression and dependence. *Journal of Affective Disorders*, 22, 221–223.

Birtchnell, J., Falkowski, J. and Steffert, B. (1992) The negative relating of depressed patients: A new approach. *Journal of Affective Disorders*, 24, 165–176.

Birtchnell, J. and Kennard, J. (1983) What does the dependency scale of the MMPI really measure? *Journal of Clinical Psychology*, 39, 532–543.

Blatt, S.J. and Shichman, S. (1983) Two primary configurations of psychopathology. *Psychoanalysis and Contemporary Thought*, 6, 187–249.

Borys, D.S. and Pope, K.S. (1989) Dual relationships between therapist and client: A national study of psychologists, psychiatrists and social workers. *Professional Psychology: Research and Practice*, 20, 283–293.

Bowen, M. (1978) *Family Therapy in Clinical Practice*. London: Aronson.

Bowlby, J. (1969) *Attachment and Loss, Vol. 1: Attachment*. London: Hogarth Press/ Institute of Psychoanalysis.

Bowlby, J. (1973) *Attachment and Loss. Vol. 2: Separation, Anxiety and Anger*. London: Hogarth Press/Institute of Psychoanalysis.

Bugental, J.F.T. (1978) *Psychotherapy and Process: The Fundamentals of an Existential-Humanistic Approach*. Reading, Mass.: Addison-Wesley.

Burns, T.A. (1973) A structural theory of social exchange. *Acta Sociologica*, 16, 183–208.

Buss, D.M. (1994) *The Evolution of Desire: Strategies of Human Mating*. New York: Basic Books.

Byrne, D., McDonald, R.D. and Mikawa, J. (1963) Approach and avoidance affiliation motives. *Journal of Personality*, 31, 21–37.

Cannon, B. (1991) *Sartre and Psychoanalysis: An Existential Challenge to Clinical Metatheory*. Lawrence: University Press of Kansas.

Carson, R.C. (1969) *Interaction Concepts of Personality*. Chicago, III.: Aldine.

Chadwick-Jones, J.K. (1976) *Social Exchange Theory: Its Structure and Influence in Social Psychology*. London: Academic Press.

Chagnon, N.A. and Irons, W. (Eds.) (1979) *Evolutionary Biology and Human Social Behavior: An Anthropological Perspective*. North Scituate, Mass.: Duxbury.

Chase, M. (1952) *Harvey*. London: Warner Chappell Plays Ltd.

Christie, A. (1936) *The A.B.C. Murders*. New York: Bantam Books, 1967.

Clark, D.H. (1965) The therapeutic community concept: practice and future. *British Journal of Psychiatry*, 111, 947–954.

Claxton, G.L. (1998) *Hare Brain, Tortoise Mind*. London: Fourth Estate.

Coopersmith, S. (1967) *The Antecedents of Self-Esteem*. San Francisco, Calif.: Freeman.

Cosmides, L. (1989) The logic of social exchange: Has natural selection shaped how humans reason? Studies with the Wason selection task. *Cognition*, 197–276.

Cory, G.A. (1998) MacLean's triune brain concept: In praise and appraisal. *Across-Species Comparisons and Psychopathology Newsletter*, 11 (No. 7), 6–19.

Davies, M., Udwin, O. and Howlin, P. (1998) Adults with Williams syndrome. *British Journal of Psychiatry*, 172, 273–276.

Deutsch, H. (1942) Some forms of emotional disturbance and their relation to schizophrenia. *Psychoanalytic Quarterly*, 11, 301–321.

Dublin, J.E. (1985) The terrorized patient as brutalized person. In E.M. Stern (Ed.), *Psychotherapy and the Terrorised Patient*. New York: Hawthorn Press.

Efran, J. and Clarfield, L. (1992) Constructionist therapy: Sense and nonsense. In S. McNamee and K. Gergen (Eds.), *Therapy as Social Construction*. London: Sage.

Eibl-Eibesfeldt, I. (1970) *Human Ethology*. New York: Aldine de Gruyter.

Eibl-Eibesfeldt, I. (1989) *Human Ethology*. New York: Aldine de Gruyter.

Ellis, A. (1986) Rational emotive therapy. In I.L. Kutash and A. Wolf (Eds.), *Psychotherapist's Casebook*. San Francisco: Jossey-Bass.

Ellis, A. and Grieger, R. (1977) *Handbook of Rational-Emotive Therapy*. New York: Springer.

Erikson, E. (1965) *Childhood and Society*. London: Penguin.

Evans, F.B., III (1996) *Harry Stack Sullivan: Interpersonal Theory and Psychotherapy.* London: Routledge.

Eysenck, H.J. (1947) *Dimensions of Personality.* London: Routledge and Kegan Paul.

Ezriel, H. (1950) A psycho-analytic approach to group treatment. *British Journal of Medical Psychology*, 23, 59–74.

Fagan, J. and Shepard, I.L. (Eds.) (1970) *Gestalt Therapy Now.* Palo Alto, Calif.: Science and Behavior Books.

Fairbaim, W.R.D. (1952) *An Object Relations Theory of Personality.* Boston: Routledge and Kegan Paul.

Feifel, H. and Eells, J. (1963) Patients and therapists assess the same psychotherapy. *Journal of Consulting Psychology*, 27, 310–318.

Feldman, L.B. (1976) Depression and family interaction. *Family Process*, 15, 389–395.

Feldman, L.B. (1979) Marital conflict and marital intimacy: An integrative psychodynamic-behavioral-systemic model. *Family Process*, 18, 69–78.

Ferriera, A.J. (1964) The intimacy need in psychotherapy. *American Journal of Psychoanalysis*, 24, 190–194.

Folman, R.Z. (1991) Therapist-patient sex, attraction and boundary problems. *Psychotherapy*, 28, 168–173.

Freedman, M.B., Leary, T., Ossorio, A.G. and Coffee, H.S. (1951) The interpersonal dimension of personality. *Journal of Personality*, 20, 143–161.

Freud, A. (1937) *The Ego and the Mechanisms of Defence.* London: Hogarth Press.

Freud, S. (1895) Project for a scientific psychology. *Standard Edition*, Vol. 1. London: Hogarth Press, 1950.

Freud, S. (1902) On dreams. *Standard Edition*, Vol. 5. London: Hogarth Press, 1953.

Freud, S. (1905) Three essays on the theory of sexuality (translated by J. Strachey). *Standard Edition*, Vol. 7. London: Hogarth Press, 1953.

Freud, S. (1911) Formulations regarding the two principles in mental functioning (translated by M.N. Searl). *Collected Papers*, Vol. 4, pp. 13–21. London: Hogarth Press, 1925.

Freud, S. (1912) Recommendations to physicians practising psychoanalysis. *Standard Edition*, Vol. 12. London: Hogarth Press, 1958.

Freud, S. (1914) On narcissism: An introduction (translated by J. Strachey). *Standard Edition*, Vol. 14. London: Hogarth Press, 1957.

Freud, S. (1915a) The unconscious (translated by J. Strachey). *Standard Edition*, Vol. 14. London: Hogarth Press, 1957.

Freud, S. (1915b) Repression (translated by C.M. Bains). *Collected Papers*, Vol. 4, pp. 84–97. London: Hogarth Press, 1925.

Freud, S. (1920) *Beyond the Pleasure Principle* (translated by J. Strachey). New York: Liveright Publishing, 1950.

Freud, S. (1923) The ego and the id. *Standard Edition*, Vol. 19. London: Hogarth Press, 1961.

Freud, S. (1927) The future of an illusion (translated by J. Strachey). *Standard Edition*, Vol. 21. London: Hogarth Press, 1961.

Freud, S. (1950) "Why war?" (translated by J. Strachey). *Collected Papers*, Vol. 5. London: Hogarth Press.

Fromm-Reichmann, F. (1959) Loneliness. *Psychiatry*, 22, 1–25.

Frosh, S. (1997) *For and against Psychoanalysis.* London: Routledge.

Frude, N. (1991) *Understanding Family Problems: A Psychological Approach.* Chichester: Wiley.

Gardner, R. (1982) Mechanisms in manic-depressive disorder: An evolutionary model. *Archives of General Psychiatry,* 39, 1436–1441.

Garrett, T. (1994) Sexual contact between psychotherapists and their patients. In P. Clarkson and M. Pokorny (Eds.), *The Handbook of Psychotherapy.* London: Routledge.

Gibb, J.R. (1961) Defensive communication. *Journal of Communication,* 11, 141–148.

Gilbert, P. (1989) *Human Nature and Suffering.* Hillsdale, N.J.: Erlbaum.

Gilbert, P. (1992) *Depression: The Evolution of Powerlessness.* Hillsdale, N.J.: Erlbaum.

Giovacchini, P.L. (1990) Regression, reconstruction and resolution: Containment and holding. In P.L. Giovacchini (Ed.), *Tactics and Techniques in Psychoanalytic Therapy. Vol. 3, The Implications of Winnicott's Contributions.* Northvale, N.J.: Jason Aronson.

Goffman, E. (1963) *Behavior in Public Places: Notes on the Social Organization of Gatherings.* New York: Free Press.

Goldberg, D.P., Hobson, R.F., Maguire, G.P., Margison, F.R., O'Dowd, T., Osborn, M. and Moss, S. (1984). The clarification and assessment of a method of psychotherapy. *British Journal of Psychiatry,* 144, 567–580.

Goldstein, A.P. and Kanfer, F.H. (1979) *Maximising Treatment Gains: Transfer Enhancement in Psychotherapy.* London: Academic Press.

Gorell Barnes, G. (1985) Systems theory and family therapy. In M. Rutter and L. Hersov (Eds.), *Modern Child Psychiatry,* Vol. 2. Oxford: Blackwell.

Gorell Barnes, G. and Cooklin, A. (1994) Family therapy. In P. Clarkson and M. Pokorny (Eds.), *The Handbook of Psychotherapy.* London: Routledge.

Grassian, S. (1983) Psychopathological effects of solitary confinement. *American Journal of Psychiatry,* 140, 1450–1454.

Greenson, R.R. (1968) Dis-identifying from mother: Its special importance for the boy. *International Journal of Psycho-Analysis,* 49, 370–374.

Grieger, R. (1989) A client's guide to Rational Emotive Therapy (RET). In W. Dryden and P. Trower (Eds.), *Cognitive Psychotherapy: Stasis and Change.* London: Cassell.

Groddeck, G.W. (1923) *The Book of the It.* New York: Mentor Books, 1961.

Guntrip, H. (1969a) *Schizoid Phenomena, Object Relations and the Self.* London: Hogarth Press.

Guntrip, H. (1969b) Religion in relation to personal integration. *British Journal of Medical Psychology,* 42, 323–333.

Guttman, L.A. (1954) A new approach to factor analysis: The radex. In P.R. Lazarsfeld (Ed.), *Mathematical Thinking in the Social Sciences.* Glencoe, Ill.: Free Press.

Hamilton, E.W. and Abramson, L.Y. (1983) Cognitive patterns and major depressive disorder: A longitudinal study in a hospital setting. *Journal of Abnormal Psychology,* 92, 173–184.

Hamilton, W.D. (1963) The evolution of altruistic behavior. *American Naturalist,* 97, 354–356.

Hamilton, W.D. (1964) The genetical evolution of social behaviour, I and II. *Journal of Theoretical Biology,* 7, 1–16 and 17–62.

Harris, A. (1959) Sensory deprivation and schizophrenia. *Journal of Mental Science*, 105, 235–237.

Harter, S. (1996) Historical roots of contemporary issues involving self concept. In B.A. Bracken (Ed.), *Handbook of Self-Concept: Developmental, Social and Clinical Considerations*. New York: Wiley.

Havens, L.L. (1986) *Making Contact: Uses of Language in Psychotherapy*. Cambridge: Harvard University Press.

Hayward, M.L. and Taylor, J.E. (1956) A schizophrenic patient describes the action of intensive psychotherapy. *Psychiatric Quarterly*, 30, 211–248.

Heard, D.H. and Lake, B. (1986) The attachment dynamic in adult life. *British Journal of Psychiatry*, 149, 430–438.

Heisey, M.J. (1982) *Clinical Case Studies in Psychodrama*. Washington, D.C: University Press of America.

Hinde, R.A. (1997) *Relationships: A Dialectical Perspective*. Hove, East Sussex: Psychology Press.

Hobson, R. (1985) *Forms of Feeling: The Heart of Psychotherapy*. London: Tavistock.

Holroyd, J.C. and Brodsky, A.M. (1977) Psychologists' attitudes and practices regarding erotic and non-erotic physical contact with patients. *American Psychologist*, 32, 843–849.

Holt, H. (1986) Existential analysis. In I.W. Kutash and A. Wolf (Eds.), *Psychotherapist's Casebook: Theory and Technique in the Practice of Modern Therapies*. San Francisco: Jossey-Bass.

Homans, G.C. (1974) *Social Behavior: Its Elementary Forms* (rev. ed.). New York: Harcourt, Brace, Jovanovich.

Horney, K. (1945) *Our Inner Conflicts*. New York: Norton.

Horowitz, L. (1979) On the cognitive structure of interpersonal problems treated in psychotherapy. *Journal of Consulting and Clinical Psychology*, 47, 5–15.

Horowitz, L.M., Rosenberg, S.E., Baer, B.A., Ureno, G. and Villasenor, V.S. (1988) Inventory of Interpersonal Problems: Psychometric properties and clinical applications. *Journal of Consulting and Clinical Psychology*, 56, 885–892.

Hudson, L. and Jacot, B. (1991) *The Way Men Think*. London: Yale University Press.

Jacobson, E. (1964) *The Self and the Object World*. New York: International Universities Press.

Jacoby, L.L., Lindsay, D.S. and Toth, J.P. (1992) Unconscious influences revealed: Attention, awareness and control. *American Psychologist*, 47, 802–809.

Janov, A. (1973) *The Primal Scream*. London: Abacus.

Jehu, D. (1994) *Patients as Victims: Sexual Abuse in Counselling and Psychotherapy*. Chichester, Sussex: Wiley.

Jones, E. (1993) *Family Systems Therapy*. Chichester, Sussex: Wiley.

Jones, M. (1968) *Social Psychiatry in Practice: The Idea of a Therapeutic Community*. London: Penguin.

Jones, P. (1996) *Drama as Therapy: Theatre as Living*. London: Routledge.

Jung, C.J. (1921) *Psychological Types. The Collected Works*, Vol. 6 (Edited by H. Read, M. Fordham, and G. Adler). London: Routledge and Kegan Paul, 1971.

Kantor, M. (1993) *Distancing: A Guide to Avoidance and Avoidant Personality Disorder*. Westport, Conn.: Praeger.

Kaufman, G. (1996) *The Psychology of Shame: Theory and Treatment of Shame-Based Syndromes*. New York: Springer.

Kennedy, R. (1986) *The Family as In-Patient*. London: Free Association Books.

Kernberg, O. (1994) Validation in the clinical process. *International Journal of Psycho-Analysis*, 75, 1193–1200.

Kiesler, D.J. (1983) The 1982 interpersonal circle: A taxonomy for complementarity in human transactions. *Psychological Review*, 90, 185–214.

Kiesler, D.J. (1986) Interpersonal methods of diagnosis and treatment. In J.O. Cavenar (Ed.), *Psychiatry*, Vol. 1, 1–23. Philadelphia: Lippincott.

King, A. (1986) Behaviour therapy. In H. Maxwell (Ed.), *An outline of Psychotherapy for Medical Students and Practitioners*. Bristol: Wright.

Klerman, G.L., Weissman, M.M., Rounsaville, B.J. et al. (1984) *Interpersonal Psychotherapy of Depression*. New York: Basic Books.

Kohut, H. (1984) *How Does Analysis Cure?* Chicago: University of Chicago Press.

Kubie, L.S. (1994) The destructive potential of humor in psychotherapy. In H. Strean (Ed.), *The Use of Humor in Psychotherapy*. Northvale, N.J.: Jason Aronson.

LaForge, R., Freedman, M.B. and Wiggins, J. (1985) Interpersonal circumplex models: 1948–1983 (Symposium). *Journal of Personality Assessment*, 49, 613–631.

Laing, R.D. (1965) *The Divided Self*. London: Penguin.

Laing, R.D., Phillipson, H. and Lee, A.R. (1966) *Interpersonal Perception*. London: Tavistock Publications.

Lambert, M.J., Shapiro, D.A. and Bergin, A.E. (1986) The effectiveness of psychotherapy. In S.L. Garfield and A.E. Bergin (Eds.), *The Handbook of Psychotherapy and Behaviour Change*. New York: Wiley.

Lange, A. and van der Hart, O. (1983) *Directive Family Therapy*. New York: Brunner/Mazel.

Lasch, C. (1984) *The Minimal Self*. London: Picador.

Lasky, E. (1979) Physical attractiveness and its relationship to self-esteem: Preliminary findings. In M. Cook and G. Wilson (Eds.), *Love and Attraction*. Oxford: Pergamon.

Lazarus, A.A. (1973) Hypnosis as a facilitator in behavior therapy. *International Journal of Clinical and Experimental Hypnosis*, 21, 25–31.

Leary, T. (1957) *Interpersonal Diagnosis of Personality*. New York: Ronald Press.

LeDoux, J.E. (1989) Cognitive-emotional interactions in the brain. *Cognition and Emotion*, 3, 267–289.

Lerner, B. (1972) *Therapy in the Ghetto*. Baltimore: Johns Hopkins University Press.

Lewicki, P., Hill, T. and Czyzewska, M. (1992) Nonconscious acquisition of information. *American Psychologist*, 47, 796–801.

Lewinsohn, P.M., Steinmetz, J.L., Larson, D. and Franklin, J. (1981) Depression-related cognitions: Antecedent or consequence? *Journal of Abnormal Psychology*, 90, 213–219.

Lewis, H.B. (1986) The role of shame in depression. In M. Rutter, C.E. Izard and P.B. Read (Eds.), *Depression in Young People*. New York: Guilford.

Liberman, R.P. (1972) *A Guide to Behavioural Analysis and Therapy*. New York: Pergamon.

Lilly, J.C. (1956) Mental effects of reduction of ordinary levels of physical stimuli on intact, healthy persons. *Psychiatric Research Reports*, No. 5, 1–9. Washington, D.C.: American Psychiatric Association.

Liss, J. (1974) *Free to Feel: Finding Your Way through the New Therapies*. London: Wildwood House.

Livesley, W.J., Schroeder, M.L. and Jackson, D. N. (1990) Dependent personality disorder and attachment problems. *Journal of Personality Disorders*, 4, 131–140.

Loftus, E.F. and Klinger, M.R. (1992) Is the unconscious smart or dumb? *American Psychologist*, 47, 761–765.

Lomas, P. (1987) *The Limits of Interpretation: What's Wrong with Psychoanalysis*. London: Penguin.

Lorr, M. and McNair, D.M. (1963) An interpersonal behavior circle. *Journal of Abnormal and social Psychology*, 67, 68–75.

Lorr, M. and McNair, D.M. (1965) Expansion of the interpersonal behavior circle. *Journal of Personality and Social Psychology*, 2, 823–830.

Lowen, A. (1967) *The Betrayal of the Body*. London: Collier Macmillan.

Luborsky, L., Crits-Christoph, P., Mintz, J. and Auerbach, A. (1988) *Who Will Benefit from Psychotherapy? Predicting Therapeutic Outcomes*. New York: Basic Books.

Macdiarmid, D. (1989) Self-cathexis and other-cathexis: Vicissitudes in the history of an observation. *British Journal of Psychiatry*, 154, 844–852.

MacFarlane, J. (1975) Olfaction in the development of social preferences in the human neonate. In M. Hoffer (Ed.), *Parent-Infant Interaction*. New York: Elsevier.

Mackie, R. (1969) Intimate and non-intimate relations in therapy. *British Journal of Medical Psychology*, 42, 371–382.

MacLean, P.D. (1973) *A Triune Concept of Brain and Behavior*. Toronto: University of Toronto Press.

Mahler, M. (1961) On sadness and grief in infancy and childhood. *Psychoanalytic Study of the Child*, 16, 332–351.

Mahler, M. (1963) Thoughts about development and individuation. *Psychoanalytic Study of the Child*, 18, 307–324.

Mahrer, A.R. (1983) *Experiential Psychotherapy*. New York: Brunner/Mazel.

Maslow, A. (1968) *Towards a Psychology of Being*. New York: Van Nostrand Reinhold.

Masson, J.M. (1989) *Against Therapy*. London: Collins.

Maudsley, H. (1867) *Physiology and Pathology of the Mind*. London: Macmillan.

Mazur, A. (1977) Interpersonal spacing on public benches in "contact" versus "non-contact" cultures. *Journal of Social Psychology*, 101, 53–58.

McBride, G., King, M.G. and James, J.W. (1965) Social proximity: Effects on galvanic skin response in humans. *Journal of Psychology*, 61, 153–157.

McLeod, J. (1990) The client's experience of counselling and psychotherapy: A review of the research literature. In D. Mearns and W. Dryden (Eds.), *Experiences of Counselling in Action*. London: Sage.

Milardo, R.M. and Murstein, B.I. (1979) The implications of exchange orientation on the dyadic functioning of heterosexual cohabitors. In M. Cook and G. Wilson (Eds.), *Love and Attraction*. Oxford: Pergamon.

Millard, D. and Oakley, H. (1994) Psychotherapeutic communities: The contemporary practice. In P. Clarkson and M. Pokorny (Eds.), *The Handbook of Psychotherapy*. London: Routledge.

Millon, T. (1969) *Modern Psychopathology: A Biosocial Approach to Maladaptive Learning and Functioning*. Philadelphia: Saunders.

Millon, T. (1981) *Disorders of Personality, DSM-III, Axis II*. New York: Wiley.

Milton, J. (1997) Psychoanalysis and the limits of education. *Newsletter of the Psychotherapy Section of the British Psychological Society*, 21, 30–37.

Mitchell, K.M., Bozarth, J.D. and Krauft, C.C. (1977) A reappraisal of the thera-peutic effectiveness of accurate empathy, non-possessive warmth and genuineness. In A.S. Gurman and A.M. Radzin (Eds.), *Effective Psychotherapy: A Handbook of Research*. New York: Pergamon.

Mitchell, S.A. (1986) Interpersonal psychoanalysis. In I.L. Kutash and A. Wolf (Eds.), *Psychotherapist's Casebook*. San Francisco: Jossey-Bass.

Moreno, J.L. (1972) *Psychodrama*. New York: Boston House.

Murray, H. (1938) *Explorations in Personality* New York: Oxford University Press.

Nacht, S. (1969) Reflections on the evolution of psychoanalytic knowledge. *International Journal of Psycho-Analysis*, 40, 32–42.

Navran, L. (1954) A rationally derived MMPI scale to measure dependence. *Journal of Consulting Psychology*, 18, 192.

Nesse, R.M. (1990) Evolutionary explanations of emotions. *Human Nature*, 1, 261–289.

Nesse, R.M. and Berridge, K.C. (1997) Psychoactive drug use in evolutionary perspective. *Science*, 278, 63–66.

Nunally, J.C. (1978) *Psychometric Theory* (2nd ed.). New York: McGraw-Hill.

Olson, D.H. (1985) *Family Adaptability and Cohesion Evaluation Scales III, Couples Version*. St. Paul: University of Minnesota.

Olson, D.H., Sprenkle, D.H. and Russell, C.S. (1979) Circumplex model of marital and family systems: 1. Cohesion and adaptability dimensions, family types, and clinical applications. *Family Process*, 18, 3–28.

Orford, J. (1986) The rules of interpersonal complementarity: Does hostility beget hostility and dominance, submission? *Psychological Review*, 93, 365–377.

Orlinski, D.E. and Howard, K.I. (1986) Process and outcome in psychotherapy. In S.L. Garfield and A.E. Bergin (Eds.), *Handbook of Psychotherapy and Behaviour Change*. New York: Wiley.

Ornitz, E.M. (1983) The functional neuroanatomy of infantile autism. *International Journal of Neuroscience*, 19, 85–124.

Ost, L.G. (1989) One session treatment for specific phobias. *Behavior Research and Therapy*, 27, 1–7.

Palazzoli, M., Boscolo, L., Cecchin, G.F. and Prata, G. (1980) Hypothesising-circularity-neutrality: Three guidelines for the conductor of the session. *Family Process*, 19, 3–12.

Parker, I., Georgaca, E., Harper, D., Mclaughlin, T. and Stowell-Smith, M. (1995) *Deconstructing Psychopathology*. London: Sage.

Perls, F.S., Hefferline, R.F. and Goodman, P. (1951) *Gestalt Therapy: Excitement and Growth in the Human Personality*. New York: Julian Press.

Pilowsky, I. (1969) Abnormal illness behaviour. *British Journal of Medical Psychology*, 42, 347–351.

Pinker, S. (1995) *The Language Instinct*. London: Penguin.

Pinker, S. (1997) *How the Mind Works*. London: Allen Lane.

Pope, K.S. and Bouhoutsos, J.C. (1986) *Sexual Intimacy between Therapists and Patients*. New York: Praeger.

Pope, K.S., Tabachnik, B.G. and Kieth-Spiegel, P. (1987) Ethics of practice: The beliefs and behaviors of psychologists as therapists. *American Psychologist*, 42, 993–1006.

Power, M. and Brewin, C.R. (1991) From Freud to cognitive science: A contemporary account of the unconscious. *British Journal of Clinical Psychology*, 30, 289–310.

Price, J. (1988) Alternative channels for negotiating asymmetry in social relationships. In M.R.A. Chance (Ed.), *Social Fabrics of the Mind*. Hillsdale, N.J.: Erlbaum.

Price, J. and Gardner, R. (1995) The paradoxical power of the depressed patient: A problem for the ranking theory of depression. *British Journal of Medical Psychology*, 68, 193–206.

Price, J. and Sloman, L. (1987) Depression as yielding behavior: An animal model based on Schjelderup-Ebbe's pecking order. *Ethology and Sociobiology*, 8, 85S–98S.

Price, J.S., Sloman, L., Gardner, R., Gilbert, P. and Rohde, P. (1994) The social competition hypothesis of depression. *British Journal of Psychiatry*, 164, 309–335.

Rank, O. (1923) *The Trauma of Birth*. London: Harper and Row.

Rapoport, R. (1960) *Community as Doctor*. London: Tavistock.

Raskin, P.M. (1985) The application of identity status and intimacy status research to counselling with couples. *Psychotherapy*, 22, 201–212.

Reiner, A. (1990) An explanation of behavior (review of MacLean's *The Triune Brain in Evolution*). *Science*, 250, 303–305.

Riding, N. (1996) Interpreting the Inventory of Interpersonal Problems. Paper read to the Annual Meeting of the Society for Psychotherapy Research (UK), Ravenscar, Yorkshire, March 23–26.

Rioux, B. (1963) A review of folie à deux, the psychosis of association. *Psychiatric Quarterly*, 37, 405–428.

Robson, P.J. (1988) Self-esteem: A psychiatric view. *British Journal of Psychiatry*, 153, 6–15.

Rochlin, G. (1961) The dread of abandonment: A contribution to the etiology of the loss complex and to depression. *Psychoanalytic Study of the Child*, 16, 451–470.

Rogers, C.R. (1957) The necessary and sufficient conditions of therapeutic personality change. *Journal of Consulting Psychology*, 21, 95–103.

Rogers, C.R. (1961) *On Becoming a Person*. Boston: Houghton Mifflin.

Rogers, C.R. (1986) Client-centered therapy. In I.L. Kutash and A. Wolf (Eds.), *Psychotherapist's Casebook: Theory and Technique in the Practice of Modern Therapies*. San Francisco: Jossey-Bass.

Rosenblatt, P. and Titus, S. (1976) Together and apart in family. *Humanitas*, 12, 367–379.

Rowe, C.E. and MacIsaac, D.S. (1989) *Empathic Attunement: The Technique of Psychoanalytic Self Psychology*. Northvale, N.J.: Jason Aronson.

Royston, R. (1995) How Humans Relate: A New Interpersonal Theory (Book Review). *British Journal of Psychotherapy*, 11, 637–638.

Rycroft, C. (1995) *A Critical Dictionary of Psychoanalysis*. London: Penguin.

Ryle, A. (1966) A marital patterns test for use in psychiatric research. *British Journal of Psychiatry*, 112, 285–293.

Ryle, A. (1995) *Cognitive Analytic Therapy: Developments in Theory and Practice*. Chichester, Sussex: Wiley.

Salkovskis, P.M. (1995) Demonstrating specific effects in cognitive and behavioural therapy. In M. Aveline and D.A. Shapiro (Eds.), *Research Foundations for Psychotherapy Practice*. Chichester, Sussex: Wiley.

Sargant, W. (1957) *Battle for the Mind: A Physiology of Conversion and Brain Washing*. London: Heinemann.

Sartre, J.P. (1969) *Being and Nothingness: An Essay on Phenomenological Ontology*. London: Methuen.

Savournin, R., Evans, C., Hirst, J.F. and Watson, J.P. (1995) The elusive factor structure of the Inventory of Interpersonal Problems. *British Journal of Medical Psychology*, 68, 353–369.

Scanzoni, J. (1979) Social processes and power in families. In W. Burr, R. Hill, F. Nye and L. Reiss (Eds.), *Contemporary Theories about the Family*, Vol. 1. New York: Free Press.

Schaefer, E.S. (1965) A configurational analysis of children's reports of parent behavior. *Journal of Consulting Psychology*, 29, 552–557.

Schafer, R. (1984) The pursuit of failure and the idealization of unhappiness. *American Psychologist*, 39, 398–405.

Scharff, J.S. and Scharff, D.E. (1988) *Object Relations Individual Therapy*. Northvale, N.J.: Jason Aronson.

Schaverien, J. (1989) The picture within the frame. In A. Gilroy and T. Dalley (Eds.), *Pictures at an Exhibition: Selected Essays on Art and Art Therapy*. London: Tavistock/Routledge.

Schjelderup-Ebbe, T. (1935) Social behavior of birds. In C. Murchison (Ed.), *Handbook of Social Psychology*. Worcester, Mass.: Clark University Press.

Schwartz, D.A., Flinn, D.E. and Slawson, P.F. (1974) Treatment of the suicidal character. *American Journal of Psychotherapy*, 28, 194–207.

Scott-Heyes, G. (1982) Analysis and revision of Ryle's Marital Patterns Test. *British Journal of Medical Psychology*, 55, 67–75.

Shepard, M. (1971) *The Love Treatment: Sexual Intimacy between Patients and Psychotherapists*. New York: Wyden.

Shlien, J.M. (1984) A countertheory of transference. In R. Levant and J. Shlien (Eds.), *Client-Centered Therapy and the Person-Centered Approach*. New York: Praeger.

Simkin, J.S. (1982) Gestalt therapy in groups. In G.M. Gazda (Ed.), *Basic Approaches to Group Psychotherapy and Group Counselling* (3rd ed.). Springfield, Ill.: Thomas.

Simons, R.C. (1987) Applicability of DSM-III to psychiatric education. In G.L. Tischler (Ed.), *Diagnosis and Classification in Psychiatry: A Critical Appraisal of DSM-III*. Cambridge: Cambridge University Press.

Skinner, B.F. (1953) *Science and Human Behavior*. New York: Macmillan.

Smail, D. (1995) Love for sale: Psychotherapy and prostitution revisited. *Newsletter of the Psychotherapy Section of the British Psychological Society*, 17, 14–20.

Smith, D.L. (1991) *Hidden Conversations: An Introduction to Communicative Psychoanalysis*. London: Routledge.

Spinelli, E. (1994) *Demystifying Therapy*. London: Constable.

Stanton, M. (1990) *Sandor Ferenczi: Reconsidering Active Intervention*. London: Free Association Books.

Steiner, R. (1995) Hermeneutics or Hermes-mess? *International Journal of Psycho-Analysis*, 76, 435–446.

Stengel, E. (1941) On the aetiology of fugue states. *Journal of Mental Science*, 87, 572–599.

Stengel, E. (1943) Further studies on pathological wandering. *Journal of Mental Science*, 89, 224–241.

Stoller, R.J. (1979) *Sexual Excitement: Dynamics of Erotic Life*. London: Marefield Library.

Stone, L. (1984) *Transference and Its Context*. New York: Jason Aronson.

Storr, A. (1983) A psychotherapist looks at depression. *British Journal of Psychiatry*, 143, 431–435.

Strong, S.R., Hills, H.I., Kilmartin, C.T., DeVries, H., Lanier, K., Nelson, B.N., Strickland, D. and Meyer, C.W., III. (1988) The dynamic relations among interpersonal behaviors: A test of complementarity and anticomplementarity. *Journal of Personality and Social Psychology*, 54, 798–810.

Strupp, H.H. (1989) Psychotherapy: Can the practitioner learn from the researcher? *American Psychologist*, 44, 717–724.

Strupp, H., Fox, R. and Lessler, K. (1969) *Patients View Their Psychotherapy*. Baltimore: Johns Hopkins University Press.

Sullivan, H.S. (1953) *The Interpersonal Theory of Psychiatry*. New York: Norton.

Sullivan, H.S. (1954) *The Psychiatric Interview*. New York: Norton.

Sullivan, H.S. (1964) *The Fusion of Psychiatry and Social Sciences*. New York: Norton.

Suttie, I. (1935) *The Origins of Love and Hate*. London: Kegan Paul.

Szasz, T. (1972) *The Myth of Mental Illness*. London: Paladin.

Tabachnick, N. (1961) Interpersonal relations in suicidal attempts. *Archives of General Psychiatry*, 4, 16–21.

Tantam, D. (1988) Lifelong eccentricity and social isolation I: Psychiatric, social and forensic aspects. *British Journal of Psychiatry*, 153, 777–782.

Taylor, G.J. (1975) Separation-individuation in the psychotherapy of symbiotic states. *Canadian Psychiatric Association Journal*, 20, 521–526.

Thibaut, J.W. and Kelley, H.H. (1959) *The Social Psychology of Groups*. New York: Wiley.

Travers, J.A. (1991) *Psychotherapy and the Self-Righteous Patient*. New York: Haworth Press.

Trivers, R. (1971) The evolution of reciprocal altruism. *Quarterly Review of Biology*, 46, 35–57.

Trivers, R. (1985) *Social Evolution*. Redwood City, Calif.: Benjamin/Cummings.

Van der Linden, P. (1988) How does the large group change the individual? *International Journal of Therapeutic Communities*, 9, 31–40.

van Deurzen-Smith, E. (1988) *Existential counselling in Practice*. London: Sage.

Vinokur-Kaplan, D. (1995) Enhancing the effectiveness of interdisciplinary mental health treatment teams. *Administration and Policy in Mental Health*, 22, 521–530.

Waldroop, J.A. and Hurst, J.C. (1982) The psychotherapist and one-way intimacy. *Psychotherapy: Research and Practice*, 19, 48–53.

Watzlawick, P., Beavin, J.H. and Jackson, D. (1967) *Pragmatics of Human Communication: A Study of Interactional Patterns, Pathologies and Paradoxes*. New York: Norton.

Webster, S. W. (1996) A historian's perspective on interviewing. In R. Josselson (Ed.), *Ethics and Process in the Narrative Study of Lives*. London: Sage.

Weiss, R.S. (1969) The fund of sociability. *Trans-Action*, 6, 36–43.

Whitaker, D.S. and Lieberman, M. (1964) *Psychotherapy through the Group Process*. New York: Atherton Press.

Whyte, L.L. (1978) *The Unconscious before Freud*. London: Julian Friedman.

Wiggins, J.S. (1979) A psychological taxonomy of trait-descriptive terms: The interpersonal domain. *Journal of Personality and Social Psychology*, 37, 395–412.

Wile, D.B. (1984) Kohut, Kernberg, and accusatory interpretations. *Psychotherapy*, 21, 353–364.

Winnicott, D.W. (1952) Anxiety associated with insecurity. In D.W. Winnicott, *Collected Papers*. London: Tavistock.

Winnicott, D.W. (1956) On transference. *International Journal of Psycho-Analysis*, 37, 382–395.

Winter, D. (1997) Everybody has still won but what about the booby prizes? *Newsletter of the Psychotherapy Section of the British Psychological Society*, 21, 1–15.

Wolberg, L.R. (1964) *Hypnoanalysis* (2nd ed.). Orlando, Fla.: Grune and Stratton.

Wolberg, L.R. (1986) Hypnoanalysis. In *Psychotherapist's Casebook: Theory and Technique in the Practice of Modern Therapies*. San Francisco: Jossey-Bass.

Yalom, I.D. and Lieberman, M.A. (1971) A study of encounter group casualties. *Archives of General Psychiatry*, 25, 16–30.

Yardley, K. and Honess, T. (1987) *Self and Identity: Psychosocial Perspectives*. New York: Wiley.

Yurkovich, E. (1989) Patient and nurse roles in the therapeutic community. *Perspectives in Psychiatric Care*, 25, 18–22.

Zung, W.W.K. (1965) A self-rating depression scale. *Archives of General Psychiatry*, 12, 63–70.

Author index

Subject index